THE SOVIET CENSORSHIP

The
Soviet Censorship

Edited by

Martin Dewhirst and Robert Farrell

Published by

THE SCARECROW PRESS, Inc.
Metuchen, New Jersey, USA
1973

In cooperation with

RADIO LIBERTY COMMITTEE
New York, N. Y.

and

THE INSTITUTE FOR THE STUDY OF THE USSR
Munich, Germany

KM
D 48

Library of Congress Cataloging in Publication Data

Dewhirst, Martin.
   The Soviet censorship.

   "[Issued] in cooperation with Radio Liberty
Committee, New York, N. Y., and the Institute for
the Study of the USSR, Munich, Germany."
   Bibliography: p.
   1.   Censorship--Russia.   I.   Farrell, Robert,
joint author.   II.   Radio Liberty Committee.
III.   Institut zur Erforschung der UdSSR.
IV.   Title.
Law   363.3'1'0947   73-9844
ISBN 0-8108-0674-6

This volume is dedicated to the memory of Arkady Belinkov (1921–1970).

Table of Contents

Introduction

There is no freedom of the press in Russia, but who can say that there is no freedom of thought?

A. S. Yesenin-Volpin, Moscow, 1959[1]

Thus the struggle for the liquidation of censorship, for freedom of speech and the press, for genuine freedom of conscience, is now the chief and most urgent task of the whole democratic movement in the USSR.

B. V. Talantov, Kirov, 1968[2]

Although the Soviet censorship system is much more extensive, demanding, thorough and efficient than its predecessor in Tsarist Russia (and probably than any other similar institutions with the possible exception of some now operating in Asia), it has been the subject of surprisingly little research in the West. Whereas one could mention dozens of books and

---

[1] Page 171 of his *A Leaf of Spring*, London, Thames and Hudson, 1961.

[2] The final paragraph of his "Sovetskoye obshchestvo 1965–68gg." (Soviet Society, 1965–68), *Posev*, No. 9, 1969, pp. 35–41.

articles devoted wholly or partly to censorship in Russia up to 1917,[3] there appears to be no detailed published study of the restrictions on freedom of the spoken and written word in the USSR.[4] This is no doubt largely due to the near impossibility of acquiring reliable information on the matter;

---

[3] For instance, Sidney Monas, *The Third Section*, Cambridge, Mass., Harvard University Press, 1961; P. S. Squire, *The Third Department*, London, Cambridge University Press, 1968; chapter 5 of Jacob Walkin, *The Rise of Democracy in Pre-Revolutionary Russia*, London, Thames and Hudson, 1963; three articles by Benjamin Rigberg in Vols. 13 (1965), 14 (1966), and 17 (1969) of *Jahrbücher für Geschichte Osteuropas:* "The Tsarist Press Law, 1894–1905" (pp. 331–343), "The Efficacy of Tsarist Censorship Operations, 1894–1917" (pp. 327–346), and "Tsarist Censorship Performance, 1894–1905" (pp. 59–76); A. M. Skabichevsky, *Ocherki istorii russkoy tsenzury (1700–1863 g.)*, St. Petersburg, Izdaniye F. Pavlenkova, 1892; M. K. Lemke, *Nikolayevskiye zhandarmy i literatura 1826–1855 gg.*, St. Petersburg, S. V. Bunin, 1909; *idem, Ocherki po istorii russkoy tsenzury i zhurnalistiki XIX stoletiya*, St. Petersburg, Trud, 1904; *idem, Epokha tsenzurnykh reform, 1859–1865 godov*, St. Petersburg, Gerold, 1904; A. Kotovich, *Dukhovnaya tsenzura v Rossii (1799–1855 gg.)*, St. Petersburg, Rodnik, 1909; *Literaturny muzeum*, No. 1, ed. A. S. Nikolayev and Yu. G. Oksman, Petersburg [sic], 2-ya Gosudarstvennaya tipografiya, n. d. [1921]; L. M. Dobrovolsky, *Zapreshchennaya kniga v Rossii 1825–1904*, Moscow, Izdatelstvo Vsesoyuznoy knizhnoy palaty, 1962; Baron N. V. Drizen, *Dramaticheskaya tsenzura dvukh epokh 1825–1881* [Petrograd], Knigoizdatelstvo "Prometey" N. N. Mikhaylova, Tipografiya Ministerstva Vnutrennikh Del [1917]; A. V. Nikitenko, *Dnevnik* [1826–1877], Leningrad, Gosudarstvennoye izdatelstvo khudozhestvennoy literatury, 1955–1956 (three vols.); V. G. Dmitriyev, *Skryvshiye svoyo imya*, Moscow, Nauka, 1970, pp. 27–47; N. Ya. Eydelman, *Taynyye korrespondenty "Polyarnoy zvezdy,"* Moscow, Mysl, 1966; V. Lakshin, "Puti zhurnalnyye," *Novy mir*, No. 8, 1967, pp. 229–245; A. F. Berezhnoy, *Tsarskaya tsenzura i borba bolshevikov za svobodu pechati (1895–1914)*, Leningrad, Izdatelstvo Leningradskogo universiteta, 1967; the entry *Tsenzura*, pp. 948–962 of Vol. 37a (i.e., 74) of the *Entsiklopedichesky slovar*, St. Petersburg, Brokgauz-Yefron, 1903; a review of one of the annual reports on letters perlustrated by the Tsarist postal censorship, "Nikolay II i samoderzhaviye v 1903," *Byloye*, No. 2, 1918, pp. 190–222; the first version of some memoirs by a postal censor, S. Maysky, "Cherny kabinet," *Byloye*, No. 7, 1918, pp. 185–197; (Maysky's booklet with the same title, Petrograd, 1922, is used by Zh. Medvedev in his study of Soviet postal censorship: see footnote 233, p. 140.) A. V. Belgard, "K istorii pervogo posmertnogo izdaniya sochineny L. N. Tolstogo," *Mosty*, No. 6, Munich, 1961, pp. 313–318; *idem*, "Pechat i Rasputin," *ibid.*, No. 9, 1962, pp. 345–351.

[4] Except for (a) articles on rewriting works of literature (see note 26, p. 13, and note 29, p. 14); (b) works on the rewriting of history, e.g., Klaus Mehnert, *Stalin versus Marx*, London, George Allen and Unwin, 1952; C. E. Black (ed.), *Rewriting Russian History*, New York, Praeger, 1956; Anatole G. Mazour, *Modern Russian Historiography*, Princeton, D. Van Nostrand Co., Inc., 1958; Konstantin Shteppa, *Russian Historians and the Soviet State*, New Brunswick, N. J., Rutgers University Press, 1962; John Keep (ed.), *Contemporary History in the Soviet Mirror*,

although it is not entirely a tabu subject,[5] anyone attempting to investigate it faces obstruction from officials in charge of archives and libraries and arouses the suspicions of many private citizens of whom he makes enquiries.

London, George Allen and Unwin, 1964; Spencer Roberts, *Soviet Historical Drama. Its Role in the Development of a National Mythology*, The Hague, Nijhoff, 1965; Marin Pundeff (ed.), *History in the USSR*, San Francisco, Chandler Publishing Company, 1967; Lowell Tillett, *The Great Friendship. Soviet Historians on the Non-Russian Nationalities*, London, Oxford University Press, 1969; Bertram Wolfe, *An Ideology in Power*, London, George Allen and Unwin, 1969; Nancy Whittier Heer, *Politics and History in the Soviet Union*, Cambridge, Mass., The M.I.T. Press, 1971; George Fletcher, "The New Party History," *Survey*, No. 57, October, 1965, pp. 162–172; Erwin Oberländer, *Sowjetpatriotismus und Geschichte*, Cologne, Verlag Wissenschaft und Politik, 1967; P. K. Urban, *Smena tendentsy v sovetskoy istoriografii*, Munich, Institute for the Study of the USSR, 1959 (occasionally Soviet writers joke somewhat bitterly about the continual pressure on historians to revise their views; see, for instance, E. Radzinsky, "Snimayetsya kino," *Teatr*, No. 1, 1966, p. 183); (c) articles about the censoring of public libraries, e.g., Bertram Wolfe, "Krupskaya Purges the People's Libraries," *Survey*, No. 72 (Summer, 1969); the Russian version of this article, with quotations in the original language, "Krupskaya chistit biblioteki," *Novy zhurnal*, No. 99 (June, 1970); pp. 143–145 of Wolfe's book *The Bridge and the Abyss*, London, Pall Mall Press, 1967; pp. 306–307 of *Harvard Slavic Studies*, Vol. 1, 1953; pp. 287–288 of *Sovremennyye zapiski*, Paris, Vol. 63, 1937; pp. 374–377 of Merle Fainsod's *Smolensk Under Soviet Rule*, London, Macmillan, 1958; the anonymous article "Censorship in Russia: A Note," *Problems of Communism*, January-February, 1963, pp. 70–72; and pp. 178–180 of Peter Maggs's article "Der nichtmilitärische Geheimschutz nach Sowjetrecht," *Osteuropa Recht*, No. 3, 1965; and (d) a detailed, scholarly work by Zhores Medvedev on Soviet postal censorship (see note 233, p. 140). The best (brief) general surveys seem to be those provided by chapter 3 of *The Politics of Ideas in the USSR*, ed. Robert Conquest, London, The Bodley Head, 1967; by Peter Maggs, "Der nichtmilitärische Geheimschutz nach Sowjetrecht," *Osteuropa Recht*, No. 3, 1965, pp. 161–181; and by Leon Twarog, "Literary Censorship in Russia and the Soviet Union," pp. 98–123 of *Essays on Russian Intellectual History*, introduced by Sidney Monas, Austin, University of Texas Press, 1971.

[5] Soviet censorship could be mentioned quite openly as late as 1928: see chapter 5 of Panteleymon Romanov's *Pravo na zhizn* (The Right to Live), p. 24 of the Prideaux Press (Letchworth) 1970 reprint. The crucial passage, as translated on p. 278 of V. Zavalishin's *Early Soviet Writers*, New York, Praeger, 1958, reads:

> Russia is the kind of hapless country that will never have real freedom. But it's beyond me how they can fail to see that they kill all culture when they seal up the sources of creative art. The USSR is the only country in the world with preventive censorship. When a writer doesn't know what will happen to him tomorrow, how can you expect him to speak his mind? No wonder none of us cares what he writes, as long as it gets past the censor....
>
> That's right.
>
> In the old times a writer fought for his convictions. They were sacred to him. The government was something alien to him and hostile to freedom. Now we've got to look on the government as on our own. To dislike it would denote conservatism, not liberalism as before. But what convictions does a writer have now? If he's told that his line is "unsuitable,"

However, the increasing production and circulation of *samizdat* materials, especially since 1966, and the interest they arouse at the present time in the West, make it opportune to reveal as much as possible about the main cause of the *samizdat* phenomenon: the immense difficulty experienced by Soviet citizens in publishing critical remarks and studies about really

he blushes like a schoolboy who has made a mistake, and is ready at once to rewrite everything and to say "white" for "black," just because he is terrified. We are so steeped in lies that we even fear one another.

Even later a devastating picture of an editor-cum-censor could be drawn: see Ilf and Petrov's 1933 story *Kak sozdavalsya Robinzon* (How Robinson Was Created), e.g., in their *Felyetony i rasskazy*, Moscow, Gosudarstvennoye izdatelstvo khudozhestvennoy literatury, 1957, pp. 114–117. For many years after 1933 it was only occasionally admitted that censorship existed in the USSR. In Volume 32 (1936), column 308, of the first edition of the *Bolshaya sovetskaya entsiklopediya*, for instance, it is mentioned that Lenin himself introduced film censorship. The entry on censorship (Vol. 60, 1934) in this edition has nothing to say on the situation in Russia after 1917, but in 1957 Vol. 46 of the second edition of the encyclopedia explained (p. 519) the difference between censorship in the USSR and censorship in bourgeois countries. The existence of *Glavlit*, the official censorship agency, is also openly, if rarely, admitted; see, for example, p. 364 of *Spravochnik partynogo rabotnika*, Moscow, Gosudarstvennoye izdatelstvo politicheskoy literatury, 1957; p. 542 of the corresponding volume for 1959; and p. 380 of *Vedomosti Verkhovnogo Soveta SSSR*, No. 20 (1211), May 13, 1964. *Glavlit* was listed in the index (p. V) of the 1966 Moscow telephone directory and its main numbers were given on p. 3. The 1968 edition provides the numbers for *Glavlit* (294 4663), *Mosoblgorlit* (Moscow Town and Country Censorship) (253 1097), and for the three main sections (scientific and technical literature; social and political literature; and artistic literature). It should be stated in connection with our note 99, p. 65, that the *Glavlit* telephone numbers were still given in 1968 under the heading *Komitet po pechati pri SM SSSR*. In the post-Stalin period it again became possible to mention or allude to editorial censorship in speeches, poems and fiction. Apart from several references by Tvardovsky one could mention V. Aksyonov's *Syurprizy* (Surprises), p. 60 of his collection *Katapulta* (The Catapult), Moscow, Sovetsky pisatel, 1964; and *Uvazhayte trud khudozhnikov* (Respect the Work of Artists), pp. 91–96 of Z. Paperny's *17¹/₂ felyetonov* ($17^1/_2$ Feuilletons), Moscow, Iskusstvo, 1966. It has recently been suggested (e.g. *Novy mir*, No. 1, 1964, pp. 266–267) that "omitted" passages should be indicated by dots or that at least it should be mentioned that the work in question is being published in a cut version. As a rule, however, the reader of Soviet works has no idea how much has been left out of the original manuscript; contrast, for instance, the beginning of chapter two of Andrey Platonov's *Sokrovenny chelovek* as published in his *V prekrasnom i yarostnom mire*, Moscow, Khudozhestvennaya literatura, 1965 (p. 127), and in his *Izbrannoye*, Moscow, Moskovsky rabochy, 1966 (p. 49). The Procurator at the trial of Sinyavsky and Daniel mentioned *Glavlit* and read out its views on Daniel's story *Govorit Moskva* (This is Moscow Speaking); see pp. 166–167 of *On Trial*, ed. L. Labedz and M. Hayward, London, Collins and Harvill Press, 1967, or p. 184 of the *Belaya Kniga po delu A. Sinyavskogo i Yu. Danielya*, comp. A. Ginzburg,

v

controversial subjects.[6] It is impossible to say whether the Soviet censorship apparatus is bigger under Brezhnev than it was under Khrushchev, but it is certainly better in quality. Younger, more highly trained and educated censors are taking over, bringing with them a more sophisticated style of work. Whereas the general trend since 1963 has been for large-circulation publications (periodicals and books) to get steadily drearier, many extremely interesting small-circulation works on specialized and relatively "safe" subjects have appeared, thus, it would seem, preventing a more widespread upsurge of active, articulate dissatisfaction at the "Stalinism with a human face" now obtaining in the USSR.

Nonetheless, in the last few years a vocal minority has been informing itself, if not the silent majority, about its views and feelings on a wide variety of subjects. To do this it has had to evade the censorship, and on the whole rely on the *samizdat* system to circulate its views. Rather than

---

Frankfurt, Posev, 1967. The Ukrainian writer O. Honchar (A. Gonchar) referred to the censor as the "invisible man" in his speech at the Fourth Writers' Congress: *Chetvyorty syezd pisateley SSSR. Stenografichesky otchet*, Moscow, Sovetsky pisatel, 1968, p. 103. However, the subject is still a delicate one and in the articles in *Izvestiya* (May 30 and August 20, 1970) and *Zvezda* (No. 12, 1971, p. 157) attacking not only the participants of the conference on the transcript of which this volume is based, but also the conference itself, the subject to which it was devoted was not mentioned or even hinted at. Soviet sensitivity on this matter makes itself felt in many ways; for instance, the 1970 Russian guidebook to the Moscow Rublyov Museum has the censor's permission number on the last page, but the similar guidebook in English, French and German (as with most Soviet books mainly intended for foreigners) does not.

[6] Under Khrushchev there was relatively little *samizdat*, perhaps in part because the censorship was tending to become more relaxed or, towards the end, because it was hoped that it would not become significantly more stringent. Compare, for example, Paustovsky's introduction to A. Grin's *Zolotaya tsep. Doroga nikuda* (The Golden Chain. The Road to Nowhere), Moscow, Izvestiya, 1960, with what he had been able to publish in his introduction to Grin's *Izbrannoye* (Selected Works), Moscow, Gosudarstvennoye izdatelstvo khudozhestvennoy literatury, 1956. Not surprisingly, criticism of the Soviet censorship system, usually presented as an appeal for more *glasnost*, is a frequent subject of later *samizdat* writings, e.g., Solzhenitsyn's open letter (*Grani*, No. 66, 1967, pp. 162–167) to the Fourth Soviet Writers' Congress and several responses to it by other authors (pp. 64–81 of *Solzhenitsyn. A Documentary Record*, ed. L. Labedz, London, Allen Lane, The Penguin Press, 1970); A. D. Sakharov's *Razmyshleniya o progresse, mirnom sosushchestvovanii i intellektualnoy svobode*, Frankfurt, Posev, 1968 (Progress, Coexistence, and Intellectual Freedom, London, Deutsch, 1968); and also G. Svirsky's speech in January, 1968 (*Posev*, No. 9, 1968, pp. 55–58; translation on pp. 283–289 of *In Quest of Justice* [see footnote 7 immediately below]); A. Antipov's essay "Ot brozheniya umov — k umstvennomu dvizheniyu," *Vestnik russkogo studen-*

vi

analyse the results,[7] the participants in the symposium which follows discuss the Soviet censorship network itself and hope thereby to shed new light on the régime and contribute to a greater understanding of the situation and atmosphere in which Soviet intellectuals live and work. All the major participants in the conference decided to settle in the West after the Sinyavsky-Daniel trial in 1966 and its aftermath made it apparent that they could work more productively here than in their native country. As very recent émigrés who still keep as closely in touch as possible with developments in the Soviet Union, they express views and attitudes which deserve serious attention. The symposium was organized by the Institute for the Study of the USSR in cooperation with Radio Liberty.

The reader will notice that the speakers are by no means in complete agreement with one another; occasionally a participant may even appear to contradict himself. They are agreed, however, that the Soviet censorship system cannot be understood if taken in isolation; it should rather be seen as a crucial part of the Soviet régime *in toto* and regarded as a section of the Soviet publishing and editorial network in particular.[8] Thus it would have been exceptionally inappropriate if any attempt had been made to "edit" or "censor" out any disagreements and contradictions which arose during the proceedings; it even seemed better to translate the verbatim report (Russian was the only language used at the conference) a shade too literally than to be too "free" in our treatment of the record.

It is hoped, nonetheless, that what follows can be read easily as well as profitably. The notes, for which the editors bear responsibility, supply references to works mentioned and provide suggestions for further reading; only the initialled footnotes were written in consultation with the speakers, but thanks are due to all the major participants for their assistance in the realisation of this project.

---

cheskogo khristianskogo dvizheniya, Paris, No. 93, 1969, pp. 89–92; and N. Aleksandrov, "Nasha korotkaya pamyat," *ibid.*, No. 94, 1969, pp. 62–65. It should however be noted that *samizdat* protests against the censorship were also made under Khrushchev: see M. A. Naritsa's letter of September, 1960 (*Grani*, No. 51, 1962, pp. 9–12); the article by 'N. Gavrilov' in *The New Leader*, December 9, 1963, pp. 14–18; and the "Letter from a Russian Writer" in *Encounter*, June, 1964, pp. 88–98.

[7] The largest collection of *samizdat* materials in English is that edited by A. Brumberg, *In Quest of Justice : Protest and Dissent in the Soviet Union Today*, London, Pall Mall Press, 1970.

[8] The considerable overlap of the editor's and the censor's functions is clear from such works as Lidiya Chukovskaya's "Rabochy razgovor," *Literaturnaya Moskva*, No. 2, 1956, pp. 752–779, and her subsequent book *V laboratorii redaktora* (second edition), Moscow, Iskusstvo, 1963.

As time goes on it becomes increasingly difficult to see any real difference between "peaceful coexistence" and the "cold war." Until the rulers of the USSR come to accept the notion of peaceful *ideological* coexistence the Soviet censorship seems bound to play a vitally important, if negative, role in the intellectual life of a large part of the world. What follows is intended to be a general survey of this problem.

Martin Dewhirst

What is the Soviet Censorship?

Max Hayward:

Our symposium opens with a talk on the nature of the Soviet censorship by Arkady Belinkov, who has considerable personal experience of the actual system. He is also the author of an excellent book on the writer Yury Tynyanov, the second edition of which was published in Moscow in 1965. This work is both a penetrating study in its own right and a brilliant piece of Aesopian art; there can be few literary critics in the Soviet Union who would have cared to run the risk of making the daring statements we find on many of its 635 pages. I cannot think of anyone better qualified to launch our discussion.

Arkady Belinkov:

It should be said at the outset that censorship as practised in the Soviet Union is a new phenomenon in the history of thought control. Before it emerged, dictatorial societies, from antiquity onwards, had been concerned merely to repress heretical opinions, whereas the Soviet Communist Party has introduced a system so thorough that it not only censors a writer but dictates what he shall say. The result is that the great Russian literary tradition has been all but destroyed: the Soviet writer has to submit to the dictates of "socialist realism" with its demand for works propagandising such utilitarian objectives as increased production in agriculture or better service in laundries. This type of "creativity," performed under the surveillance of the censor, has debased literary standards and brought onto the scene one of the most stultifying influences on Soviet writers, namely, the "positive hero." Official insistence that Soviet authors must create positive characters who are successfully engaged in the construction of communism and who, as glowing examples of the new "Soviet Man," inevitably triumph over their adversaries, has produced this hitherto-unknown form of censorship entrusted with the function not merely of forbidding a writer to say certain things or restricting his activity, but of actually shaping the entire literary process. On top of this comes the fact that from the very beginning the writer is surrounded and conditioned by the ideology that has spawned this censorship. If someone sets out to write a book with the best intentions, but knows in advance that it will be banned or mutilated because of its subject or plot, or because of the way in which the plot is resolved, or because the conflicts which arise in the course of the development of the plot are "unsuitable," he is confronted not by censorship in the usual sense of the word, but by the all-embracing phenomenon of the Soviet dictatorship itself. Indeed, it is not the Soviet censorship that has destroyed one of the greatest literary traditions any nation has ever produced—it is this Soviet dictatorship. The censor has only played a minor role. The overwhelming majority of books which have not been published in the Soviet Union were not destroyed by the censor, but were ruined during the very process of their creation, either at the manuscript stage or when they reached the editor's desk. I know of countless occasions when manuscripts have been destroyed by editors, but I can only count on my fingers the number of cases, all publicized internationally, of direct persecution by the censor.

As we embark upon our discussion of the nature of the Soviet censorship, we need to remember that it is both an instrument created by a dictatorship and a reflection of that dictatorship; it is impossible to dissociate the two.

I think the entire history of Soviet literature illustrates clearly enough the effects of this new Soviet form of censorship which arrogates to itself the right to "recommend" or prescribe what an author shall write if he is to be regarded as ideologically reliable. This attempt to dragoon Soviet writers reached its peak after the literary purge introduced by the Party Central Committee resolution of August 14, 1946, the purpose of which was expounded by Andrey Zhdanov at a subsequent meeting of Leningrad writers.[1] Each period of a nation's history is to a certain extent a continuation of its previous history, but Soviet history has one unique feature. Until the October Revolution of 1917, Russia, a country sharing many features common to all monarchical systems, was still fairly remote from the democratic ideals current in the West. But from the beginning of Alexander II's reign up to World War I (with some exceptions during the Pobedonostsev period), the country was alive with high hopes for democracy. Even during the reigns of Alexander I and Nicholas I there had been a positive, reformist movement, pitting itself against sheer negative reaction. Yet the Soviet system insisted on salvaging from the past that most repulsive of reactionary institutions—the censorship.

At this point perhaps I may offer some historical parallels. In 1826, for example, when the manuscript of "Boris Godunov" was presented to Nicholas I with the help of the poet Vasily Zhukovsky, the monarch inscribed in his own hand: "I would consider the aim of Mr. Pushkin to be

---

[1] See *Bolshevik*, Nos. 17–18, 1946.

accomplished if he cleaned up his comedy and rewrote it as an historical tale or novel in the manner of Walter Scott."[2] Another example which shows that this Tsar was a direct ancestor of the Soviet orthodox literary critic who upholds "socialist realism" is provided by a letter he wrote to the Tsarina in 1840. (It was published for the first time in Russian a century later in *Literaturny kritik* (Literary Critic), which was closed down shortly afterwards.[3]) This incredible letter deals with Lermontov's *A Hero of Our Time*. The august critic found the work "repulsive, every bit as bad as contemporary foreign novels, and likely to corrupt its readers' morals and character. The author, no doubt because of his perverted mind, makes one despite and hate humanity! The hero of the novel is of course Maksim Maksimych, and there are many 'real' people like him in the Caucasian corps, but the writer was incapable of showing him in all his nobility and simplicity. Lermontov is more concerned with contemptible and uninteresting characters about whom it would be better not to write anything at all." Nikolay Pavlovich ends by suggesting that Lermontov might "clear his head" if he found himself in Maksim Maksimych's company and wishing him a good journey to the Caucasus [into exile].

Soviet history chose what it wanted from the past: it chose Ivan the Terrible, Peter the Great, Nicholas I and various outstanding patriotic figures from such fields as sociology and liberalism. Soviet literary scholars have accomplished a great deal in fifty years, not all of it repugnant, although things of true merit are few and far between. Textual studies of Pushkin, for example, have been developed almost into a science and can be credited with important achievements. Soviet scholars have restored more meaningful forms to classical Russian literature, which began in, say, the 1730s with Trediakovsky's *Novy i kratky sposob k slozheniyu rossiyskikh stikhov* (New and Brief Method for the Composition of Russian Verses) and Lomonosov's *Pismo o pravilakh rossiyskogo stikhotvorstva* (Letter on the Rules of Russian Versification), and continued up to 1917. The original texts of works by Herzen and Turgenev have been restored, freeing them from the distortions of the Tsarist censorship, and it is now planned to do the same for Dostoyevsky and many other Russian classics. Nowadays this work is highly sophisticated and scientific, even including the use of computers, which greatly facilitate the handling of texts. Many of the

---

[2] See p. 612 of Vol. 5, 1957, of *A. S. Pushkin. Polnoye sobraniye sochineny v desyati tomakh.*

[3] See B. Eykhenbaum's article "Nikolay I o Lermontove," *Literaturny kritik*, No. 2, 1940, pp. 32–34, for a partial translation from the German of this letter. For a better and fuller translation see pp. 100–102 of Emma Gershteyn, *Sudba Lermontova*, Moscow, 1964 (the French original is on pp. 467–468 of this book).

Tsarist censors' deletions have been restored, and this has added to the lustre of Russian nineteenth-century literature, which still, of course, remains essentially the same, as the original censors had interfered relatively little with these works.

If, however, the same painstaking method of correcting the censor's distortions were to be applied to Soviet literature, different works would emerge, because Soviet censorship has consistently mutilated manuscripts to such a degree that it has transformed them into works quite opposed to their authors' intentions. Here I must remind you that the Main Board for the Protection of Military and State Secrets in the Press (*Glavlit*)—which was formally and finally established in 1922 with Lebedev-Polyansky as its first director, initially as a division of the People's Commissariat of Enlightenment under Lunacharsky—is merely *one* of the institutions in the total Soviet system of censorship and thought control.[4] Let me rather give you an example of the *unofficial* censorship, which I consider to be much more important than such official institutions as *Glavlit*.[5] In the autumn of 1956, after failing to get in to hear a discussion of Dudintsev's novel

---

[4] For (1) the 1922 Statutes (*Polozheniye*) of *Glavlit*, (2) the Instruction from *Glavlit* to its local organs, (3) the Rules (*Postanovleniye*) governing the maintenance of typographies, (4) the decree (*Postanovleniye*) on "The Method of Opening Printing Enterprises and their Surveillance" and (5) the 1923 Instruction (*Instruktsiya*) from the People's Commissariat of the Interior "On the Manner of the Issuance of Permits for Trading in Printing Machines and Type and the Opening of Printing Enterprises," see pp. 307–314 of *Letters from Russian Prisons*, published for The International Committee for Political Prisoners, London, 1925. (These translations are imperfect.) The originals of (1), (3), (4) and most of (2) are published in L. Fogelevich, *Deystvuyushcheye zakonodatelstvo o pechati*, Moscow, Yuridicheskoye izdatelstvo NKYu RSFSR, 1927, pp. 31–33, 160–161, 161–162 and 33–34 respectively. (5) was superseded in 1926 by a document (*Instruktsiya*) published by Fogelevich (1927 edition) on pp. 162–165. See also pp. 3–5 of this edition on the functions at this time of the *Otdel Pechati TsK* and the *Komitet po delam pechati pri SNK SSSR* (until then this Committee had been attached to the *Narkomtorg*). For circulars and orders issued between 1929 and 1935 calling on *Glavlit* employees (plenipotentiaries) to tighten up their control of works submitted for publication, see pp. 115–117 of L. Fogelevich, *Osnovnyye direktivy i zakonodatelstvo o pechati*, Moscow, OGIZ, 1935.

[5] For the Secrets Law of 1956 (which now appears to be the ostensible *raison d'être* of *Glavlit*) see Supplement 47 of B. Gorokhoff's *Publishing in the USSR*, Indiana University Publications, 1959, or pp. 61–63 of *The Politics of Ideas in the USSR*, ed. Robert Conquest, London, The Bodley Head, 1967. (Russian text in *Ugolovny kodeks RSFSR*, Moscow, 1957, pp. 143–145; see also pp. 116–118.) Note the entry *Gosudarstvennaya tayna* on pp. 76–77 of the *Entsiklopedichesky slovar pravovykh znany*, Moscow, 1965, and article 75 (*Razglasheniye gosudarstvennoy tayny*) on p. 37 of the *Ugolovny Kodeks RSFSR*, Moscow, 1970 (this edition does not contain the apparently still valid 1956 Secrets Law, which may itself now be

Ne khlebom yedinym (Not by Bread Alone),[6] I walked slowly with a group of other people to the Arbat underground station, discussing the usual literary subjects. Among us was an old and very famous author who remarked to me: "What I'm going to say will not be published in my memoirs, although I might write it down. But perhaps in ten or fifteen years you will write about it or tell someone." Some fifteen years have passed and I am telling you. The author related the following incident:

> In 1954 we were all sitting in my dacha in a state of confusion, unable to grasp what was happening. Things were being written that we ourselves were writing thirty years before; everything was strange and unfamiliar. How should one write? What should one write? Everything was incomprehensible. And then Kostya, Viktor and Sasha said to me, "Listen, go to *him* and explain. Let *him* tell you." I went to *him* and said, "Look, some write this, others write that. We are at a loss to know what to do. Guide us, as we have always been guided." And he replied, "No, that's your business. You are master in your own literary house. Do what you think is necessary. The time of the personality cult is over and will never return."

The "business" referred to was Soviet literature, Kostya was Fedin, Viktor was Shklovsky and Sasha was Bek. The person who told me this story was Ilya Ehrenburg, and *him* was Khrushchev.

I quote this incident to show that the writers themselves share the blame. The tragedy of Soviet Russian literature exists, it is not just a consequence of the censorship, and the latter's misdeeds should not be exaggerated. Most of the blame attaches to the Soviet dictatorship which created the censorship along with the rest of the system, and which is mainly responsible for the vices of Soviet literature.

Now I shall sketch in some historical background. It was quite a long time after the outbreak of the French Revolution of 1789 before the first decree on censorship came out.[7] The October Revolution and the resulting Soviet régime were, of course, more radical than the French and succeeded in accomplishing much more in a shorter time: the Soviet régime imposed

---

regarded as secret). For the Decree on State Secrets of April 27, 1926, see L. Fogelevich, *Deystvuyushcheye zakonodatelstvo o pechati*, Moscow, 1927, pp. 34—35 (also in L. Fogelevich, *Osnovnyye direktivy i zakonodatelstvo o pechati*, Moscow, OGIZ, 1935, p. 113). Since 1966 *Glavlit* has stood for the Main Board for the Protection of State Secrets in the Press (see note 99 on page 65), but this does not seem to be generally known even to participants at this conference.

[6] *Novy mir*, Nos. 8–10, 1956. Since then only a recensored edition has been published in the Soviet Union. For a report on the discussion see *Literaturnaya gazeta*, October 27, 1956.

[7] See for instance Henri Welschinger, *La Censure sous le Premier Empire, avec documents inédits*, Paris, Charavay Frères Editeurs, 1882, and the review of this book by A. Gradovsky, *O svobode russkoy pechati*, St. Petersburg, Gershunin [1905], chapter 8.

censorship by the third day after it came to power, and the first decree was published on October 28, 1917 (old style) by the Council of Peoples' Commissars and applied to everything printed after this date. Part of the decree reads:

> It is common knowledge that the bourgeois press is one of the most powerful weapons in the hands of the bourgeoisie. Especially at this critical moment, when the new government of workers and peasants is consolidating its power, it is impossible to leave this weapon wholly in the hands of the enemy, because at the present time it is no less dangerous than bombs and machine-guns. For this reason, we have taken these temporary and extraordinary measures for the suppression of torrents of filth and slander in which the yellow and green press would gladly drown the young victory of the people.[8]

Although the decree listed everything that was to be suppressed, it was still considered inadequate, and a week later Lenin stated: "We announced earlier that if we took power we would close the bourgeois newspapers. To tolerate the existence of these newspapers means to cease being socialist."[9]

---

[8] See the Decree on the Press, signed by Lenin and dated October 27, 1917 (old style), published in *Pravda* the following day. (Also on pp. 24–25 of *Dekrety sovetskoy vlasti*, Vol. 1, Moscow, 1957.) Almost fifty years later A. Bek suggested that it was time to end these "temporary and extraordinary measures," permit all citizens to express all their opinions, and introduce a law on the press, perhaps modelled on the one in Czechoslovakia, so that writers would know what was and what was not permitted (*Zhurnalist*, No. 2, 1967, p. 15). A cut version of the Czechoslovak law of October 25, 1966, was published on pp. 48–49 of *Zhurnalist*, No. 6, 1967, but no progress appears to have been made on this matter in the USSR even before events in Czechoslovakia in 1968 indicated that political censorship of the mass media is essential if the present Soviet and Soviet-type systems are to be preserved.

[9] Lenin's speech on the press at the meeting of the All-Russian Central Executive Committee on November 4, 1917 (old style). See V. I. Lenin, *Polnoye sobraniye sochineny*, 5th edition, Vol. 35, Moscow, 1962, pp. 53–55 and also pp. 51–52. English translation in his *Collected Works*, Vol. 26, Moscow, 1964, pp. 284–286; and also p. 283 and note 111 on p. 558. The Revolutionary Military Committee decided on October 26 (old style), i.e., the day after the October Revolution began, to close down a number of "bourgeois" newspapers like *Rech* and *Den*. The Council of People's Commissars adopted the Decree on the Press (see note 7 above) the following day. For a good idea of the arguments about censorship at this time see *Dekrety sovetskoy vlasti*, Vol. 1, Moscow, 1957, pp. 43–44, and John Reed, *Ten Days That Shook the World*, New York, Vintage Books, 1960 (this edition includes documents and helpful notes by Bertram Wolfe), especially pages 230, 249–252, 353–358, 365 and 391–392. Pp. 391–392 have an almost complete translation of the exceedingly important Decree on the Introduction of a State Monopoly of Advertisements, published on November 8, 1917 (old style). The Decree (also printed on pp. 210–211 of *Sovetskaya pechat v dokumentakh*,

But even this was not enough, and it was not long before the "Revolutionary Tribunal for the Press" was set up.[10] At once ideological and political dissenters began to be put on trial and imprisoned, and the censorship became a punitive organ, transformed from an ordinary ideological instrument into one of the instruments for suppressing opposition to the state. The decree announcing the establishment of this Tribunal openly proclaimed: "As part of the Revolutionary Tribunal, a Revolutionary Tribunal for the Press is to be established. The crimes and misdemeanours committed against the people through the medium of the press are to be under the jurisdiction of this Revolutionary Tribunal for the Press."[11] This was subsequently formulated in the Criminal Code of the RSFSR (at present as Article 70), and social and political protests thereby became ideological offences and criminal acts. The result was a series of exiles, deportations and executions, including the deportation abroad of such well-known figures as Berdyayev and Frank, the execution of Gumilyov and the emigration of numerous other writers. In the course of fifty years the system has been refined and perfected, but despite an occasional slackening of the reins it is no less obvious that Soviet power and ideological persecution are inseparable.

Moscow, Gosudarstvennoye izdatelstvo politicheskoy literatury, 1961) forbade on pain of closure any Russian non-Soviet publications to accept payment for printing any advertisements. Further details on this on pp. 54–57 of *Dekrety sovetskoy vlasti*, Vol. 1, Moscow, 1957.

[10] Enacted on January 28, 1918 (old style). Published on pp. 432–434 of *Dekrety sovetskoy vlasti*, Vol. 1, Moscow, 1957. For examples of the forcible closure in December 1917 and March 1918 of "slanderous" and "bourgeois" newspapers see *ibid.*, p. 549 and *ibid.*, Vol. 2, Moscow, 1959, p. 569. By April 1918 all newspapers had to publish all the decrees and orders (*rasporyazheniya*) of the Central Executive Committee and the Council of People's Commissars (*ibid.*, Vol. 2, p. 50). See also A. A. Goncharov, "Borba sovetskoy vlasti s kontrrevolyutsionnoy burzhuaznoy i melkoburzhuaznoy pechatyu (25 oktyabrya—iyul 1918 g.)," *Vestnik Moskovskogo universiteta. Zhurnalistika*, No. 4, 1969, pp. 13–22.

[11] *Dekrety sovetskoy vlasti*, Vol. 1, p. 432. For more on the early period of Soviet censorship see: "Rasprostraneniye pechati v pervy god Sovetskoy vlasti" in E. G. Golomb and Ye. M. Fingerit, *Rasprostraneniye pechati v dorevolyutsionnoy Rossii i v Sovetskom Soyuze*, Moscow, Svyaz, 1967; A. Okorokov, "Leninsky Dekret o pechati" and Ye. Dinershteyn, "Reforma izdatelskogo dela 1921 goda" in Vol. 20 of *Kniga* (1970); Ernest J. Simmons, "The Origins of Literary Control," *Survey*, Nos. 36 and 37, 1961; and the summary of the *samizdat* collection of documents from 1917–22, *Sushchestvuyet li v Sovetskom Soyuze tsenzura?...* (Does Censorship Exist in the Soviet Union?...), in *Khronika tekushchikh sobyty* (Chronicle of Current Events), No. 14 (June 30, 1970). There is an interesting survey, "Zakonodatelstvo o pechati za pyat let," by M. Shchelkunov on pp. 172–188 of *Pechat i revolutsiya*, No. 7, 1922.

Dictatorship and censorship are one and the same in their broad and varie-
gated manifestations, and it is in the light of this that they should be studied.

The Soviet literary climate does, of course, vary. My generation wit-
nessed the gradual reimposition of ideological controls begun after the
appearance of Ehrenburg's novel *The Thaw* in 1954,[12] and the subsequent
alternating period of relaxation and repression lasting up to the May 1966
plenary session of the Party Central Committee, at which it was decided to
eliminate all manifestations of "sedition," particularly in Soviet literature,
in preparation for the forthcoming fiftieth anniversary of the October
Revolution.[13]

The essential change in the censorship after 1954, and even more so
after Khrushchev's revelations at the Twentieth Party Congress in 1956,
was that reprisals against an author were now primarily confined to literary
sanctions: an author was no longer imprisoned for something already
edited and passed by the censorship. This was extremely important because
it encouraged the writer to look for methods of getting past the censor. If
he succeeded, then at least his physical safety was guaranteed, and even
expulsion from the Writers' Union or destruction of the printer's type to
prevent a second edition, and so on, was trivial and insignificant. Now
that the writer has less fear of imprisonment and thinks mainly about how to
circumvent the censor, how does he go about it, and what punishment is
he likely to incur if detected? I would like to answer these questions by
quoting from personal experience.

I was ordered to write an article on Aleksandr Blok for the *Kratkaya
literaturnaya entsiklopediya* (Short Literary Encyclopedia), five volumes of
which have now been published. At that time, however, the project was in
its early stages; the general layout of the encyclopedia was being prepared
and so-called "model articles" were being written, among which was one
of mine. It had to be rewritten countless times so that together with a
number of other articles it could serve as a standard against which to
measure later contributions. At the end of the article I included a quotation
from a letter which Blok, already critically ill, had written to Chukovsky
on May 26, 1921, three months before his death, and which read in part,
"But now I have neither soul nor body. I am more ill than I have ever
been before.... But vile, snorting Mother Russia has gobbled me up like
a sow gobbling its piglet."[14] As this was a "model article" it naturally

---

[12] *Znamya*, No. 5, 1954.

[13] There is a good general survey by Maurice Friedberg of censorship during
the Khrushchev period: "Keeping Up with the Censor," *Problems of Communism*,
November-December, 1964.

[14] Aleksandr Blok, *Sobraniye sochineny*, Vol. 8, 1963, p. 537.

landed first of all, along with eight other "model articles," on the desk of the chief editor of the encyclopedia, Aleksey Surkov. Surkov then summoned Vladimir Zhdanov, head of the Section for Russian Literature, and a senior academic editor, Aleksandr Belkin, together, naturally, with the author of the article. The only one left to summon was Blok, but he had died about forty years before, so we had to answer for him and for Chukovsky, to whom this outrageous (from an official standpoint) letter had been addressed. Surkov reddened and with a sweeping gesture struck out the page containing this quotation. They then took the article out of my hands and gave it to Oleg Mikhaylov (a very talented young Soviet literary critic) to finish, whereby it lost its continuity and came to consist of two dissimilar parts joined together.[15] But at least I was not thrown into prison.

Thus, the most important thing is to get round the editor and censor, and if you succeed, you appear in print. A third edition of my book on Tynyanov did come out in June 1968, but since I had left the country it was confiscated. I know for a fact that six copies survived; when a book is banned, they never succeed in destroying every single copy. For example, from the window of the new *Novy mir* (New World) building we saw the issue of this journal for October 1966, which contained some of Simonov's war notes, being burned in the yard of the old *Izvestiya* (News) building. Nevertheless, some copies of this issue are still extant. Books are stolen in the printing houses and then sold, and several copies of the third edition of my book on Tynyanov have been stolen, of course. I am waiting with interest to see if anything may come of it. When the second edition of this book appeared, it had acquired the 200 pages that I had not succeeded in having printed in the first edition[16]—I had given up hope of ever seeing them printed, even in the sixteenth edition. The reason was this: if a second edition has been expanded and revised, the rule is that such alterations must be indicated on the title page, and the passages in question specially marked. The censor then checks these only. So we had to find ways of preventing the censors from reading these additional pages. When the time came to arrange the pages in the proper order for printing, friends removed the title page, so this second edition went to the censor to be approved for printing without one. The censor merely telephoned to check the name of the book, and everything was in order, but when it went to the censor a second time to be approved for publication there had to be a title page, so my friends took the usual typographical block and, instead of "expanded and revised edition," simply put "second edition." And this

---

[15] See Vol. 1 of the encyclopedia, cols. 642–645.
[16] Moscow, 1960.

is how the book appeared—with a title page saying only "second edition," although it is 200 pages longer than the first.

There are also other ways of hoodwinking the censor. Once, for example, I wanted to quote from an article by the poetess Zinaida Gippius (who left the Soviet Union after the Revolution) published in the émigré—and therefore suspect—newspaper *Russkaya mysl* (Russian Thought). In the footnote indicating the source, which was: "*Russkaya mysl*, ed. P. B. Struve, Sofia, 1921," I simply mistyped the date to read 1912, knowing full well that the censors pay little attention to works that pre-date the Soviet period. After it had passed the censor I made a note in the margin changing the date back to 1921, and because minor corrections of this sort are seldom sent back to the censor for approval, although strictly speaking they should be,[17] the footnote was published in full. When I was later asked which Struve it referred to, I said it was the astronomer.[18]

Writers evade censorship in completely unexpected ways. Take the *Kratkaya literaturnaya entsiklopediya*, on which I worked with people like Aleksandr Belkin, Vladimir Zhdanov and Yu. G. Oksman. The fifth volume came out very late because it contained three articles by my wife and one by me, and we had committed the treasonable offence of fleeing from the Soviet Union. When it finally appeared in print, these four articles all appeared under other names, since ours were anathema.[19] Leafing through this new volume, however, I came across an excellent article written by a very talented person named Ivlev, and in the bibliography relating to this article[20] I discovered my name. In Stalin's days you might have been purged for such a "slip."

There are, in fact, no insurmountable barriers and nothing which cannot be attempted in post-Stalin Soviet literature. Even today, however black the picture is painted, I maintain that if the censor makes some radical change in a work, one has to blame both the censor and the author who permits this to happen. Resistance is still possible; if one wants to do something, one can. If they delay publication of a volume for eight months in order to remove all mention of my name, and my name nevertheless appears, then all is not lost.

---

[17] See *O perepechatkakh i ispravleniyakh* (On Reprintings and Corrections), *Glavlit* circular of November 29, 1932, as published on p. 119 of L. Fogelevich, *Osnovnyye direktivy i zakonodatelstvo o pechati*, Moscow, OGIZ, 1935.

[18] 1793–1864.

[19] Mr. Belinkov's article, on Yulian Oksman, appeared in a cut version and signed "B. I. Kolosova" (the name of the cook of the encyclopedia's deputy chief editor, V. V. Zhdanov). Mrs. Belinkova's articles were attributed to various non-existent male writers, V. Savelyev, L. V. Akimov and N. V. Semyonov.

[20] *Obovaz.* cols. 448–451 of Vol. 5.

In conclusion, I would like to add one significant detail to my story about Ehrenburg. As we continued to walk along the road he suddenly stopped, took out his dentures and held them in the palm of his hand. This was somewhat unexpected and strange in the middle of a literary conversation. "Look," he said, clamping his jaws together, "all my teeth have gone. Why? Because I was afraid. All my life I have been afraid. I never went to the dentist." This is somehow symbolic of Soviet writers. They are frightened all their lives and end up with artificial limbs—because you might call Soviet literature an artificial limb of literature.

Herman Achminov:

Did ways exist of evading the censor or exerting direct pressure on him during the Stalin era? In your talk you somehow jumped from the beginning of the Soviet régime to the post-Stalin era,[21] but books were, after all, published during Stalin's time too. They were not printed as they had been written, but neither were they printed in exactly the form demanded by the censor. For example, I remember that there were a number of changes made in Virta's novel *Odinochestvo* (Loneliness),[22] and I should like to know how pressure was exerted on such a writer from above. And what pressure might have come from below, from the writer himself,

---

[21] For the decree (*polozheniye*) of June 6, 1931, on, and explaining the functions of, *Glavlit* see pp. 110–111 of L. Fogelevich, *Osnovnyye direktivy i zakonodatelstvo o pechati*, Moscow, OGIZ, 1935. For an important article on Soviet censorship in the 1930s see R. Gul, "Tsenzura i pisatel v SSSR," pp. 438–449 of *Sovremennyye zapiski*, 66, Paris, 1938. Gul distinguishes between four main controls over publication, *Glavlit*, *Kultprop* (culture and propaganda department of the Central Committee), *Litkontrol* OGPU (i.e., secret police surveillance and supervision both of writers and of officials employed in *Glavlit* and *Kultprop*), and Stalin (who keeps an eye on everyone). Other details, e.g., on the 1939 decree on the registration and ringing of carrier-pigeons (which presumably the postal censors found difficult to control) are on pp. 229–232 of I. Yevtikhiyev and V. Vlasov, *Administrativnoye pravo*, Moscow, 1946; pp. 387–388 of this book summarize the functions of *Glavlit* during the Stalin era. For a survey of the information on censorship at this time, as provided by the Smolensk Archives, see M. Fainsod, "Censorship in the USSR—A Documented Record," *Problems of Communism*, March-April 1956, and chapter 19 of the same author's *Smolensk under Soviet Rule*, London, Macmillan, 1958. See also A. Inkeles, *Public Opinion in Soviet Russia*, Cambridge, Mass., Harvard University Press, 1950, chapter 13, and also p. 233 for a note on the censorship of Soviet radio broadcasts, a subject not discussed at this conference. Soviet attempts to jam, censor and reduce or stop foreign broadcasting to the USSR also await study by future scholars. For an introduction to this subject see *The Politics of Ideas in the USSR*, ed. R. Conquest, London, The Bodley Head, 1967, pp. 58–61. There is a revised version of Gul's article in *Novy zhurnal*, 109, New York, 1972, pp. 240-257.

[22] Compare the 1937 (Goslitizdat) and 1957 (Molodaya gvardiya) editions.

during Stalin's day, let us say from 1927, when the Left Opposition was destroyed?

Arkady Belinkov:

Of course something was achieved even under Stalin. A chill darkness enveloped Soviet letters, but something was nevertheless created and there was some sort of literature. But I also think of what happened to such writers as Babel and Mandelshtam. Osip Mandelshtam wrote an anti-Stalinist poem[23] for which he was banished, and he died on the way to a concentration camp. No one was immediately imprisoned and no one died for composing an anti-Khrushchev poem.

As far as the facts about interference from censorship are concerned, if you look at the fourth collection of articles in the series called *Voprosy tekstologii* (Questions of Textual Criticism) published by the Gorky Institute of World Literature in 1967,[24] you will see something utterly appalling. It is quite understandable when they censor us, the participants at this conference who recently arrived in the West from the Soviet Union, but you would be staggered if you knew what torments they inflicted on loyal communist writers such as Furmanov, Serafimovich, Gladkov and Fadeyev. And so in the mid-1930s the almost complete destruction of Russian literature took place.

Many people still harbour certain illusions, assuming that it is the Central Committee or the KGB, the militia and the fire brigade, etc., who tell the writers what to write. This is not true. In the 1920s literature was bossed by commissars, but all that is past and it is now the writers themselves who give the orders. No one in the Central Committee takes a serious step without having sought the advice of certain writers and without having some sort of a proposal from them. My friend Andrey Sinyavsky was arrested on September 8, and Yuly Daniel on September 12, 1965. Daniel was brought to Moscow after long sessions of the presidium of the Central Committee. Two persons showed up at the Union of Writers before a high-level tribunal (one member was Voroshilov, the head of the seventh investigatory board for especially important cases, and the other was the man directly in charge of the Sinyavsky-Daniel case), together with their colleagues from the militia, to seek advice. They asked: "What do you think should be done? You are writers and you know better whether it is worth it or not and what sort of an impression it will make on world

---

[23] Osip Mandelshtam, *Sobraniye sochineny*, Vol. 1, Washington, D.C., 1967, p. 202.

[24] *Tekstologiya proizvedeny sovetskoy literatury*, ed. V. Nechayeva and A. Dementyev, Moscow, Nauka, 1967.

public opinion." The writers present answered with one voice "crucify them," and thereby sealed the fate of Sinyavsky and Daniel.

These high-ranking officials came to confer with the writers rather than just request a report because there had been a very unfortunate precedent in this respect, with dire consequences for Aleksey Surkov. When Belgrade radio (the first source of information on this subject in the Soviet Union) announced on October 23, 1958, that Boris Pasternak had been awarded the Nobel Prize for literature, Surkov was summoned to Khrushchev, who questioned him about Pasternak. Surkov said that Pasternak was a scoundrel and God knows what else, that his poems were always terribly anti-Soviet and his influence on Russian literature baleful. On the basis of this report the vicious Soviet campaign against Pasternak was launched, and of course it incensed world opinion. When the whole scandal erupted Khrushchev summoned Surkov, grabbed him by the collar, shook him fiercely and gave him a terrible dressing-down for failing to mention that Pasternak was a world-famous author.

Leonid Finkelstein:

There was an excellent article by Lakshin in *Novy mir*[25] on volume four of *Questions of Textual Criticism* in which the author writes that it would be good to see some work published on the "history of the text" of such works as Sholokhov's *Tikhy Don* (The Quiet Don), Fadeyev's *Molodaya gvardiya* (The Young Guard), Bulgakov's *Master i Margarita* (The Master and Margarita), and of some other works. How right he was!

Arkady Belinkov:

There has been textual criticism of both *Tikhy Don* and *Molodaya gvardiya*. Yu. Lukin wrote about the former;[26] he was the editor of *Tikhy Don*, and practically the author, so much time did he spend on it. In the last years of Stalin's rule the great task was to ennoble man, and according

---

[25] No. 2, 1969, pp. 247–252.

[26] See his *Mikhail Sholokhov*, Moscow, Sovetsky pisatel, 1952. See also on this, and for other examples of rewriting, two articles by Maurice Friedberg: "Soviet Literature and Retroactive Truth," *Problems of Communism*, January-February, 1954, and "New Editions of Soviet Belles-Lettres," *The American Slavic and East European Review*, February, 1954. The same author's book, *Russian Classics in Soviet Jackets*, New York, Columbia University Press, 1962, *inter alia*, analyses the publication and non-publication of nineteenth-century authors in the USSR. Dr. Friedberg's article "Soviet Books, Censors and Readers" (in *Literature and Revolution in Soviet Russia 1917–1962*, London, Oxford University Press, 1963, ed. M. Hayward and L. Labedz) contains some interesting data on the publication of Western fiction in the USSR. His survey "What Price Censorship?" (*Problems of Communism*, September-October, 1968) considers the *samizdat* phenomenon a

to Zhdanov Soviet man had to be depicted as a beautiful and noble creature, whereas Mikhail Zoshchenko had depicted him as mean-spirited and nasty.[27] That was false; all this "rubbish" had to be swept out of the corners of Soviet literature. Lukin did exactly this with Sholokhov's novel: he threw out 862 bits of rubbish, and the novel was purged by the injection of good everyday newspaper language. This was the transformation to which the novel was subjected in the spirit, *inter alia*, of Stalin's classic work *Marxism and Questions of Linguistics*.[28] This is how the Russian language came to be changed.

As you know, there are three versions of *Molodaya gvardiya*, and the fact that Fadeyev was forced to rewrite this work twice was a contributory, if not the main, cause of his suicide. The first edition of the novel was a fairly straightforward account, taken from real life, of a group of young people who organized underground resistance in the town of Krasnodon during the German occupation and were subsequently betrayed and executed. But the Party and Stalin himself did not figure prominently enough, so Fadeyev was compelled to revise the book, correcting these "errors." Unfortunately for the author Stalin died shortly afterwards and the book had to be rewritten yet again in a third version. This was too much even for Fadeyev. In the end, he shot himself in the heart at his dacha in Peredelkino on May 13, 1956.[29]

Yuri Demin:

I would like to add something to what you have just said. Once I was drinking vodka with a lawyer, a most interesting fellow of peasant origin

---

natural consequence of the oppressive control and censorship of the Soviet press. On the various versions of *Tikhy Don* see also D. M. Stewart, *Mikhail Sholokhov. A Critical Introduction*, Ann Arbor, The University of Michigan Press, 1967, Appendix B; C. G. Bearne, *Sholokhov*, Edinburgh, Oliver and Boyd, 1967, chapter 4; and G. Yermolayev, "Politicheskaya pravka 'Tikhogo Dona,' " *Mosty*, No. 15, 1970, pp. 265–289.

[27] See the "Doklad t. Zhdanova o zhurnalakh 'Zvezda' i 'Leningrad' " in *Bolshevik*, Nos. 17–18, 1946, and Rebecca Domar, "The Tragedy of a Soviet Satirist," pp. 201–243 of *Through the Glass of Soviet Literature*, ed. Ernest J. Simmons, New York, Columbia University Press, 1953.

[28] See "Marksizm i voprosy yazykoznaniya," pp. 114–171 of I. V. Stalin, *Sochineniya*, Vol. 3 [XVI], Stanford, 1967.

[29] *Pravda*, May 15, 1956, p. 3, gave alcoholism as the cause of his death. This newspaper later (August 29, 1956, p. 4) rebuked K. Simonov for suggesting (*Novy mir*, No. 6, 1956) that the first version of *Molodaya gvardiya* was better than the second. On the rewriting of this novel see V. Aleksandrova, "'Chistyat' verneyshikh" and "Posmertnyye ispytaniya 'Molodoy gvardii,' " *Sotsialistichesky Vestnik*, No. 1, 1948, pp. 15–17 and No. 1–2, 1952, pp. 20–22, B. Shub, "Humanity Deleted," *Problems of Communism*, No. 2, 1952, and V. Boborykin, "Biografiya romana," *Voprosy literatury*, No. 5, 1971, pp. 129–143. See also pp. 23 and 31–32 in this volume.

who had himself been in prison, and who was later employed as legal adviser by the Union of Writers. The conversation turned to Fadeyev, the lawyer telling me that the writer was terrified because people had started returning from prison, and the majority of arrests had of course taken place during his term of office as general secretary of the Union.

Arkady Belinkov:

Among those returning from the camps was an old friend of Fadeyev's called Ivan Makaryev. He was a very poor writer, so they put him in charge of the Union funds. Makaryev squandered all the money on drink, and Fadeyev rebuked him severely. In the course of their heated exchange Makaryev asked: "Did they give you a lot of trouble over my case?" "No, they didn't give me any trouble at all," Fadeyev replied. "Well, if they didn't give you any trouble, how did they find out anything about me in the first place?" The next day, at 52, Vorovsky Street, premises of the board of the Union of Writers, Makaryev waited for Fadeyev in the long corridor where the latter's office was situated, and when he appeared Makaryev slapped his face in front of a most dignified gathering. Fadeyev survived the slap in the face, but many other people were beginning to come back and since he was unable to face them, he shot himself. This was not the only factor contributing to his suicide, but it did play an important part.

To return to methods of evading the censor: One trick is to place something in a historical context, although this is not a foolproof device. You can say as many uncomplimentary things as you like about the age of Pericles, for example, but on the other hand there are many things you cannot say about other periods. If I write a harsh piece about Tsar Paul (1796–1801) or Nicholas I, for instance, the censor smells a rat and writes on my manuscript: "Why are you getting so emotional about Paul I?" or "Why are you getting so vehement about Nicholas I?" Here I should like to mention something that always annoys me. When people refer to what I have written in various articles or books, they usually stress my *penchant* for the Aesopian method, but I assure you that it was never my principal aim to criticize the present by writing about the past, and, indeed, no particular skill is required to write about Ivan the Terrible using a certain phraseology and certain similarities in order to suggest an analogy with Stalin. Anyone can do that. One ought to write about Ivan the Terrible as a forerunner of Stalin. It must be remembered that Soviet history is only a new chapter in Russian history, from which it has subsumed negative features. I never tried to draw an analogy between Paul I and Stalin or anyone else; there is the authentic Paul, with a direct line of historical development leading from him to Stalin. Therefore I urge you to distinguish me from writers of fables; I have never used Aesopian allusions or even associations. What I have written about is actual history and not just something similar to history.

Wasyl Miniajlo:

Perhaps you could explain one aspect of so-called Soviet "controversial works." A discussion on such works may appear in the Soviet press, the controversy seems to be approaching a climax, then it abruptly ends and you hear no more about it. One has no idea from the Soviet press how these controversies end. Perhaps the literary circles know, but the Soviet reader does not. Oles Honchar's novel *Sobor* (The Cathedral)[30] is a case in point. The literary critics gave it very favourable reviews, and then, in *Izvestiya* of June 13, 1968, appeared an article by N. Fed sharply attacking both the work and its author. After this the whole affair petered out. Apparently nothing happened to Honchar, but what finally happened to *Sobor?* If we assembled here do not know, then obviously the ordinary Soviet reader does not either.

Arkady Belinkov:

The Soviet reader knows much less. I have no information on the fate of the novel *Sobor* because I was not interested.[31] But I would like to mention that there was a serious open discussion concerning a literary work even in the late 1930s, in *Literaturny kritik* and *Literaturnaya gazeta* (Literary Gazette). The book in question was *K istorii realizma* (On the History of Realism) by Georg Lukács. Controversies have continued ever since, but none has ever reached a definite conclusion. This is quite normal, because if a book is considered really controversial it is condemned and withdrawn, and if it is not bad enough to be condemned, the discussion just fades out. The decision is taken by the Union of Writers and the Party Central Committee. I give them this order of precedence because I want to stress again the very important role played by a certain group of people within the Union without whom the Central Committee takes no action. The proceedings are quite informal and intimate; everyone concerned sits around in the office of, say, Suslov or Demichev in the Central Committee building, and it is Surkov, for example, who advises Demichev what to do, not vice versa, because Surkov knows more about it.

---

[30] First published in *Vitchyzna*, Kiev, No. 1, 1968. See also p. 30 in this volume.
[31] But see p. 30.

Herman Achminov:

How were such decisions arrived at before the death of Stalin? Take Valentin Ovechkin's *Rayonnyye budni* (District Workdays), which was published under Stalin.[32] How was it possible for this work to appear?

Arkady Belinkov:

On personal orders from Stalin, who decided what should or should not be published. I was in prison at the time, but I read later in the information bulletin of the Union of Writers[33] that Viktor Nekrasov, after strong opposition, had been awarded a Stalin Prize for his novel *V okopakh Stalingrada* (In the Trenches of Stalingrad), which was published under the title "Stalingrad" in *Znamya* (Banner) in 1946.[34] He received the prize in Stalin's office from Stalin himself, who had at first decided to award him a "First Class" prize, but then changed his mind and made it a "Second Class" one, saying, "I failed to take something into account."

Max Hayward:

Yes, it is well known that Stalin personally censored manuscripts. Leonov recalls how Stalin censored the manuscript of his *Russky les* (The Russian Forest)[35] and annotated it in red ink in the margins. He even had the copy that Stalin altered. But were there cases when censorship was evaded, that is, when a "subversive" book navigated all the obstacles and saw the light of day?

Arkady Belinkov:

Possibly, but I am not sure. I do know that certain books were permitted to pass the censorship so that they could serve as examples of how not to write. This apparently occurred in the case of *Dvoye v stepi* (Two People in the Steppe) by Kazakevich, which was printed[36] at the personal request of Stalin in order to show what could be done with a writer. Mikhail Zoshchenko told me this, and also expressed his belief that his own story *Priklyucheniya obezyany* (The Adventures of a Monkey) was passed for the same reason.[37]

---

[32] *Novy mir*, No. 9, 1952.

[33] On the little-known *Moskovsky literator* see G. Avis, "Moskovsky literator and the Dudintsev Debate," *Journal of Russian Studies*, Bradford, No. 18, 1969.

[34] Nos. 8–10.

[35] Published in *Znamya*, Nos. 10–12, 1953.

[36] In *Znamya*, No. 5, 1948.

[37] In *Zvezda*, Nos. 5–6, 1946. Zoshchenko had earlier got into trouble because of his "Freudian" reminiscences, "Pered voskhodom solntsa" (Before Sunrise), published in *Oktyabr*, Nos. 6–7 and 8–9, 1943.

Wasyl Miniajlo:

In 1961 Khrushchev was in Alma-Ata and made a speech in which he talked at length about Lysenko in a very approving way. The speech was not printed until three days later in *Pravda* (Truth),[38] and the passage referring to Lysenko and the justification of his agricultural theories had been omitted. The Party apparatus had obviously censored Khrushchev.

Arkady Belinkov:

Such things happened under Stalin as well. If I am not mistaken, it was in one of his first speeches at the end of 1941 that Stalin said, "Without our allies we shall not be able to vanquish the enemy." This remark was published in the press but never appeared in any subsequent collections of his *dicta*, not even in the monumental work which minutely records all his orders and decrees.[39] Shortly after the war he made a similar statement at a banquet: "Without the allies we would not have won the war." This, too, has never appeared in print.

Anthony Adamovich:

I am neither a Western-born sovietologist nor a recent arrival from the Soviet Union—I left my country a good many years ago. But I feel a great affinity with our new colleagues from the Soviet Union. I have also had

---

[38] August 26, 1961. His successor is also sometimes censored: see *The Daily Telegraph*, April 27, 1971, about two passages in Brezhnev's speech at the 24th CPSU Congress which were dropped from the version printed in *Pravda*. However, books by Brezhnev are now published without a censor's number in them. After the leadership change in 1964 substitute pages for 1965 desk calendars were distributed, marking Brezhnev's and Kosygin's birthdays and omitting Khrushchev's (BUP report in *The Guardian*, January 11, 1965). On the other hand the post-Khrushchev edition of Ozhegov's *Slovar russkogo yazyka* does not restore the sentence explaining the meaning of the word *khrushch* (cockchafer) printed in the 1952 edition but dropped in 1960 (*Khrushch—vreditel selskogo khozyaystva*, "The cockchafer is a wrecker of agriculture"). Khrushchev's "Secret Speech" has never been put on sale in the Soviet Union, which suggests that "de-stalinization" was always kept well under control. Even Lenin is censored, in the sense that not all of his works have been published in the USSR. For an example (though it is misdated) see a letter he wrote in 1922 to the Politburo, published with a commentary in *Vestnik russkogo studencheskogo khristianskogo dvizheniya*, No. 98, Paris-New York, 1970, pp. 54–60.

[39] I. V. Stalin, *O Velikoy Otechestvennoy voyne Sovetskogo Soyuza* (On the Great Patriotic War of the Soviet Union), Moscow, Izdatelstvo literatury na inostrannykh yazykakh, 1946. For some kindly references by Stalin to his Western allies see his *Sochineniya*, Vol. 2 [XV], Stanford, The Hoover Institution, 1967, pp. 8–9, 15, 19, 26–28 and 215.

some experience in the field of letters in the Soviet Union, in Belorussia, to be precise. From 1927 to early 1930 I worked for one of the Belorussian literary journals and it was part of my job to carry manuscripts to *Glavlit*. At that time things were much simpler and resistance to censorship was greater, and I am very keen to learn at this symposium what the situation was like afterwards. Perhaps I may be permitted to make a few observations relevant to the theme of this session, the task of which is to define the peculiarities of Soviet censorship.

When I was giving a course of lectures at Columbia University on the history of Russian literary criticism, I pondered on this question and decided that the best way to approach a definition of censorship might be to take as my point of departure the place that censorship occupies in the literary process. Two figures are involved here—the author and the reader. A reader who expresses an opinion about literature is *ipso facto* a critic; a critic who has the authority to alter the text of a literary work is an editor. An editor who is a government official with authority not only to alter but to ban the text of a literary work completely, is a censor. In the Soviet Union you have the editor fulfilling the functions of a censor, while the actual censor, himself an editor as well, has taken on a new function, that of "recommending" or "directing." Of course, censors performed this function before the Soviet period. As far back as the eighteenth century, Catherine the Great, who dabbled in literary criticism, was the first to introduce the concept of the "positive hero" (though she did not use this term), even issuing a directive indicating the traits she considered important in a positive hero of her day.[40]

---

[40] See the polemics between Catherine the Great and Novikov, especially Catherine's *Vsyakaya vsyachina* (All Sorts and Sundries) for July 3, 1769 (e.g. in *Russkaya proza XVIII veka*, Moscow-Leningrad, 1950, Vol. 1, pp. 300–301). The following translation of the crucial passage is taken from pp. 273–274 of Vol. 1 of *The Literature of Eighteenth-Century Russia*, ed. Harold Segel, New York, Dutton, 1967:

> The good-hearted author, in all of whose intentions, activities, and deeds there shines the beauty of the soul of a virtuous and chaste person, rarely touches on vices in order not to give offense to humankind by such an example. But proposing his instructions to others, he sets an example in the person of a man embellished with various perfections, that is, with virtue and fairness; he describes a devout observer of faith and law, praises the son of the fatherland burning with love for and loyalty to his sovereign and society, characterizes the peace-loving citizen, the true friend, the faithful protector of a secret and a given word. To this he adds the benefits flowing therefrom, and the sweet satisfaction felt by the person who preserves virtue in the fact that neither repentance nor the gnawing of conscience have a place in the heart of such a person. Here is the finest way to correct human frailties! Reading such a composition each person feels an inner exultation, adheres to virtue, having disdain neither for himself nor for the author. Without an accuser he himself attacks vices that he had followed out of imprudence. The prime object of the malicious person is to

Natalia Belinkova:

I agree with you completely when you mention the link between the reader and the censor, and as evidence I can quote an interesting statement made by the chairman of the "Lenin" collective farm in the Rostov Oblast, who, in his capacity as reader-*cum*-censor, helped to decide the fate of *Dr. Zhivago* and Boris Pasternak in the same way that some of the secretaries and members of the Union of Writers influenced the fate of Sinyavsky and Daniel. When they were hounding Pasternak in 1958, this collective farm chairman, whose name was G. Sitalo, wrote the following letter to the press under the heading *Pravilnoye resheniye* ("A Correct Decision"):[41]

> This year, our kolkhoz alone sold the state 1,250,000 poods of grain [1 pood = 36 pounds] and 200,000 poods of oil seed. In only nine months we have milked over 2,070 litres from each cow. From our total sown area of 17,000 hectares under cereals we have harvested an average of 24 centners [1 centner = 100 kilograms] per hectare. Our income...has already reached 41 million rubles.

> These figures may seem boring to an outsider, but to us they sound like a marvellous symphony. They represent a victory unprecedented in the history of our village, a victory for the toilers in the fields, our cattle-breeders, agronomists, livestock experts, engineers, mechanics, veterinary workers... who are serving their people and beloved country faithfully and loyally.... And now we have just heard the news that in his book Pasternak has slandered our country, our people, which was the first in man's history to build a new, socialist society. We love our literature, and we love our writers, and we are proud of their successes. Therefore we are happy to learn that Pasternak has been deprived of the high calling of a Soviet writer and has been expelled from membership of the Union of Writers of the USSR.

Wasyl Miniajlo:

When you say that the reader himself is linked to the censor, I think you mean here not the ordinary reader of novels, but the person who has been inspired or incited to criticize, such as the collective farm chairman you have just quoted. Are there no spontaneous critics who state their genuine opinions independently of the Party line?

---

vilify his fellowmen, to add to their vices his own, to abuse others and to rejoice in wounding others.

    We ourselves shall endeavor to follow this principle, and we invite others to do the same who feel that it is entirely just...

On censorship under Catherine the Great see chapters 3 and 4 of A. Skabichevsky, *Ocherki istorii russkoy tsenzury* (*1700–1863 g.*), St. Petersburg, 1892.

[41] *Literaturnaya gazeta*, November 1, 1958.

Natalia Belinkova:

I think that this other type of reader does exist, but I would say that the bulk of readers in the Soviet Union are "inspired," that is to say, they have been brought up to expect a book to reflect the virtues claimed for the Soviet socialist society by the authorities.

Martin Dewhirst:

Of course, this collective farm chairman had probably never read any of Pasternak's works.

Natalia Belinkova:

Do you think that even one of those writers who screamed for the blood of Sinyavsky and Daniel in the presence of the KGB and condemned their writings as anti-Soviet would have admitted that he had read them, even if he had? In order to denounce a writer it is not at all necessary to read his work.

Albert Parry:

They say that even Khrushchev never read *Dr. Zhivago*.

Herman Achminov:

Arkady Viktorovich [Belinkov], in fairness to the censor you pointed out that he himself is subjected to a higher-level censorship. But I would like to know if you intentionally refrained from stating that this superior censorship is the doctrine of Marxism-Leninism itself, which I feel is an independent factor tying the hands of the censor, just as it tied the hands even of Khrushchev.

Arkady Belinkov:

I did not ignore it. I took it to be part of the dictatorship to which I referred, and when I say "dictatorship" I assume that the main ingredient is Marxism-Leninism. I would even say that the Soviet Union is a theocracy, implying that Marxism-Leninism is a religion. Marxism-Leninism is naturally the most important factor in the censorship.

Leonid Finkelstein:

Natalia Aleksandrovna [Belinkova] was correct when she said that the reader in the mass has been deformed, and that the objective reader is in the minority. Half a century of Soviet literature, Soviet censorship, Soviet editing, or Soviet dictatorship—call it what you like—has so ruined the reader's taste that today he can no longer appreciate real literature.

Yuri Demin:

There was no need to ruin the taste of such readers—they did not have any. The younger reader in the 1930s was born a cripple, but later things changed, and after the war a new generation appeared with more feeling for literature. At least the young today have some understanding. They are seeking good literature, but are simply given so little of it. It is no coincidence that poetry readings by Yevtushenko and Voznesensky are so popular and fill auditoriums to bursting point. But take the person who went to the Rabfak [workers' faculty, to prepare workers and peasants for higher education] after the Revolution to learn to read, but afterwards worked on building sites, underfed and struggling to keep body and soul together. What use had he for literature? Today's reader, on the other hand, is fully literate and quite different. For his sake it is worth making an effort.

Wasyl Miniajlo:

What proportion of the masses can be classed as having some discernment, and what sort of person is easily induced to make such statements as came from the collective farm chairman quoted earlier?

Yuri Demin:

That man represents the very stratum of the population I was talking about first. These are people whose lives have been hard, who have toiled and believed in the Soviet ideal. In the Soviet Union as a whole, the cultural centres are only islands in the vast expanse of provincial Russia, where people still have faith in the Soviet régime. They do not particularly like the leadership, but they believe in the Soviet idea of equality and brotherhood, in all the slogans dating back to the French Revolution and displayed all over the country as part of the régime's propaganda. In the provinces they still believe in these concepts, not as much as before, but much more than the inhabitants of the major cities, which are hot-beds of radicalism. These "inspired" or, let us say, indoctrinated readers represent the bulk of the population, a complex mass to whom we give little thought, and about whom we know even less. What does "inspired" mean? It means that a person has faith in the Party and someone prompts him to say something, urging him, "Speak out! Don't be ashamed to speak your mind." We writers frequently suffer because workers and peasants, without realizing what is really at stake, simply support any measures proposed by the Party. It is not that the farmer or worker has to be induced to say something—he actually believes it; it comes from within.

Anatol Popluiko:

To digress a moment: I wonder if Mr. Belinkov can throw some light on Fadeyev's suicide. From what was published in the Soviet press shortly after his death, it appeared that the reason was the whole affair of his unfinished novel *Chernaya metallurgiya* (The Ferrous Metal Industry), which he was compelled to rewrite several times.[42] And my second question: you mentioned in conversation that you received many letters from readers after publication of the second edition of *Tynyanov*. Could you tell us briefly what they wrote and what your reaction was?

Arkady Belinkov:

The same thing happened with *Chernaya metallurgiya* as with *Molodaya gvardiya :* Fadeyev was constantly forced to rewrite it. Everyone had to do this, and some did not live long enough to finish the task. Pogodin, for instance, died before he had finished rewriting *Kremlyovskiye kuranty* (Kremlin Chimes) for the fourth time. The first version of this play largely centred on Stalin, the second on Lenin, but the third time it had to give equal prominence to both Stalin and Lenin. The fourth time it was not clear to Pogodin what he was supposed to do, but he died in 1962 before he could finish it, and only a few fragments were published. By then it had become an absolutely worthless work, bearing no resemblance whatsoever to literature.

In answer to your second question, I must confess that the letters I received from readers frightened me, because they did not grasp the metaphors in the book, though they did grasp the sociological and political essence, to put it delicately. I received many letters from readers and was always disappointed because they never asked me if I had succeeded in writing what I wanted to write. Instead, they asked, "How did you manage to get it past the censor?" Here is an example: the journal *Baykal* was to publish extracts from my book *Sdacha i gibel sovetskogo intelligenta. Yury Olesha.* (The Surrender and Destruction of a Soviet Intellectual. Yuri Olesha),[43] one of which contained the following sentence:

> In our day, contradictions arise between the artist and society. To disregard these contradictions would be rash. They are a product of the discord between socialist realism and an extremely realistic socialism.

---

[42] Chapters from this novel were published in *Ogonyok*, Nos. 42–45, 1954 and the *Biblioteka "Ogonyok"* series, No. 42, 1959. See also S. Preobrazhensky's article in *Neva*, Nos. 3 and 4, 1971.

[43] See *Baykal*, Nos. 1 and 2, 1968.

The publishing house in Ulan-Ude telephoned me in Moscow and asked me to remove this particular passage, although in fact it was much less provocative than certain other phrases. I did not omit it; I changed it to read:

> Even in our time, in exceptional cases of course, certain particular contradictions sometimes arise between the artist and society. Of course, they are immediately resolved, but to disregard them entirely would be premature. These insignificant contradictions, which are, of course, easily resolved, most frequently arise in connection with an insignificant discord occurring somewhere between socialist realism and an extremely realistic socialism.[44]

I added so many of these reservations that the statement acquired a completely different tone, and I even put brackets around it to make it appear less conspicuous. This illustration, incidentally, is one method that can be used to circumvent the censor. And the readers understood what I was getting at. In all the letters I received about this extract from my book the same question was asked: "How did you do it?" Only one person, here in the West, asked me: "Why didn't you say it openly?"

Herman Achminov:

Who was responsible for this censorship in Ulan-Ude?

Arkady Belinkov:

The deputy chief editor, Badmayev, a worthy individual who asked me to make these alterations with the best intentions. He did not censor my article; in fact he saved it from being scrapped altogether. This incident reminds me of what one might call the *regional* idiosyncrasies of the Soviet censorship. In Moscow you can write the name Genghis Khan, and, as long as you do not identify it with a specific period, no one bothers about it. In Ulan-Ude, however, which is very close to China, the name Genghis Khan would immediately attract attention, and so it is not usually permitted. In four cases I gave in and struck out this name, and once they left it in.[45]

When I say we succeeded in getting certain things past the censor I do not want to create the impression that we were victorious in the running battle with the censorship. I would certainly not consider myself a victor, because I received a death sentence for my first book, and for my three subsequent books I was sentenced to fifteen years' imprisonment. You cannot speak of "victory," but nevertheless books do appear, articles are published, and something is achieved.

---

44 *Ibid.*, No. 1, 1968, p. 104.

45 *Ibid.*, No. 2, 1968, p. 105, where he is compared to Hitler for the sincerity with which he believed in his own ideas.

The first defeat I suffered after returning home from prison was at the "Sovetsky pisatel" (Soviet Writer) publishing house, where I had to complete the personnel record card required of all Soviet writers. Apart from your surname there is also a space for a pseudonym, so I filled out the card and put "Belinkovich" as my pseudonym. I am a Jew, but I have a Russian surname—Belinkov—inherited from my great-grandfather. I was living in an anti-semitic country, so I decided to do what Sinyavsky did—I adopted a Jewish-sounding pseudonym. I fought for this pseudonym for about two years, but in the end had to capitulate, as I was faced with the choice of either abandoning my pseudonym or having a book suppressed.

J. René Beermann:

Open falsification of public opinion is also resorted to. When, for example, Aleksandr Yashin's *Vologodskaya svadba* (Vologda Wedding), published in *Novy mir* in December 1962, was severely criticized for its "negative" descriptions of life in a contemporary kolkhoz village, a letter appeared in the press,[46] purporting to come from Vologda collective farm workers and condemning Yashin for writing this story. The letter was a fabrication.[47]

Arkady Belinkov:

Yes, they do such things. Even the names of Party officials are sometimes appended to letters and articles in their absence, and so there are occasional scandals if they object to this when they return.

Max Hayward:

I think it is now time to end this discussion. I want to thank Arkady Belinkov for his excellent talk, which served as a most informative introduction to our symposium.

---

[46] *Komsomolskaya pravda*, January 31, 1963.

[47] See G. Radov, "Za napechatannoy strokoy," *Zhurnalist*, No. 6, 1967, pp. 16–18, and "Pishet selsky khod" in *Literaturnaya gazeta*, November 1, 1967. Something similar happened with F. Abramov's *Vokrug da okolo* (Round and About), *Neva*, No. 1, 1963: see the letters in *Sovetskaya Rossiya*, April 13, 1963, p. 2, and *Izvestia*, July 2, 1963, p. 3; with Ye. Dorosh's *Dozhd popolam s solntsem* (Rain as Much as Sun), *Novy mir*, No. 6, 1964: see the letter in *Selskaya zhizn*, October 7, 1964, p. 4, and Tvardovsky's reply in *Novy mir*, No. 1, 1965, p. 7; and with V. Tendryakov's *Podyonka — vek korotky* (The Ephemeron's Life is Brief), *Novy mir*, No. 5, 1965: see the letter in *Selskaya zhizn*, August 17, 1965, p. 4. On similar cases see the last page of L. Ivanov's article "O pravdivosti i printsipialnosti," *Sovetskaya pechat*, No. 3, 1965, and F. Kuznetsov, "Kritika nachinayetsya s kritika," *Zhurnalist*, No. 4, 1968.

Self-Censorship

Leopold Labedz:

We will now continue our conference with a session on self-censorship. Anatoly Kuznetsov will open the discussion.[48]

Anatoly Kuznetsov:

Self-censorship, in one form or another, operates in every writer. In the West it is simply self-discipline, but in the Soviet Union it is an ugly and unavoidable form of self-torment.

When I was still a "Soviet writer," I once experienced the great pleasure of writing without an inner censor, but it required a tremendous effort to cast off my chains and completely free myself. This was in 1967–68, when I was living in Tula.[49] I would bolt the door in the evenings and make absolutely certain that no one could see or hear me—just like the hero in Orwell's *1984*. Then I would suddenly allow myself to write everything I wanted to. I produced something so unorthodox and so "seditious" that I immediately buried it in the ground, because they used to search my apartment when I was away. I consider what I wrote at that time to be the best of anything I have ever written. But it was so extraordinary, so insolent, that to this very day I have not dared to show it even to my closest friends. In any case, this was a feast, an artist's spiritual feast. I do not know whether I will ever succeed in doing this again, but it was utter bliss. It pays to go on living for the sake of such moments.

In my novel *Babi Yar* there are three chapters called "They Burned Books," but only one was published in the Soviet Union.[50] I wrote about the burning of books in 1937, again in 1941 under the Germans, and then in 1946–47, after the Germans, but when the novel was published in

---

[48] A. Anatoli (Kuznetsov) has himself edited and published in Russian his contributions to this conference: see *Zarubezhye*, Munich, June 1970, pp. 7–15. See also his important statements in *The Daily Telegraph*, August 1, 4 and 7, 1969, and in *The Sunday Telegraph*, August 10 and 24, 1969.

[49] See *The Sunday Telegraph*, London, of August 17, 1969 for examples of what Kuznetsov was writing in his secret diary in 1967.

[50] See A. Anatoli (Kuznetsov), "Babi Yar," Posev edition, Frankfurt, 1970, pp. 126–131, 157–160 and 463–465.

Yunost (Youth) the censor included only the chapter about book-burning under the Nazi occupation. In my rejected chapter referring to 1937, my mother, while pushing dangerous books and papers into the stove, says to me, a young boy then, that it is terrible when they make bonfires of books in the public squares, but it is even more terrible when everyone begins to burn them in every home, out of fear. This happened all over the Soviet Union, and in our humble home as well. We destroyed everything, including Gorky, so that if there was a search they would not find a scrap of anti-Soviet literature. Under the Germans it was just the opposite—we burned everything Soviet. After the Germans we burned anti-Soviet literature again. It is loathsome when a political censor tears books to shreds, but it is even more so when every writer, out of fear, cultivates and develops this censorship within himself, and then starts to apply it to others.

Everything, without exception, that has been published in the Soviet Union bears the stigma of two censors: first the internal self-censor and then the external official censor. Only quite recently have I known the pleasure of seeing my work published as I wrote it; usually only half of what I submitted for publication was printed, and that was only a third or less of what I would have put to paper if there had been freedom of speech and the press. I was also at fault for being too cautious at the outset. But not everyone wants to commit suicide, and I was born and raised in a world where one must lie constantly simply in order to survive. I was very tenacious and have survived up to now, although my whole life has been a series of narrow escapes. This is apparent in my writings, where I have communicated ideas by means of allusions and images; yet, even after this self-censorship some of these allusions fell victim to the censor's scissors.

I will give an example of how this works in practice. Here is a passage from *Babi Yar*, describing the Nazi occupation of Kiev. I am travelling on a wagon through the forest to a village, along with a fugitive prisoner, Vasily. I wrote:

> I lay face upwards in the straw, watching the tree-tops float by, sometimes catching sight of a brown squirrel or a brightly coloured woodpecker, and thinking, I suppose, about everything at once: that the world is a vast place; that Vasili turned out to be right, that the murderous, all-destroying locusts kept to the main roads and centres, such as our city, where goodness knows what was going on—Babi Yar, Darnitsa, orders, starvation, Aryans, Volksdeutsche, book-burning; yet close at hand the fir trees were swaying gently in the breeze as they had done a million years ago, and the earth, vast and blessed, was spread out beneath the sky, neither Aryan, nor Jewish, nor gypsy, but just the earth intended for the benefit of people. That was it—for PEOPLE. My God, either there aren't people in the world any more, or else there *are* some somewhere but I don't know about them.... How many

thousands of years has the human race been living on the earth, and people still don't know how to share things out.

If only there was something worthwhile sharing. But in fact one beggar would hang out his old socks to dry and another beggar would come along and murder him for the sake of those socks. Can it really be true that the only thing people have learnt to do to perfection in the whole of their history is to murder each other?[51]

The editors of *Yunost* said to me: "Take back this manuscript, run home, and correct it quickly. Bring it back to us in a different form. It can't possibly be shown to anyone as it is." For the life of me I couldn't see any seditious allusions, but I crossed out the last paragraph about sharing socks and killing, and then brought the manuscript back to *Yunost*. Boris Polevoy, the chief editor, his assistant, Preobrazhensky, and others just laughed at me. They crossed out half the first paragraph and also discarded everything after "the fir trees were swaying gently." I began to argue and to defend every word. They would restore a word, cross it out again and then discuss it, and finally they risked including the next two lines in the paragraph, putting the final period after "for PEOPLE."[52] Anything further would be outright treason, they insisted. This happened to the entire book. There was nothing left of the broader humanistic idea, and the Soviet edition was just one more indictment of German Fascism.

A little further on in my story, after we arrive in the village and recount the events in the city, I described life in the village:

> They had had, it appeared, some good luck—there were no more collective farms. They had simply collapsed, and good riddance to them.
>
> There were no more farm bosses, nor any of the various officials and hangers-on who had made an easy living off the farms at the expense of the peasants. As for the Germans, once they had passed through no one had seen them again. There was just the village of Litvinovka and there were the peasant families, just as they were, and they didn't belong to the landowners or the Soviets or the Germans. Good God, when had things ever been like that before?
>
> So everybody started to live according to his own ideas. All around were fields which had not been harvested, and everyone selected a patch of land for himself, cut the corn, dug the potatoes and carried the hay. There wasn't enough room to store it all. And they ate and ate. Even the old folk could not recall it ever happening before that the village of Litvinovka had eaten its fill.
>
> They laid in stores for years ahead; the cellars were bursting with vegetables, the attics were piled high with apples and pears, and strings of dried fruits

---

[51] "Babi Yar," Posev, 1970, pp. 187–188. Translation by David Floyd, London, Jonathan Cape, 1970, p. 187.

[52] *Yunost*, No. 8, 1966, p. 40.

hung under the eaves; nobody forbade anybody to do anything, nobody took anything off anybody and nobody forced anybody to go anywhere.... The old folk crossed themselves and said the end of the world must be at hand.

In the evenings they would gather in the light of a taper for a get-together, chewing sunflower seeds till they were drowsy, and distilling spirit from beet. In the daytime you could hear the sound of chains clanking; the old men and women, the girls and the children were busy threshing the wheat. Then they would grind the grain between two big stones and pass the flour through a hand sieve. The village of Litvinovka was simply revelling in its good fortune.[53]

When I presented them with this they were naturally appalled, exclaiming: "Don't show that to anyone!" I deleted quite a lot, including such phrases as "the landowners or the Soviets or the Germans," and "officials and hangers-on...," etc., but the editors were still horrified and began to cross out a lot more. Their final version read as follows:

As for the Germans, once they had passed through no one had seen them again. So everybody started to live according to his own ideas. All around were fields which had not been harvested, and everyone selected a patch of land for himself, cut the corn, dug the potatoes and carried the hay.... There wasn't enough room to store it all. They laid in stores for years ahead; the cellars were bursting with vegetables, the attics were piled high with apples and pears, and strings of dried fruits hung under the eaves; the old folk crossed themselves and said the end of the world must be at hand.[54]

This is how Boris Polevoy edited it with his own hand; not one vivid scene was spared in the whole novel, and when this happens one loses heart. I published four novels under these conditions, and by the time I wrote my last novel, *Ogon* (Fire),[55] I was weary; it seemed as though these years of self-censorship had frozen my soul. Then, to cap everything, the censors treated *Ogon* even more ruthlessly than all my previous works. My inner censor had proved to be weak.

You can, of course, do a deal with the censors if you sacrifice your principles. For the right to leave a certain phrase in your work, or in order to have it published at all, you agree to "neutralize" it by inserting something edifying, hoping that the reader will sort out the wheat from the chaff. Thanks to this method, my first novel, *Prodolzheniye legendy* (Contin-

---

[53] "Babi Yar," Posev edition, pp. 192–193. Floyd translation pp. 192–193.

[54] See *Yunost*, No. 8, 1966, p. 41.

[55] *Ibid.*, Nos. 3–4, 1969. The author had become an unperson by the end of the year and so this novel is omitted from the index of works published in the journal in 1969 (see *Yunost*, No. 12, 1969, p. 108). (This had happened the previous year to Mr. Demin, another participant at this conference: his story *Odinoky los* (The Lone Elk) was printed in *Nash sovremennik*, No. 7, 1968, but is not listed in the contents for that year because its author decided to remain abroad.)

uation of a Legend), was published.[56] Although it is a realistic portrayal of
the hardships and horrors of the life of a building worker in Siberia, it ends
on a high-pitched, intensely optimistic note. The orthodox critics praised
the novel, and honest, intelligent people told me that they had enjoyed it and
realized that the "happy end" had been a condition of publication.

When *Babi Yar* was published as a book,[57] I wanted to restore some
inoffensive passages previously deleted by *Yunost*. The publishing house,
"Molodaya gvardiya" (Young Guard), at first protested, but later agreed to
some minor insertions, on condition that I added some anti-semitic nuances.
In *Yunost*, for example, the young narrator and a friend are looking for the
remains of the death camp at Babi Yar. Meeting an old man, they ask him
exactly where the Jews were executed and he rejoins with the sharp question:
"And how many Russians are buried here, and Ukrainians, and other
nationalities?"[58] The old man is merely reminding the narrator that it was not
only Jews who perished at Babi Yar. But the version suggested by the
"Molodaya gvardiya" editors had the old man *scream* his question[59] and,
spluttering with rage at the word "Jew," end it with a vehement "Pah!" It was
only at the last minute that I managed to have this final exclamation eliminated.

Another way of occasionally beating the censorship and communicating
something of value to the reader is to swallow your pride and cultivate the
acquaintance of influential people, even though you may secretly despise
them. Yevtushenko is quite adept at this, and on many occasions his work
has been published only because of his connections. Oles Honchar, the
former head of the Ukrainian Union of Writers, extricated himself from a
tight corner in the same way. He was under attack because of his novel
Sobor (The Cathedral),[60] but the Festival of Ukrainian Literature and Art
in the Russian Federation, to which he had been chosen as a delegate long
before, cropped up just in time. The delegation was headed by the former
notable scientist and member of the Ukrainian Party Central Committee,
Ovcharenko. Honchar made friends with Ovcharenko, who may be a sort
of minor Sakharov, and the *Sobor* affair was hushed up.

Aleksandr Solzhenitsyn and Iosif Brodsky do not cultivate friendships
with the high and the mighty. Yevtushenko does, as a matter of tactics,
and it enabled him to publish a poem branding the heirs of Stalin with the

---

[56] *Yunost*, No. 7, 1957.

[57] By Molodaya gvardiya in Moscow, 1967.

[58] *Yunost*, No. 8, 1966, p. 8.

[59] Page 6 of the 1967 book edition.

[60] Published in *Vitchyzna*, Kiev, No. 1, 1968. See also p. 16 in this volume.

help of these very heirs.[61] But there are dangers involved in prostituting yourself, of bartering away your conscience in that strange world of perpetual intrigues and constant self-censorship. It is the road to destruction, because the official, external, censorship, by engendering self-censorship and compromise, destroys the soul, destroys the artist and destroys the human being. I, personally, have gone down the road of surrender to the very brink of destruction, where I felt like either committing suicide or going out of my mind. I fled from the Soviet Union like an animal saving itself from a natural calamity: anywhere, but only away, away; otherwise—destruction.

A truly great Soviet literature cannot exist, because although there are many gifted artists, true genius is squandered. Genius is uncompromising, genius and villainy are incompatible, and that crystal purity, without which there is no genius, is absolutely impossible in the Soviet Union.

Aleksandr Fadeyev's suicide shook me to the core. His novel *Razgrom* (The Rout), 1927, proved that he had great talent, and who knows what an artist with his potential strength might have been able to accomplish under conditions of freedom. But he became the first assistant to the chief executioner of Soviet literature. The two versions of *Molodaya gvardiya*[62] and his unfinished *Chernaya metallurgiya* are good material for an analysis of his personality, warped by the system.

Pravda's explanation that Fadeyev's suicide was a result of alcoholism was a cynical lie.[63] I was among the first to arrive on the scene and his housekeeper told us that he had not had a thing to drink for two or three weeks. He had worked and taken many walks, deep in thought. On the morning of his death he told the gardener to prune the trees, and then retired to his study, where he shot himself. One of those close to Fadeyev was ·S. Preobrazhensky, the present assistant to the chief editor of *Yunost* and Fadeyev's biographer. He arrived before us and went into the study with the militia, who saw two thick envelopes addressed in the novelist's handwriting to "the CC CPSU" and "My Family." Preobrazhensky wanted to take the envelopes, but the police would not allow it, and they subsequently disappeared. No one, not even Fadeyev's family, knows their contents. Judging from the circumstances, a lot was written in these letters,

---

[61] See *Pravda*, October 21, 1962. For an account of how Yevtushenko published his *Babi Yar* see *A Precocious Autobiography*, Penguin Books, 1965, pp. 129–133.

[62] Compare the 1946 and 1947 editions with the rewritten version of 1951 and later. See also pp. 14–15 and 23 in this volume and also A. Bek, *Novoye naznacheniye* (The New Appointment), Frankfurt, Posev, 1971, pp. 114–123 and 153–154.

[63] *Pravda*, May 15, 1956.

and they were not composed in one day. The suicide had been soberly thought out long before.[64] I talked a lot about this with Preobrazhensky. He believes, and I agree with him, that fear of vengeance by rehabilitated writers whom Fadeyev had helped to repress under Stalin was only the last straw. The main reason for his suicide was the horror he felt towards himself. He had prostituted his talent and his feeling for humanity, and all that was left to him were the barren clichés of socialist realism. His conscience caught up with him and life simply became unbearable. His was a truly Shakespearean death.

Some writers turn absolutely cynical, of course, and self-censorship and dishonesty in their creative work become a part of their very flesh and blood. This breed of writers regards genuine literature with a pathological hatred, and the more honest and talented a writer they see, the greater is the fury with which they are prepared to stifle him. Others, realizing that they cannot survive without making compromises, resort to self-censorship, intrigues and concessions, but always within the limits of their conscience. They do this in order that at least something shall be communicated to the reader in their crippled works. By communicating anything, however little, they fulfil their mission. The third sort of writer is the one who makes great demands on himself. Refusing to make concessions, he does not play games with the censor, nor (so he thinks) does he practise self-censorship. His only chance of getting into print is the existence of *samizdat*, but far from all the extant manuscripts are printed even in this way. I spent a lot of time searching for such underground writings and discovered some excellent literature by certain young writers in Leningrad who do not recognize *samizdat*. They are an isolated, closed, circle who seem to write only for their own pleasure. They secrete their work somewhere in their desks and only if you have earned their deepest trust are you permitted to read one or more of their manuscripts. But you cannot take the manuscript away with you, nor are you allowed to make copies. They work only for the sake of creativity, but unfortunately this usually leads to the gradual extinction of their creative powers, because to enable his talent to develop and progress a writer must not only be free from any kind of censorship, he must also have readers. An audience nurtures talent, and if a writer does not have an audience his talent finally dries up.

This also happens to writers who at first succeed in their struggle to appear in print and acquire a public, but are deprived of it later by increasing censorship of their works. Promising writers whose work has deteriorated

---

[64] Preobrazhensky discusses Fadeyev's suicide in *Neva*, No. 4, 1971, p. 186. On this and on the attempted suicides of other Soviet writers see Yu. Krotkov's article in *Bulletin*, Institute for the Study of the USSR, Munich, No. 4, 1968.

almost beyond recognition because they have been forced to write for the "desk-drawer" include my friend Anatoly Gladilin, the Ukrainian poetess Lina Kostenko, whom many considered a second Lesya Ukrainka, and Vladimir Maramzin, a young Leningrad writer.[65]

So we see how the repressive influence of the Soviet régime pollutes even the bulk of "desk-drawer" literature. Even these noble projects are compromised by self-censorship, and only by comparison with the savagely censored published literature could these manuscripts be considered unrestrained. Although they write more freely than recognized authors, the majority of these clandestine writers cherish the secret hope that one day their works will suddenly be published, and they impose considerable restrictions on themselves. Whether it is submitted for publication and refused, or not submitted at all, much "desk-drawer" literature is subjected to the author's own censorship. He is aware that his home may be searched, and he censors his writings accordingly. Part of this underground literature appears in *samizdat*, but it is candid only within certain limits set by self-censorship. If the KGB were to assess a work that appeared in *samizdat* as anti-Soviet agitation, the author would most certainly dispute this. No matter where one looks, one sees varying degrees of self-inflicted censorship. In the topsy-turvy Soviet world some walk steadily on their hands, while others try to be semi-normal and walk on all fours. No one, or hardly anyone, walks on his own two feet.

One way of escaping self-censorship is to employ the oblique approach, cloaking the real meaning with allusions and images—the so-called Aesopian method. In no other literature is this device so prevalent as in Soviet literature, and at no time in history has the ability to speak or read between the lines, which many Russians learn in their early childhood, been developed to such a fine art as in the USSR. Indeed, by reading between the lines, the Soviet reader is able to discover things that the author never meant to say, while even the experienced reader can miss the point of an allusion. When I was still living in the Soviet Union, for example, I happened to come across a poem about a people named "I."[66] As I read the poem I thought

---

[65] Gladilin's latest book is *Yevangeliye ot Robespyera* (The Gospel According to Robespierre), Moscow, Politizdat, 1970; contrast his first major work, *Khronika vremyon Viktora Podgurskogo*, Moscow, Sovetsky pisatel, 1958. For a large collection of Kostenko's works see her *Poeziyi*, Smoloskyp, Baltimore-Paris-Toronto, 1969. Contrast Maramzin's stories in *Prostor*, No. 11, 1969, with the rather better "Ya s poshchechinoy" in *Molodoy Leningrad*, 1965, pp. 206–210. See also the *samizdat* works by Gladilin (*Prognoz na zavtra*, Posev, Frankfurt, 1972) and Maramzin ("Proch ot mesta katastrofy," *Russkaya mysl*, No. 2924, December 7, 1972, p. 4).

[66] See S. Lipkin's poem "Soyuz" in *Moskva*, No. 12, 1968, p. 197.

that the "I" people, whose praises the poet was singing, must be the smaller nations in general. After I came to London someone pointed out to me that the country in question was Israel! Even with my experience, I had completely missed the point of the poem. Not only had the censor failed to grasp the point, but I, the reader, had missed it too. I am sure that in my own works most readers failed to grasp what was being said between the lines. Take these extracts from *Babi Yar*, for instance:

> ...How dare they, what right have they, to claim to decide the question of MY life or death—
> of HOW LONG I should live
> of HOW I should live
> of WHERE I should live
> of WHAT I should THINK
> of WHAT I should FEEL
> and of WHEN I SHOULD DIE?
>
> I want to live so long that there will be no trace left of those people!
> I loathe you all, [dictators,] enemies of life; I scorn you as the most loathsome things which the earth has ever given birth to. You are cursed! Cursed! CURSED!
> ... Today one [two-legged] scoundrel arbitrarily makes one rule; tomorrow another one comes along and adds a second rule, and so on, until five or ten, and God knows how many more, may be conceived in the murky minds of the Nazis, [the N.K.V.D., the royalists, Marxists, Chinese and Martians, and all our other uninvited benefactors whose name is legion.]
> But I want to live!
> To live as long as is permitted me by Mother Nature and not by the two-legged degenerates. [67]

The entire novel is an indictment of all dictatorships and any kind of coercion of human beings. It is aimed not only at the former Nazis, but also against the present Soviet dictatorship. Yet from letters and discussions with many people I gained the impression that *Babi Yar* was generally taken only at its face value, that is, it was interpreted as an anti-Fascist novel revealing new facts about the atrocities committed by German Fascism and expressing concern lest revenge-seeking Germans might raise their heads again. But how could it be otherwise when I did not dot the "i's" and cross the "t's?" It is worse, of course, if your allusion passes over the head of the ordinary reader but is understood by the KGB, as

---

[67] *Yunost*, No. 10, 1966, p. 38. (Posev edition, pp. 427–428 and Floyd translation p. 421.) The first two words in square brackets were censored by *Yunost*. The sentence in square brackets was added later.

[68] In *Novy mir*, No. 4, 1968. The uncensored version, with a note on the interest shown by the KGB in this story, is published in *Novy zhurnal*, New York, No. 100, 1970.

happened to me after publication[68] of my story *Artist mimansa* (The Extra), which is an allegory in defence of the common man tortured by the state machinery.

In the Soviet Union you can never declare "the king is naked!" The closest you come to the truth is to say something like this: "By the way... the king is rather poorly dressed...that is to say, he has practically no clothes on." And they will most likely get you for that: "How dare you say that the king has practically no clothes on?" The desire to be able to say "the king is naked," the desire to be free, not only from official censorship, but above all from self-censorship, developed into an obsession with me. I did and do not see any possibility of writing freely in the USSR without being destroyed. Either they strangle you, or you strangle yourself. And here I would like to risk expressing some controversial ideas about things that it may be thought blasphemous to doubt. Believe me, I have thought about this a great deal, and I do have doubts. So before I proceed, let me stress my admiration for Aleksandr Solzhenitsyn, Sinyavsky, Daniel, and all the other writers who have so valiantly struggled and so tragically suffered.

Yet even these courageous writers exercise self-censorship. The high price (including prison for some) they pay is not for complete liberation from self-censorship, only for partial liberation. A writer in the Soviet Union is never completely free; he is always somehow choking himself and it is simply a matter of how tightly he fastens the noose. Utter cynics, such as the Mikhalkovs, Alekseyevs, Sobolevs and Polevoys,[69] tie the noose as tightly as possible. Others, such as Yevtushenko, Aksyonov, Vladimov and Bykov, are tormented by this noose and desperately thrash about, trying to loosen it. There are also writers who seem not to practise self-censorship and who are not persecuted. This is because they live in a state of loyal co-existence with the régime. The quiescent Konstantin Paustovsky appeared to be such a writer, but this is actually an illusion, and people who knew Paustovsky well said that his fate caused him great sorrow. He was constantly stifling himself. I saw him shortly before his death, and he said he desperately needed time to write a book about himself and his life, about how he had wanted to live, not how he actually had lived. He had experienced cruel times, surrounded by continuous horror, but he took no part in it. He remained aloof and wrote about eternal values. To write about eternal values while living under such conditions may be noble and heroic, but is it not somehow a terrible course for an artist to take—to observe and remain silent, to put one's hand over one's mouth in order not to scream? What is that if not the most cruel form of self-censorship?

---

[69] Soviet hack-writers.

I regard my own past silence as a crime. My own self-censorship was motivated by cowardice and the instinct of self-preservation. It is nothing to be proud of; I would even go further and say that no writer in the Soviet Union has anything very much to be proud of, not one writer! Even the great—Pasternak, Tsvetayeva and Akhmatova—practised at least the self-censorship of silence. And the contemporary poetess Bella Akhmadulina, who is near to greatness, writes almost only about eternal values and does not reveal her attitude to the Orwellian horrors surrounding her: the invasion of Czechoslovakia, the imprisonment of Sinyavsky, Daniel, Ginzburg and Marchenko, and much else.

Perhaps the greatest living Soviet writer, Aleksandr Solzhenitsyn, has every right to be proud of his work, but can we say this entirely without reservation? He speaks as an anti-Stalinist, revealing shocking details about the Soviet régime, but about the nature of the régime itself—the naked king himself—he says nothing. He allows us to draw our own conclusions from the complex pattern of images and allusions which he weaves, but by not stating his own conclusions he exercises self-censorship. At one time the Party allowed some of Solzhenitsyn's works to be published because they fitted in with the official policy of discrediting Stalin. When he began to take too many liberties they muzzled him, and he became a martyr for exposing the evils of Stalinism. But what about Lenin and Leninism, and communism in general? Solzhenitsyn employs rigid self-censorship when dealing with these questions.

I am only going to such extremes in order to show that no one in the Soviet Union, not even such an outstanding and seemingly daring writer as Solzhenitsyn, is free from the dictates of self-censorship. I sincerely hope that I am not interpreted as criticizing other writers in order to vindicate myself. In a letter that Amalrik wrote to me[70] he makes just such a charge—that I criticize everyone but myself. This is a misunderstanding. I have spoken about the horrors of Soviet reality and about the impossibility of writing creatively under these conditions. I have given examples of what happens to writers, including myself, who live under these conditions. I renounce all my books published in the Soviet Union, and also my tarnished surname under which these books appeared. I, too, was a dishonest, cowardly and compromising author.

I do not judge other Soviet writers; I only say that it is impossible in the Soviet Union to create without censorship, particularly self-censorship. It was because of this compulsory self-censorship that I was no longer able to live there.

---

[70] November 1969. English translation in *Survey*, Nos. 74–75, 1970, pp. 95–102.

Yuri Demin:

I would like to instil some optimism into what has become a rather sombre atmosphere. Every writer exercises self-censorship in some form or another; it may be either simply a manifestation of the writer's desire to comply with the existing norms, or the result of his instinct for survival. In the Soviet Union it is most often the instinct for survival.

Soviet writers can be classified into three groups. The first group, which I would describe as right-wing, accepts unreservedly and even justifies the prescriptions of the régime. As a result of this attitude, these writers live at peace with the system. The second group consists of those who do not agree with the prescriptions of the régime, but reconcile themselves outwardly, while trying at the same time to circumvent the rules and evade the censorship. The Russian liberals belong to this group. The third group, consisting of such writers as Solzhenitsyn, Akhmatova and Pasternak, rejects the régime and struggles defiantly against all that it represents. Although they are "rebels," these writers, too, are constrained by self-censorship. I do not see, however, that the quality of Solzhenitsyn's writings, for example, has suffered because of self-censorship. Self-censorship is most often simply a form of self-perfection that enables a good writer to write well rather than poorly. Every writer in his own way exercises self-censorship, but only inferior and vulgar writers suffer from it, because they fear the truth rather than vulgarity.

Because the term "self-censorship" is somewhat abstract, a discussion of it is inevitably rather general. But if one speaks of the Soviet Union in particular, it is true to say that people there live under very dangerous conditions. We live well here in the West; everything is peaceful and no one threatens us. Here, philistines can create brutal sex films or novels without exercising self-censorship, and no one does more than reproach them for it. But in the Soviet Union it is different. That country is controlled by a régime with dictatorial powers over every aspect of life. Censorship is a logical corollary of this régime, because without it the dictatorship would collapse within a week.

In the Soviet Union certain rules exist, with which some comply, which others try to circumvent, and still others defy. The most interesting thing for us to consider is how a writer evades censorship. The system of censorship does not operate according to set rules, because it is constantly adapting itself to new circumstances; this means that new methods of evading it are constantly arising. Here is an example: immediately after Solzhenitsyn wrote his letter on censorship,[71] I was told on good authority

---

[71] To the Fourth Writers' Congress. See pp. 64–69 of *Solzhenitsyn. A Documentary Record*, ed. L. Labedz, London, 1970, for full English translation. Russian text in *Grani*, No. 66, 1967, pp. 162–167.

that *Glavlit* had been abolished and that the editor was to be the only censor. This came as a shock, because the censors are laden with work, each one having at least ten manuscripts on his desk and too busy to process everything properly. But when the editor working on your manuscript becomes a censor, he deletes things that would normally be overlooked. Nevertheless, there will still be writers who try to find ways of conveying what they want to say to the public.

Kuznetsov said that literature cannot exist in the Soviet Union. I disagree: literature can exist anywhere. Incidentally, I think that the task of literature is by no means to *say* that "the king is naked;" that is the function of journalism. The writer's task is to *show* that the king is naked, and this is exactly what Solzhenitsyn, Pasternak and many others do. Literature can exist under any conditions. Soviet literature has been driven underground, but it continues to exist. Life under these conditions acquires its own specific character, which is reflected in the literature. Some writers survive in such an environment, others do not, but literature itself continues to live; it is suppressed, yet fights back. A kind of natural selection occurs. If a writer is a genius, he remains a genius, even in the Soviet Union. I am not concerned here with geniuses—there is a huge galaxy of literary talent in Russia. Take, for example, Leonid Martynov, a fine poet. During the years after 1945 when he could not print what he wanted to, he did not publish anything. Then, in 1955, he began to publish again, and it was as if he had been reborn.[72] Martynov possesses the great art of expressing himself through implication, which one might say is a product of a self-censorship imposed by difficult circumstances. The art of expressing oneself through allusions is completely different from journalistic writing. The writer does not state bluntly that the king is naked; he tries to tell the truth in a different manner, and each person does this in his own way. Some are successful and some are not.

There are a multitude of devices used by writers, apart from direct evasion of the censor. Some write about "eternal values," and I think this is precisely what a writer's task should be. But if all literature were to concern itself solely with eternal values and nothing else, there would be grounds for criticism. To speak about eternal values objectively and honestly is nevertheless one of the tasks of literature. Paustovsky, for instance, lived in fear but was never in trouble, because he wrote only about eternal values. When he became older he understood that a writer

---

[72] See the letter by Ilya Ehrenburg and others, *Literaturnaya gazeta*, November 27, 1956, p. 3.

should be more active,[73] and he eventually gained recognition for his public activity. He gathered a group of young people around him and taught them various things. Paustovsky behaved somewhat like Tvardovsky, who, although he did not reveal his true feelings in his writings, nevertheless felt the need to be honest and to struggle. This is not easy to do in literature, so he tried to accomplish it through public activity.

A war is going on in the Soviet Union and, as always during war-time, there are many ways of resisting the régime; accommodating oneself to the régime while simultaneously resisting is no worse a way than any other, and one means of doing this is to cultivate friendly relations with the authorities. I remember the pleasure we used to derive from trying to plant one of our people in a key post. After Bulat Okudzhava returned from Kaluga and had been working for a time at the "Molodaya gvardiya" publishing house, a position with *Literaturnaya gazeta* (Literary Gazette) suddenly became vacant. He was not well-known at that time, and they wanted to appoint someone else whom we considered rather dangerous, but with the help of various intrigues—they made someone drunk, called another on the telephone, chatted with someone else—Bulat Okudzhava was given the job at *Literaturnaya gazeta*. This happens quite often. A system of mutual help and informal connections with people in high positions can serve a common purpose.

I do not think the picture is as black as Anatoli Kuznetsov paints it. It is true that life is difficult and taxing in the Soviet Union. There are many hardships to be endured; those who cannot endure them do not survive. For those who survive life is hard, but life goes on and the literary process continues.

We were speaking earlier about writing for the desk-drawer. This also has its advantages. After the death of Stalin, for example, there was something of a literary revival; conditions became easier and there were more opportunities to have things published. But it turned out that the old literary masters could not rise to the occasion because they had nothing in their desks to submit. There was hardly a single new, daring or "seditious" phrase to be found. It might be asked: what about Ehrenburg? But I would not consider his novel *Ottepel* (The Thaw) to be either "seditious" or daring; it was only the beginning of an inevitable development. I have in mind the kind of "seditious" manuscript that might appear in *samizdat*. *Samizdat* could not exist under Stalin, so at the very moment when it

---

[73] See his defence of Dudintsev in 1956 in *The Year of Protest 1956*, ed. H. McLean and W. Vickery, Vintage Books, New York, 1961, pp. 155–159. (This is a very early piece of post-Stalin *samizdat*.)

would have been possible to get something published, none of the old guard was ready, and this provided young writers such as Yevtushenko with a good opportunity. Nowadays, however, there is *samizdat* and plenty of manuscripts in desk drawers. It is highly reassuring that so many young people have entered the literary field, although if arrests begin again writers will naturally become frightened and take steps to protect themselves. Surely there is nothing reprehensible in this? The main thing is that after taking measures to ensure survival, a writer continues his activity, nurturing his ideas and waiting for his hour to come. Under the Soviet régime no one knows what will happen tomorrow—any change in the Party Politburo could bring in a new leader who might slacken the reins. A writer must be prepared to take advantage of such circumstances, and if he happens to have a manuscript in his desk, he has the chance to use it. Thank God there are manuscripts in desk drawers; under Stalin there were very few, and it required great courage of a writer. Now it is not so dangerous.

The constant struggle in which Soviet writers are engaged gives rise to many new methods of resistance, and I believe it is the task of this conference to discuss these various methods. The country is vast, but the only breeding-grounds of culture are the large cities. Culture emanates from the progressive liberal intelligentsia living in these cities and then spreads throughout the country. Maybe we can somehow help them, but most probably Soviet literature will gradually be able to cope with its own problems by itself, and any kind of help will come from within the Soviet Union, not from outside.

Leonid Finkelstein:

Although the last two speakers differed greatly from each other, it seems to me that Demin strongly corroborated Kuznetsov. Regardless of his intention, Demin has illustrated the terrible plight of Soviet literature, which is not simply struggling—it is going through convulsions. If Soviet writers are having to ingratiate themselves with the authorities in order to appear in print, and having to resort to stringent self-censorship, no one can calculate the vast quantity of potentially good literature that has been ruined. What if instead of the slack censorship of Nicholas I there had been the sort of censorship during the nineteenth century that there is now? Who knows what would have been left of the great classical Russian literature? Perhaps very little. Maybe there would not even have been a Dostoyevsky.

We have among us here several representatives of Soviet literature who were incapable of reconciling themselves to this Soviet censorship and who defected to the West. There are many more writers in the Soviet Union who would pay dearly for a chance to escape, and therefore I feel there is no basis for discussing any positive aspects of Soviet censorship or assuming that any sort of progressive struggle can take place under these conditions. Self-censorship as a reflection of the external censorship has taken a hold over the Soviet writer, and no one will ever be able to estimate the damage.

Anatoly Kuznetsov spoke with emotion because he spoke from the heart. Of course there are means of evading the censor that many writers use and will continue to use; of course there are people who survived Babi Yar. But how many people perished? That is all I wanted to say.

Anthony Adamovich:

It has been mentioned more than once today that self-censorship operates in every writer, who is the first reader of his work, his own first critic, censor and editor. But the Soviet totalitarian régime demands such a complete and thorough censorship that it becomes the decisive factor in the entire literary process, leaving its imprint on everything, including literary criticism, which emerges in a special form. I once called Soviet literary criticism "censorial criticism" because it acts as a watchdog for the system, sniffing around and pouncing on anything the censor has missed or let through. Censorship leaves its stamp on the editor and the editing process, and the task of an editor-censor is a most unenviable one.

I agree with what Anatoly Kuznetsov said about Solzhenitsyn, and I am not the only one. I will give one example of Solzhenitsyn's self-censorship. You all know the two *zeks* [Soviet slang for prison camp inmates] in *The First Circle*—Rubin and Sologdin. Solzhenitsyn portrays them as diametrical opposites in an almost systematic manner: Rubin is the loyal communist who blindly adheres to his beliefs in spite of everything, while Sologdin is an anti-communist. At the beginning of the novel the author maintains an equal distance from both, and I expected that Solzhenitsyn would either preserve this distance from both characters throughout the novel or show more partiality for Sologdin. But he did just the opposite by making Rubin the more sympathetic character. Sologdin did not stand firm; he made concessions, whereas Rubin remained steadfast until the end of the novel. It seems to me that Solzhenitsyn was guided by self-censorship when he did this, possibly hoping that it might give him a chance of somehow having his novel published [in the Soviet Union].

Now I would like to talk about a form of self-censorship I feel within myself as a literary critic, a different kind from that practised by writers. I once wrote a book, published later in English, in which I mentioned all the facts and the people I knew connected with resistance to Sovietization. But suddenly I had doubts; some of the people I referred to were still living in the Soviet Union and my disclosures could harm them, so I had to leave out many important facts. This is how self-censorship developed within me. I still practise this form of self-censorship and will probably continue to do so until the end of my days.

Albert Parry:

I see a difference between the negative expression "self-censorship" and the positive expression "self-restraint." If we were to make a clear distinction between these two terms, I think we would reach the more balanced conclusion that there is such a thing as self-restraint, which is not at all a negative phenomenon; all of us employ self-restraint, not only in political relations, but in personal relations as well. By making this distinction we might avoid the needless self-reproach that is being voiced at this conference.

Natalia Belinkova:

We are not only confusing "self-censorship" and "self-restraint;" we are also failing to distinguish between self-censorship, as a negative phenomenon, and the positive devices employed by Solzhenitsyn or some other author to deceive the censor. Writers who live under abnormal conditions are compelled to use abnormal literary devices unfamiliar to the rest of the world. This method of deceiving the censor is positive, whereas self-censorship is completely negative: the writer cripples himself and his works by complying with the laws and requirements of the very ideology which is crushing him and his fellow-writers. I think this distinction should lend some clarity to our discussion. Certainly these two phenomena are closely related, but the Soviet régime does not confuse them.

Herman Achminov:

There is another aspect we have not yet discussed—the material incentive to accommodate oneself to the demands of the régime. Financial considerations surely have an important bearing on whether a writer says that the king is "naked" or only that he is "poorly dressed." I would, therefore, like to ask some specific questions. What is known about the financial situation of such writers as Sholokhov, Fadeyev, Yevtushenko, Ovechkin, and other lesser-known figures? What are their living conditions like? Do they have cars and chauffeurs? To what extent does the financial situation of a writer depend on the devotion he shows to the Party? What financial disadvantages result when an author is expelled from the Union of Writers? How is a writer financed before and after the publication of a book, and during a *tvorcheskaya komandirovka*?[74]

Arkady Belinkov:

In the Soviet Union there is a set scale of author's fees which is standard for all the major publishing houses. For the first edition of a book the author receives one hundred per cent of the fee, which for a Stalin or Lenin Prize laureate is about 500 rubles, and for a normal, good writer about 300 rubles per printer's sheet. This is in the central publishing houses; in the provinces they pay somewhat less. For subsequent editions an author receives progressively less, perhaps sixty per cent of the basic rate for the second and third editions, forty per cent for the fourth edition, and so on. For the eighteenth edition of his *Ot dvukh do pyati* (From Two to Five), for example, Korney Chukovsky received only about 27 rubles per sheet. Sholokhov enjoys special privileges, however, and is paid one hundred percent for all editions: for the fortieth edition of *Tikhy Don* (The Quiet Don) he received 500 rubles per sheet instead of the kopeks or so that would have been paid to lesser mortals. He must be fabulously wealthy by Soviet standards; he even has a private aircraft.[75]

Expulsion from the Union of Writers does not directly affect a writer's income from his publications because his fees are not paid by this body. The number of writers who are non-members far exceeds the 5,600 members,[76] and non-members receive exactly the same author's fees. But loss of membership does have economic disadvantages. Members receive passes to the "Houses of Creativity" (clubs where writers congregate for informal discussions, lectures, relaxation, etc.), which are considerably more expensive for non-members, and they enjoy the services of a special polyclinic. The Union of Writers also sponsors a Literary Fund, mainly for

---

[74] This expression means literally "creative mission" and refers to the trips an author makes in order to gather information or study conditions in a certain area about which he is writing.

[75] On authors' royalties during the first fifteen years after the Second World War see pp. 69–71 and 255–256 of Boris Gorokhoff, *Publishing in the USSR*, Indiana University Publications, 1959. On financial (and other) ways of ensuring that the overwhelming majority of Soviet authors write in ways acceptable to the authorities see the chapter "Bureaucratic Controls and Literary Production" in Harold Swayze's *Political Control of Literature in the USSR, 1946–1959*, Cambridge, Mass., Harvard University Press, 1962. See also Mikhail Alekseyev and Boris Dyakov, "Pisatel i izdatel," *Literaturnaya gazeta*, November 13, 1965, p. 2.

[76] In early 1971 there were 7,103 members ("Gorizonty nashey literatury," *Izvestiya*, March 17, 1971, p. 3). By July there were 7,290 (Ye. Dolmatovsky, *Literaturnaya gazeta*, July 7, 1971, p. 4).

members, in order to help authors who are in financial straits.[77] Sometimes the writer must reimburse the money later, sometimes not. This fund has existed for over a century and was created by Nekrasov and a number of other writers. Most important of all, however, is the fact that the Union of Writers is the gateway to the publishing houses. Officially, members of the Union are accorded no special preference by the publishing houses, but although non-members have the formal right to have their works published, this seldom happens.

Anatoly Kuznetsov:

The Literary Fund is supported by ten percent deductions from authors' fees, regardless of whether an author is a member of the Writers' Union or not. A member of the Literary Fund pays a ten-ruble subscription per year. This is a small amount in comparison to the money he can receive from the fund, which is in direct proportion to the degree of devotion he shows to the Party.

Advances paid to impecunious writers by publishing houses also serve as a form of blackmail, because you are then compelled either to accept all the changes and corrections made by the editor on your manuscript or return the money.

Leonid Finkelstein:

As Arkady Belinkov has just stated, the Soviet régime pays its hirelings very well. In the autumn of 1965, shortly before the trial of Sinyavsky and Daniel, I met the now popular Soviet writer, Arkady Vasilyev, in the offices of the journal *Moskva* (Moscow). He had come to pay his Party dues to the assistant secretary of the local Party organization, a *Moskva* employee, and when I heard the amount he was paying I almost jumped out of my chair. His dues for the previous month amounted to 360 new rubles, which meant that he had earned 12,000 rubles in one month. This is equivalent to the earnings of a skilled worker over ten years. He claimed that he had received the money for writing a film script, but I soon suspected what he had been paid for when the trial of Sinyavsky and Daniel took place—he was one of the two "writer-prosecutors."[78]

---

[77] See the entry *Literaturny fond* in Vol. 4 of the *Kratkaya literaturnaya entsiklopediya*, and V. Sazhin, "Bratstvo pisateley," *Zvezda*, No. 10, 1971, pp. 187–191. Its membership is slightly larger than that of the Writers' Union.

[78] See his speech for the prosecution on pp. 241–244 of *On Trial*, ed. L. Labedz and M. Hayward, London, 1967. (In Russian on pp. 284–286 of *Belaya Kniga po delu A. Sinyavskogo i Yu. Danielya*, comp. A. Ginzburg, Posev, Frankfurt, 1967.)

Leopold Labedz:

Perhaps Mr. Belinkov can add something on the subject of self-censorship, which, it seems to me, can be practised both consciously and subconsciously.

Arkady Belinkov:

Censorship is only one of the many institutions of the dictatorship, which begins to exert its all-pervading influence in the kindergarten. It creates a certain atmosphere in the country regarding personal expression, and people know quite well what they can and cannot say. Self-censorship begins in the home, when parents are sitting with friends discussing certain features of the Soviet régime and the moment the daughter walks in to say good-night the conversation suddenly switches to food. If they continued to talk about sensitive matters in front of their daughter, she might begin to ask her parents questions or, even worse, she might do the same at school, thereby arousing the suspicions of her teacher, who would alert the authorities.

I think the position Anatoly Kuznetsov adopts on self-censorship and the internal obstacles which a writer places in his own path is somewhat extreme, but from personal experience I can understand why. He talked about Solzhenitsyn and how it was impossible for good literature or geniuses to survive in the Soviet Union on account of this self-censorship. Well, there have been earlier writers who were geniuses and who lived under far less oppressive conditions, but who nevertheless practised self-censorship. I was engaged for a long time in a professional study of the work of Pushkin and I can attest to the fact that Pushkin, undoubtedly with the best of motives, wrote poems bearing obvious traces of self-censorship. He himself wrote, in his poem *Druzyam* (To My Friends): "No, I am not a flatterer when I compose verses in praise of the Tsar."[79] There is reason to believe that the poet conformed in the hope of securing the release of the Decembrists. But it was probably a bit of both, as he said himself [i.e., sincerity was mixed with calculation].

If you read what Tolstoy wrote in his notebooks about his works you will see that even he, the man who wrote the impassioned article "I Cannot Remain Silent,"[80] which might serve as the epigraph for our discussion, could and did remain silent on occasion, although what he did say was

---

[79] 1828. According to Benkendorf the Tsar liked the poem but did not want it to be published. For Pushkin's references to censors and censorship see pp. 866–867 of *Slovar yazyka Pushkina*, Vol. 4, Moscow, Gosudarstvennoye izdatelstvo inostrannykh i natsionalnykh slovarey, 1961.

[80] In 1908, on the death penalty.

more than enough. I believe, therefore, that even if Solzhenitsyn constantly censors and edits himself, what he actually says deserves an honourable place both in the history of world literature and in the history of Russian liberal thought.

Leonid Finkelstein:

The important thing here is to consider the times in which Pushkin lived, rather than Pushkin himself. As you rightly said, he lived under easier conditions, yet he once cried: "The devil caused me to be born in Russia with a soul and with talent!"[81] If Pushkin had been subjected to the present Soviet censorship it is difficult to imagine how he would have written. Solzhenitsyn is no weaker, either morally or spiritually, than Pushkin was; perhaps he is even stronger, and it is not for us here to judge him, but rather to try to see whether even he, or, say, Sinyavsky practises real self-censorship to any great extent.

In one of his works, Sinyavsky says outright that when he speaks about Soviet power he thinks of the rattling of the machine-gun carts, bread rationing and the defence of Petrograd, and it is repugnant to him to speak irreverently about Soviet power, which he distinguishes from the socialist state. Logically, says Sinyavsky, the Soviet régime and the socialist state are one and the same, yet whilst he has nothing against the Soviet régime, he does object to the socialist state.[82] He attributes this to romanticism, but it is not romanticism, it is the purest form of self-censorship. It is particularly terrifying because it is subconscious and therefore doubly insidious: the writer imagines he is faithfully committing all his thoughts to paper, not realizing that he has been brain-washed.

When Adzhubey left *Komsomolskaya pravda* (Komsomol Truth) and became the chief editor of *Izvestiya* in 1959, he summoned the entire staff and announced: "Dear friends, we must publish a good paper. In order to do this one thing is essential: kill the internal censor within you. Write everything that you believe is necessary. Don't worry, we ourselves will remove anything that might be superfluous."

This, of course, was an extremely cynical approach, but Adzhubey's words prove that the existence of self-censorship is widely acknowledged. However, there are writers who are not aware that they are employing self-censorship because it is too deeply embedded in their subconscious.

---

[81] See the end of his letter of May 18, 1836, to his wife.

[82] "Chto takoye sotsialistichesky realizm" in *Fantastichesky mir Abrama Tertsa*, New York, 1967, p. 437. In English: A. Tertz, *On Socialist Realism*, New York, Pantheon Books, 1960, pp. 80–81.

Yuri Demin:

The writers who are unaware that they exercise self-censorship—and there are many—are the same bad writers as exist in every country. It is those who can struggle with themselves who are able to create, and this is true of all writers, regardless of whether they live in the Soviet Union.

I detect a tendency here to adopt a journalistic approach to literature. Certain passages from Solzhenitsyn have been alluded to where a character speaks in a certain way, but no one pointed out that there are many other passages in which the same character speaks differently. It must not be demanded of the character, or of Solzhenitsyn, that he always spell everything out. We must not extract passages from his works in order to prove the validity of our own ideas about him; that is what they do in the newspapers. We must consider a work like *Cancer Ward* as a whole, because Solzhenitsyn, like all great writers, deliberately leaves a great deal unsaid. It would be much worse if he started to write shallow anti-Soviet articles in which he announced that "the king is naked." He writes symphonically—the anti-Soviet message arises willy-nilly, implicitly, when the conversation turns to important and serious topics. This is true of Solzhenitsyn and also of Pasternak and other great writers. They have their own general philosophical outlook, but what they write is bound to be anti-Soviet as well. And the régime and the censor understand this approach better than we do.

If one looks hard enough one can find self-censorship in any work, even in *Doctor Zhivago*. There is no point in taking a truly great and honest work and saying that because of self-censorship the author did not accomplish all he could have done; everyone exercises self-censorship to some extent. In my opinion, it is much more interesting and much more important to talk about the system of censorship as such, and about the methods of evading it. What we have been discussing belongs rather to the realm of psychology.

Aleksey Yakushev:

I personally think that Solzhenitsyn is a completely honest writer who practises no self-censorship. The brick-laying scene in *One Day in the Life of Ivan Denisovich*, for instance, was surely not put in to please the censor? It is just one of many places where Solzhenitsyn seems to idealize the "simple people" and looks to them for the basic human values. One can find this in all his works. He presents his own ideas and his own views about how society should develop and about the values on which it should be based. He tells us how he sees things. Why should we not believe that these are his real convictions? We may not agree with them, but we must allow Solzhenitsyn to have them. Lev Tolstoy evolved all sorts of theories about history, art, etc., with which some people agreed, while others did not. But no one concluded that he was practising self-censorship. He simply viewed things in a certain way. It seems to me that we have taken our conception of self-censorship too far; if a writer holds certain views and then suddenly completely changes these views for no good reason, we can rightfully say that he has censored himself. But we should not make our definition of self-censorship too broad.

Anatoly Kuznetsov:

I do not understand why one has to close one's eyes to certain blemishes, even in a genius like Pushkin. I ask myself why should one not strive to get rid of such blemishes. I admire Solzhenitsyn; he is a great writer, and he is accomplishing great things. But would he not be an even greater writer if these blemishes were not there? Does this not prove the destructiveness of self-censorship, a phenomenon arising out of the official system of censorship in the Soviet Union? Does this self-censorship not detract even from Solzhenitsyn's greatness?

Once in my life I engaged in *samizdat*. I duplicated on very thin cigarette paper fifteen copies of the version of *Babi Yar* that I had originally submitted to *Yunost*. I sent these copies of this more or less honest work to fifteen of the people whom I respect most in the Soviet Union. I sent the first copy to Solzhenitsyn, the second to Tvardovsky, and so on. In the ensuing correspondence between Solzhenitsyn and myself I asked him to compare this original version with the mutilated version in *Yunost*, pointing out that I had no choice but to make these concessions. He wrote me back an excellent letter saying that a writer may, of course, make concessions, but in doing so he should not go beyond a certain limit. This limit remains completely unclear to me, and I am afraid it always will. Each writer probably sets his own limit for himself, and even if Solzhenitsyn considers it necessary to make concessions to the censorship, he is still our hero. Okudzhava also makes concessions to the censorship, relying on hints and allusions. He never states outright that "the king is naked" (incidentally, this expression comes from a work of literature, not from journalism), yet Okudzhava also is a hero to a certain extent. Yevtushenko makes considerable concessions to censorship. Is he a hero or not? He used to be, but it looks as though he is one no longer. Paustovsky made concessions, and he is a hero; Tvardovsky is a hero. What about Katayev? Simonov? Fedin? Are they heroes or not?

Boris Polevoy once said to me: "How can you possibly be offended? Go down on your knees and give thanks for the fact that we publish your works at least in some form." And he was absolutely right: another month or two and it would have been too late to publish *Babi Yar* in any version. In the Soviet Union they are all heroes. Even the censors probably consider themselves to be heroes and revel in their complexes. I no longer know how far one can go in making concessions, so would it not be best to have no self-censorship at all?

Anatol Popluiko:

When you arrived in the West you began to prepare your works for publication here. Do you feel you are now completely free from censorship in the guise of editing?

Arkady Belinkov:

I do feel pressure from censorship. My one-and-a-half years' experience here has taught me that in the West it is much easier to publish a Soviet or pro-Soviet than an anti-Soviet book. I might add that my 936-page book *Sdacha i gibel sovetskogo intelligenta. Yury Olesha* (The Surrender and Destruction of a Soviet Intellectual. Yury Olesha) would have been published in the Soviet Union if I had sacrificed about forty pages. Doubleday Publishers cut the book by about 400 pages. I agreed to this simply because I was not interested in the English-language edition but only in the same publisher's Russian edition, where, under the contract, it is to be printed in its entirety. This is not self-censorship but external censorship. Sometimes it is prompted by commercial considerations, but often the reason is the difficulty of publishing and selling a genuinely anti-Soviet book in the West. Italy is something of an exception; there an editor offered to publish my book, omitting only what they would omit in the Soviet Union, but I refused because I was not particularly interested.

The System of Formal Censorship

Alec Nove:

I have pleasure in giving the floor to Mr. Finkelstein, who is an expert on the subject of formal censorship.

Leonid Finkelstein:

It is not my intention to deal with every aspect of formal censorship in the Soviet press, for certain sides of the problem have already been touched on by other participants.[83] Furthermore, the subject will be dealt with later by Igor Yeltsov in his talk about censorship in the Soviet cinema.

Journalists in the Soviet Union come into contact with the censorship twice in the course of any one issue of a newspaper or journal. Essentially, the censor is bound to look at any printed matter twice: on the first occasion before it is sent to the press, and again after it comes from the press. The reason for the second examination is to prevent editors and publishers from making alterations after the first inspection. You submit to the censor two copies of the material before sending it to press; one the censor keeps for himself, and when you come to him for the second time with the first printed copy he compares it with the one he has retained. Having satisfied himself that there are no unauthorized changes, he applies his stamp for the second time.

All the years I worked for the Soviet press I never ceased to be astonished that among all the incredible chaos there was one sector that worked with

---

[83] Mr. Finkelstein [L. Vladimirov] has himself written extensively on Soviet censorship: see *The Sunday Telegraph*, September 11 and 18, 1966, and his book *Rossiya bez prikras i umolchany* (Frankfurt, Posev, 1969), especially chapters 5 and 6. See also the section called "Publishing Procedures," pp. 52–56 of B. Gorokhoff, *Publishing in the USSR*, Indiana University Publications, 1959; Leo Gruliow, "How the Soviet Newspaper Operates," *Problems of Communism*, March-April 1956; and several books in English on the Soviet mass media which discuss, if only briefly, the problem of censorship: Theodore Kruglak, *The Two Faces of TASS*, New York, McGraw-Hill Book Company, Inc., 1962; Antony Buzek, *How the Communist Press Works*, London, Pall Mall Press, 1964; James Markham, *Voices of the Red Giants*, Iowa State University Press, 1967; and Mark Hopkins, *Mass Media in the Soviet Union*, New York, Pegasus, 1970. (The last named is the best.) The English version of Mr. Finkelstein's book (L. Vladimirov, *The Russians*, New York, Praeger, 1968) is an excellent example of Western editorial censorship of Russian works, a subject not discussed in detail at this conference and a rich field for future research.

unfailing efficiency—the censorship. It can work erratically, and delays occur, but one thing is certain: you can't get by without the censorship. Everything hinges on the eight years' imprisonment to which any printer is liable if he prints more than ten copies of any edition without the censor's approval.[84]

Well, what is the organizational structure of the censorship? The nerve-centre, the headquarters, is housed on the fifth floor of the building of the Ministry of Power Stations, No. 7, Kitaysky proyezd, Moscow.[85] It is generally referred to as "*Glavlit* of the USSR," although this is the old name and officially no longer exists. The official name, displayed downstairs, is "Main Board for the Protection of State and Military Secrets in the Press. State Committee for the Press under the Council of Ministers of the USSR." Naturally, this name is too much of a mouthful,[86] and so the old, convenient name of *Glavlit* is used everywhere—not only orally, but in writing too; even up there on the fifth floor you will find a sign saying "*Glavlit* of the USSR." It is an all-Union organization, headed by a man called Pavel Konstantinovich Romanov, who in the past was in charge of the department of heavy industry at the Party Central Committee. His first deputy is called Zorin, and another deputy is an agreeable young man named Nikolay Glazatov whom I knew well for a long time when he was senior censor of the "Nauka" (Science) publishing house. He was in charge of the group of censors at "Nauka" who worked in an office which, as is usual in the Soviet Union, simply had a small notice on the door stating "Unauthorized persons not admitted."

Romanov's deputy from roughly 1963 to 1966 was a certain Ivan Agayants, who from the very beginning earned a bad reputation as a real martinet who always went by the book. He summoned the chief editors to a number of meetings and told them they were too lax, that people were trying to get round the censorship and should not think that the censors were unaware of it. In 1966 he was transferred back to the KGB where, it turned out, he had been working for a number of years before joining the

---

[84] Article 75 of the RSFSR Criminal Code provides for up to eight years' deprivation of freedom for divulging a state secret without intention to commit treason or espionage.

[85] On the *Ministerstvo stroitelstva elektrostantsy SSSR* as it was until the autumn of 1962 see *Moskva 1962. Kratkaya adresno-spravochnaya kniga*, Moscow, Moskovsky rabochy, 1962, p. 23. On September 26, 1962, it was transformed into the Union-Republican *Ministerstvo energetiki i elektrifikatsii SSSR*, which almost from the start has been headed by P. S. Neporozhny (see *Vedomosti Verkhovnogo Soveta SSSR*, No. 40 (1127), 1962, p. 1002, art. 416, and No. 48 (1135), 1962, p. 1114, art. 499).

[86] It was in fact somewhat simplified in 1966, just after Mr. Finkelstein left the USSR: see footnote 99 on p. 65.

censor's office. He was, in fact, a major-general in the State Security Department.

Max Hayward:

Was he in charge of the department of misinformation?

Leonid Finkelstein:

Quite possibly. We all knew about the existence of department "D" in the Central Administration of the KGB. "D" probably stood for the word *dezinformatsiya* (misinformation), because the employees of this department specialized in spreading rumours. It is quite possible that Agayants was transferred to this department from the censors' office.

Apart from the chief censors themselves there is another group of people who exercise what is called "supercontrol." They are like the technical control sections (OTK) in industry which are not directly connected with the quality-control of products but are empowered to examine at random any batch of components or any material produced by a workshop or department. They are actually controlling the controllers. The offices of "supercontrol" are also situated in the Kitaysky proyezd, and I had to go there on three or four occasions when it was said that *upstairs* disagreed with a decision of the censor with whom I was dealing. In addition to these two groups there is a third body of people in the building in the Kitaysky proyezd. These are ordinary censors, some thirty to forty in number, whose job it probably is to deal specially with the individual publications that come under particular suspicion. *Znaniye — sila*,[87] when I was working there, had the honour of experiencing this twice, and twice passing under the authority of the central office of *Glavlit* of the USSR. When this happens, you have to present your work directly to Kitaysky proyezd.

It is impossible simply to walk into the central offices of *Glavlit*. The "Nauka" publishing house, or any newspaper, has a censors' room with the sign "Unauthorized persons not admitted" outside, but you can just open the door and walk in. If you want to go to *Glavlit*, however, you have to obtain a permit, although this is not difficult. You just ring the censor and announce your impending arrival. When you get there you receive a permit

---

[87] Knowledge is Strength (or Power). According to M. Bulatov (*Krylatyye slova*, Moscow, Detgiz, 1958, p. 53) and N. S. Ashukin and M. G. Ashukina (*Krylatyye slova*, Moscow, Khudozhestvennaya literatura, 1966, p. 256) this expression comes from Francis Bacon. See No. 11, "De Haeresibus," of his *Meditationes Sacrae :* nam et ipsa scientia potestas est ("Of Heresies," in *Religious Meditations :* for knowledge itself is power).

from a uniformed militiaman and are directed to a particular room. It is not advisable to poke your nose through any other doors.

The first time we were put directly under *Glavlit* headquarters was because of an article in the twelfth issue of *Znaniye — sila* for 1959 (the readers never suspected any irregularity because the issue was completely reset and reprinted before publication). The article, by a certain Vladimirov (real name: Sergey Altshuler), was called "If the Visionaries Will Not Play the March" and dealt with the relationship between science and fantasy. The author considered that science-fiction writers have a positive influence on the development of science, and he sought to prove his theory with examples from Jules Verne. There were no initial objections from *Glavlit*, so the issue was approved by the censorship and went to press. But *Glavlit* suddenly phoned before it was distributed and said that a "higher body" considered that the article belittled the role played by Soviet science and amounted to ideological sabotage. The article had to be taken out, and the 80,000 (old) rubles needed to reprint the issue were provided without delay by some unknown source.

The main result, however, was that we immediately came under the direct authority of *Glavlit* for three months. We also learned that *Glavlit* had had an eye on us for some time. Lev Zhigarev, our deputy chief editor, was summoned to the *Agitprop* department at the Central Committee, where he was given a reprimand and shown a report from *Glavlit*, written six months before, which said that the periodical *Znaniye-sila* was publishing science fiction stories containing political allusions. We had already blotted our copy-book once, also with regard to science fiction, so this time *Glavlit* decided to take us in hand. (I should add here that Soviet science-fiction writers are generally regarded with great mistrust.) We sat out the three months in the *Glavlit* headquarters and were then sent back to the "Nauka" publishing house for censoring there.

The second occasion when we fell foul of *Glavlit* was in 1965, and this time the results were more lasting. We had published a brilliant short story by the American writer Clifford Simak, called *Pokoleniye, dostigsheye tseli*.[88] I do not know how this story was interpreted in America, but in the Soviet Union it was regarded as a call to revolt and a patently anti-Soviet work. Whether it was cleared for publication because of the lack of 80,000 (8,000 new) rubles or because the censor somehow thought it was all right, is difficult to say, but in any event we were directly subordinated to *Glavlit*

---

[88] *Znaniye — sila*, No. 1, 1965. (The original is called *Target Generation*.) On this cut translation see G. Altov, "Fantastika i chitateli," *Problemy sotsiologii pechati*, No. 2, Novosibirsk, 1970, p. 90.

for the second time, and this was still the case when I left the Soviet Union in June 1966.

Let me now explain the censorship procedure in detail. First of all you submit two copies of your material to the censor, who then spends several days reading it. For us, as a monthly periodical, this was supposed to take place within nine days, and we reckoned with this in our schedule, but apart from one or two occasions *Glavlit* always took longer. Once it took two months, but this was an exception; the usual period is two weeks. The printers are always breathing down your neck because they have a schedule, too, and if it is upset they always blame the publishing house, never the censor! If you ring the censor—the *Glavlit* telephone is tapped, incidentally —to inquire what progress has been made, you will be given some excuse for the delay and the promise that they will get in touch with you later. You ring the next day and it is the same story; on the day after that you ring again, but this time the tone is less cordial and you are told that you are only distracting them, that they will ring you when the material has been read through. There is nothing you can do about it and it is pointless to complain. Eventually the censor calls you and invites you to come and discuss any dubious points with him. This is the crucial meeting with the censor. I should add that, according to *Glavlit* regulations, only the chief editor of a publication, his deputy, or the responsible secretary, may deal directly with *Glavlit*, and as I was none of these I was actually contravening the instructions by going in person to see the censor. But whereas on the newspapers only the responsible secretaries (or their personal assistants) speak with the censor in the normal course of work, where periodicals are concerned *Glavlit* tacitly ignores the instructions because the departmental editors work a rota system, taking turns to produce an issue. Obviously, whoever is duty editor for that month's issue knows more about it than any of the three people I have mentioned, and so he is allowed to see the censor in person.[89]

---

[89] But there is one rule which, as far as I know, has never been violated. This is that under no circumstances may there be any direct contact between the censor and the author. Notes and corrections made by the censor should where necessary be communicated to the author as though they came from the editors. The rules of the game are such that the author is not even supposed to know that his work is censored. The words *"Glavlit"* and "censorship" are officially banned from editorial correspondence or official telephone conversations. When informing our printers about the latest corrections made by the censor we had to speak and write about the resetting made necessary by "authors' corrections." There are some cynical editorial boards which even now deduct from the author's fees expenses for "authors' corrections" though these in fact cover nothing more than expenses for resetting caused by the censor's "suggestions." (It is pointless

After exchanging the customary greetings, you take a seat next to the censor and converse for a couple of minutes about the weather, football, chess and the like, and then get down to business. (Incidentally, one of our colleagues on *Znaniye — sila* was the chess Grand Master Yury Averbakh. He once played several members of the top *Glavlit* staff simultaneously in a demonstration game, so before he set off for it we begged him, "Yury, have a heart and lose!") Anyway, you start to look at the issue, and the censor's first query might concern, say, an aerial picture of a town on the cover. He wants your assurance that you had the KGB's permission to use this photograph. The next point might concern a reference in the text to a process for the extraction of polypropylene. He wants to know if it is a Soviet or an American process. You tell him it is an American process, described in the journal *Science*, such-and-such a number, and he says: "Aha! Well, be a good fellow and give me the source." This does not mean that a reference to this effect is to appear in the text. It is better not to quote the source; then the reader might think it is a Soviet process, another achievement of Soviet science. The censor simply has to be certain that no state secrets are being divulged.

You often have to give him the source for some information, and a lot depends on your relationship with the censor. If he knows you are reliable and would not let him down he takes your word on trust and does not ask for documentary proof. You just tell him that it is from the journal *Science*, from the reports of the Academy of Sciences or from a Khrushchev or Brezhnev speech, and he believes you. But this is only half the business, because you also have to check things against the "list." This is a thick, green book, familiarly referred to as the "Talmud," which lists all the information that it is forbidden to publish. It is stamped "secret" on the cover and is kept in the safe with other secret documents.[90] Well, let us say

---

for the editor to argue about these "suggestions." If he does he will be told: "The *Glavlit* organs do not have the right to demand the withdrawal of a text if it does not contain military or state secrets. We only recommend that it be removed. If you wish to print it despite our recommendation, you take the responsibility on yourself. We will issue our authorizing stamp and pass on our point of view to the Central Committee." After such a "liberal" answer any editor would almost always immediately back down. I know of only one case where an editor of a newspaper demanded a censorship stamp against the "re-commendation." He got his stamp and the newspaper came out the way he wanted it to, but soon afterwards he was dismissed.) [L.F.]

[90] Its full title is "Index of Information Not to be Published in the Open Press." It contains the following sections: General Information; Military Information; Industry and Construction; Agriculture; Transport, Economics and Finance. At the end of the book there is an alphabetical index, still a rarity in

there is a reference in the text to a factory known simply as "P.O. Box
No. 22, Kazan." The censor checks with the "Talmud" and finds that it must
not be mentioned at all. You protest that you mentioned it three years

Soviet publications. The first section is of special interest. From it we learn
that without special permission in every single instance it is forbidden to publish, *inter alia*,

1. Information about earthquakes, avalanches, landslides and other natural
disasters on the territory of the USSR;

2. Information about fires, explosions, aeroplane, naval and mine disasters,
train crashes;

3. Figures about the earnings of government and Party workers;

4. Any comparison of the budget of Soviet citizens and the prices of goods;

5. Information about even seasonal or local price increases;

6. Reports about increased living standards anywhere outside the socialist camp;

7. Reports of food shortages in the USSR (it is possible only to speak about
local bottlenecks in the delivery of specific items);

8. Any kind of average statistics about the country as a whole not taken
from Central Statistical Bureau reports;

9. The names of any KGB operatives apart from the Committee's Chairman;

10. The names of employees of the former Committee for Cultural Relations
with Foreign Countries, again, apart from the Chairman of the Committee;

11. Aerial photographs of Soviet cities and the precise geographical co-
ordinates of any populated point on Soviet territory;

12. Any mention of Glavlit organs and the jamming of foreign radio broadcasts;

13. Names of political figures on a special list, to which belong five of the
eight Soviet "prime ministers," Rykov, Molotov, Malenkov, Bulganin and
Khrushchev.

The industrial section of the "Index" bans publication of any absolute figures
on the number of workers and the productivity of enterprises (in reporting
"successes and achievements" one has to manipulate relative figures), while the
agricultural section forbids the publication of absolute figures about the harvest
of any specific crop in specific regions of the USSR or in the country as a whole.
It also forbids specific reports about harvest failures and comparisons, even
indirect comparisons using percentages, of the harvest or total yield of the current
year with that of previous years, if figures for the current year are only the same
or lower. It is forbidden to write specifically about damage and losses caused by
erosion, drought, dust storms, floods, cattle disease. One may not mention the
number of tractors on any given farm if the size of its acreage is also given,
and so on.

All these are, of course, only isolated examples. They can be extended
indefinitely. It is forbidden to mention the existence in the country of "hard
currency" or closed retail shops, special government dachas and sanatoriums, the
opening or closing of churches, the number of churchgoers, the state of the gold
reserves or other valuable ores in the country, any figures describing the assets
held by the Soviet State Bank, the number of crimes in any category for the
country as a whole or for large areas, and so on. The "Talmud" contains over
300 pages filled with rather small print. [L.F.] On this see also K. Kipiani,
"Sovetskaya tsenzura," *Nashi dni*, Frankfurt, No. 6, 1959, pp. 28–38.

ago, and he replies: "So what? Three years ago there was one 'Talmud,' now there is another." And he is quite right, of course. Actually, there are three categories of enterprises: those which are not secret and can be mentioned freely (therefore not listed in the "Talmud"); those which can be named, but without specifying what they produce; and those which must not be mentioned at all. The second and third types of enterprise are listed in the "Talmud." You can easily make a mistake in all innocence, because a factory may suddenly be put on the restricted or secret list if it starts to manufacture certain products. As a rule, you can't say anything about the factories described as "boxes," although there are exceptions. For example, you can refer to the Tula Armaments Factory (TOZ) even though it is now called "Box No. 535." There are, of course, many other things apart from plants and factories which cannot be mentioned at all, or only with special permission.

Everything forbidden by the "Talmud" the censor has marked or marks on your text in red pencil, and you must either obtain permission to print it, strike it out or change it. He has also noted his own queries in blue or green pencil, usually by putting two parallel lines next to the suspect paragraph, and he then goes through these points with you systematically. He might express surprise that you did not realize that this or that paragraph is not suitable, but though you may ask why, you never get a straight answer. Obviously something has to be done, so you ask the censor for his "suggestion." You never ask him for "instructions;" this would not be tactful because the censor is (in theory, at least) there to offer advice and not to give orders. He will probably opt for the removal of the whole paragraph. You then ask how to join the text together again and he says: "Let's think. Ah, yes! If we put the words 'but in general' after that full stop and then go on to the next paragraph but one, everything will be fine. Nobody will notice anything." As you see, the censor is terribly fond of creative work! And so it goes on, right through the whole issue.

Finally you arrive at the references. If you have not got them all with you, you have to run back to the editorial office for them. Sometimes you can even read them to the censor over the telephone; if he is satisfied, he agrees to clear the issue for printing and you can then send a messenger to collect it. When you get it back it has the censor's personal stamp on every printer's sheet (one printer's sheet equals sixteen pages of text), i.e., at the top of page one, page seventeen, page thirty-three, and so on. When the chief editor sends the issue to the censorship he signs every printed sheet, so the censor does the same. This is necessary because in the print shop the issue is taken apart, and the head of the printing shop would sooner hang himself than put the sheets into the printing machine without the *Glavlit* stamp in the corner. If he finds that one of the printed sheets does not carry the *Glavlit* stamp, he just refuses to print it: "My freedom is more precious to me," he remarks.

One thing has always puzzled me: although the number of censors in the Soviet Union must run into at least five figures, the personal number of each censor, which appears on his stamp, always consists of only two digits.[91] Another thing I must explain is that in the Soviet Union the censors do not check manuscripts. The only exception is when you yourself ask them to give a manuscript a preliminary reading because you suspect something might be rejected and you do not want time and money to be wasted unnecessarily in the type-setting room. Otherwise, what you send to the censor the first time is a mock-up or dummy issue consisting of the galley proofs with the illustrations pasted onto them. The *compositors*[92] do not need the censor's stamp, you see; they will set up anything and then make a few copies. This dummy issue has still not been "printed," of course. A maximum of ten copies (*ottiski*) are made on a hand machine in the composing room, but only up to ten copies, because more than that would constitute a printed edition. The eleventh copy would mean prison for those responsible.

So, after the censor has cleared the dummy issue for printing and it has been collected by the messenger, it goes to the printing shop, where about ten "signal" copies (advance copies of a book or journal, signature of which authorizes its publication) are made. These are then distributed: one copy to the censor, two to the Lenin Library, one to *Agitprop*, one to

---

[91] This is not to be confused with the censor's approval number which eventually appears in the published copy. The censor's personal stamp is applied to every printer's sheet or every newspaper double page and looks like this:

Permanent	Approved ....
Personal	Number .... Date................................
Number of Censor	Glavlit Representative ....
	(Signature)

On the top line, after the word "Approved," the censor adds, in his own hand, "For Printing." Then he takes from his logbook the next available approval number and adds this, together with the current date. This number will be reproduced in the publication data and can be seen on nearly all Soviet publications except special ones, e.g., those destined only for abroad. On the last line the censor adds his signature. [L.F.]

[92] As opposed to the printers.

Glavlit, one to the KGB, and so on.[93] The censor compares his "signal" copy with the copy of the dummy which he retained, and makes sure they are identical. Then he again applies his personal stamp but now, instead of "For Printing" [see footnote 91] he writes "For the Public." Now the printer has the right to release the copies which have already been prepared and held in stock. In our case matters were rather complicated because our printing works was in Kaunas, a thousand kilometres from the Moscow editorial office. The duty editor responsible for that month's issue practically lived in a "TU-124."

Everything happens much faster with newspapers and the procedure is different. Only the responsible secretary (or perhaps his assistant) has dealings with the censors. He comes in and makes a dummy of the first page, which consists of TASS reports, the leading article, photographs of leading workers, etc. It is not difficult for the secretary to find something on a leading worker, because the print shop usually has a stock of features on various workers already set up in type, and offprints of them are kept in the newspaper's information department. I used to see Vavilov, the responsible secretary at *Pravda*, quite often and he boasted that he had as many as forty editorials in reserve, or "in the pen" (*v zagone*), as they call it. He had editorials on science, a selection on agriculture, etc., which he used as the occasion required. Sometimes he would decide that some of them were obsolete and ring the print shop to tell them to "pour away" such-and-such an article. The print shop would then melt down the metal type—there is always a shortage of metal in the print shop—and use it for other articles.

This is not usually the procedure with a major newspaper such as *Pravda*, however, where the question of which editorial to publish is decided at Central Committee level, between *Pravda's* chief editor and *Agitprop*, or even the CC secretaries. But the less important newspapers do decide for themselves. The responsible secretary gathers the department heads around him and after half an hour of wrangling they decide which leading article is to go in. Each department writes leaders on its own speciality and each one wants to see *its* leader published in the newspaper, because this is regarded as a feather in its cap. Short, impromptu meetings (*letuchki*) are held in the editorial office, at which previous issues of the newspaper are analysed and evaluated and, say, the department responsible for writing

---

[93] For details of which institutions in the 1930s were obligatorily to be sent sample copies of various types of published material see pp. 119–120 and 133–143 of L. Fogelevich, *Osnovnyye direktivy i zakonodatelstvo o pechati*, Moscow, OGIZ, 1935. On the more recent period see Melville J. Ruggles and Raynard C. Swank, *Soviet Libraries and Librarianship*, Chicago, American Library Association, 1962, pp. 37–39.

about education is praised for having had two leading articles published that month. Also, an author is always paid more for a leading article than for an ordinary one of the same length, even in provincial newspapers.

Finally, one of the articles is accepted, and it takes about forty-five minutes to make up the front page, using material from TASS and APN. If it is a morning paper work usually begins at eleven a.m., and if it is an evening paper, at eight a.m. Let's assume it is a morning paper. It is not yet noon; neither the chief editor nor his deputy is present because there is nothing for them to do, so the responsible secretary or his assistant rings the censor and tells him that he is sending along the first page with one of the girls. This is actually a breach of all the rules, including the cardinal rule that the censor has no right to look at anything in print until it has passed through the hands of the head of the publication: the chief editor has signed nothing, and here you have the censor asking all sorts of questions. But in practice these questions are settled quickly with the responsible secretary by telephone.

As a rule, the censor and the secretary hardly meet one another in the course of their work. They sit in different offices in the same building and communicate by telephone. The censor says, for example: "Look here, in the editorial, fourth paragraph, second column, there's something I don't like." "Very well," replies the responsible secretary, "throw it out. We can join it up." Or sometimes the censor says that he has been given an article on some aspect of Party life which is already outdated—it does not contain the latest nuances, so it has to come out. "All right," answers the responsible secretary, "how many lines?" If it is 225, he opens a drawer, takes out a sheaf of material on the Party and lops off a piece about 225 lines long. It only takes a couple of minutes, and then a girl sends the censor the galley proofs of this "new" material which he trims to size and pastes on to the page. The rejected proofs are then returned to the responsible secretary. Time is short, he has to get the newspaper out, so he simply throws them into the bottom drawer. Later, when he has more time, he may ring the head of the department dealing with Party affairs and invite him to come in and look at the rejected piece. But perhaps the censor has written nothing on it, so the department head goes to see him personally, and this is the reason why a department head meets the censor more often than the responsible secretary who deals directly with him. He calls on the censor and together they examine the article to see if it is possible to salvage it. If so, it is published the following week.

When the last page is ready the chief editor arrives. He looks at all the pages—four, six, whatever it is—and signs them. By this time the censor has almost finished his work and the newspaper can be sent immediately for printing. After everything has been sent to the print shop a number of questions arise which have little to do with censorship: the reimposition of pages, rearrangement of the layout, etc. Nonetheless, every time something is rearranged, a wet galley proof is handed in to the censor at once and he is informed, for example, that a paragraph on the output of chairs has been transferred from one place to another, that this photograph of skaters has been moved from here to there, and so on. There are reasons for this. There exists the so-called "displacement" technique of saying in print something that is forbidden. It works like this: you juxtapose two phrases so that they are separated by the dividing line between two columns but can be read as one continuous phrase. Alternatively you print two items, the title of one being intended to relate to the other. When Pasternak died, for example, someone inserted a small column saying that Boris Pasternak, a member of *Litfond*, had died, and on the same page there was a big article called *Volshebnik poezii* (A Magician of Poetry) about the Czech poet Nezval—but probably alluding, at any rate in the title, to Pasternak as well.[94] This is why the censor checks every page for the slightest alteration in the lay-out; otherwise there could be trouble.

Well, when everything has been finally settled and the newspaper has gone to press, everyone leaves except the assistant secretary and a duty censor. When the assistant secretary gets the signal from the print shop he goes to the censor, who gives the word to start the presses rolling. Then they both go home and the paper is printed and distributed.

---

[94] See *Literaturnaya gazeta*, June 2, 1960. In the 1930s censors were expected to ensure that there were no incongruous juxtapositions on either side of a page. A. Gaev (*Tsenzura sovetskoy pechati*, Institute for the Study of the History and Culture of the USSR, Munich, 1955) gives an example (p. 23) of an undesirable combination in an issue of *Trud* for 1937: on one side a portrait of Stalin, on the other a picture of a worker swinging a hammer. If the newspaper is held up to the light the worker appears to be hitting Stalin on the head. At this time, according to A. Finn (*Experiences of a Soviet Journalist*, Research Program on the USSR [Mimeographed Series No. 66], New York, 1954), censors were expected to check materials by looking at them upside down as well as back to front; there was a famous scandal in Moscow when it was discovered that the picture of a torch on a matchbox label resembled the face of Trotsky if looked at the wrong way up (p. 6). Finn also relates the case of the night editor of a newspaper who through "lack of vigilance" committed a "seditious act" by not noticing that a comma had been left out of a quotation from Lenin (pp. 5–6). For an amusing recent misprint of a quotation from Lenin see E. G. Golomb and Ye. M. Fingerit, *Rasprostraneniye pechati v dorevolyutsionnoy Rossii i v Sovetskom Soyuze*, Moscow, Svyaz, 1967, p. 92, line 9 ("Parazitelno malo" instead of "Porazitelno malo").

I think the censors are so suspicious for two reasons. First, there are the almost daily compulsory seminars about which they are always grumbling. I was never present at these seminars and have no idea what takes place, but I imagine the censors are given pep-talks by some of the big-wigs such as Romanov or Zorin. The second reason was explained to me by Nikolay Glazatov, who said, tapping his nose: "One must have political flair, Leonid. You know what I mean." The censor must have an intuitive "feel" for the political situation and at the same time not be overcautious. It is an affliction if you are landed with an overcautious censor who hacks away to left and right. But this type does not last very long; he is a square peg in a round hole—a censor must also know what is permissible, not only what is forbidden. The editors might put up with him for a month or two, but then they will write to Romanov, and if he does not reply they write again. Finally the censor is replaced, but where he goes to is usually a complete mystery. He just vanishes into thin air.

Albert Parry:

But where do they materialize from in the first place?

Leonid Finkelstein:

I know where many censors came from, but where they disappear to is absolutely obscure. In the words of Tvardovsky's poem "Vista Beyond Vista":

> And if I were a superstitious person,
> I think I could assert
> That the smell of sulphur from that berth
> Has slowly drifted out through the ventilator.[95]

I once had a wonderful friend in the censorship, a fine young man with whom I got on famously at work. His name was Igor Batamirov, a progressive, open-minded former Komsomol official. We worked well together and it was easy to settle any infringements of the censorship with him quite amicably. I used to go to football matches with him, or to the House of Journalists, or just to have a drink. One day he simply disappeared. I asked if he was ill, and was told that he had been transferred. "Where to?" I asked, and, after a long pause, Nikolay Glazatov replied: "Out of the business." I never met him or heard of him again. It was as though he no longer existed. I enquired whether he was now in the Komsomol apparatus or in journalism, but nobody knew. The man just did not exist.

---

[95] This is the last stanza of chapter six, "Literaturny razgovor" (A Literary Conversation) of *Za dalyu — dal*, as published in Moscow, 1960, by the Gosudarstvennoye izdatelstvo khudozhestvennoy literatury. First printed in *Novy mir*, No. 6, 1953, p. 79.

Yuri Demin:

I would like to put in a word for the censors. Do you know how difficult it is to be a censor? They disappear for all sorts of reasons, sometimes because of what censors themselves sardonically refer to as a "political misprint." I knew a case, during the Stalin era, where the letter "l" was left out of a headline containing the word *Glavnokomanduyushchy*.[96] The man responsible disappeared immediately. Or, for example, the headline: "The Fishing Season in the Far East—Into the Sea with All Communists!" The man who passed this was chased out so fast his feet did not even touch the ground. Sometimes their plight is pitiable. They must watch out for everything and be exceptionally vigilant, and frequently they concentrate so hard on the small print in the text that they overlook a howler in a headline. And, curiously enough, almost every one of these blunders concerns political material, with fateful consequences for the censors.

Leonid Finkelstein:

One military censor even committed suicide. This was General Kandaritsky, head of the atomic censorship. I knew him slightly, but I have no idea whether his suicide had anything to do with his job.[97] Many things

---

[96] This results in what is known in Russian as an uncensorable (*netsenzurnoye*) word, i.e., a word that has to be (*NOT* cannot be) censored. The play on words cannot be conveyed in English, but relates to the offensive word *govno* (sometimes spelt *gavno*).

[97] This was to vet all materials, including science fiction stories, which made any mention of atomic energy. The atomic censorship is housed in a building of the State Atomic Energy Committee on Staromonetny pereulok. The atomic censors, who work extremely slowly and uncooperatively, have been headed since 1966 by Valery Kalinin. There is also the Commission for Research on and the Exploitation of Cosmic Space at the USSR Academy of Sciences. This is no more than a specialized censorship group, very closely associated with *Glavlit* and working in the Academic Institutes Building at 18, Vavilov prospekt. This office has been headed since its inception in 1957 by Candidate of Technical Sciences Mikhail Galaktionovich Kroshkin. Each book, article, radio or TV broadcast in any way connected with space flights must have authorization from Kroshkin's censorship office. At the press conferences given after each flight by Soviet cosmonauts Kroshkin sits behind them and "corrects" their replies on the spot.

Other specialized censorship groups also exist, for radio electronics, chemistry, and State Security. The last named is still known as the "KGB Censorship." If questions entering the domain of one of these specialized offices crop up in the text it must immediately be sent in to obtain the stamp of the appropriate censor, before the material is sent to *Glavlit*. This rule is inapplicable only to the KGB censorship—materials are sent to them by the *Glavlit* censors where necessary, and the board of editors is informed at the same time. [L.F.]

slip through in headlines, and for this the censors are held responsible. But not for this alone, of course. They are continually walking a tight-rope; all the time they keep repeating, *"you* have an easy time of it." This is the censors' stock phrase. But I must say that in recent years responsibility has somehow shifted. The authorities have shown more understanding towards them and become more lenient. Now the censor does not always have to answer for a mistake, whereas the editor always does! This is good for the censor, who feels himself freer, but bad for the editor.

Let me turn to the recruitment of censors. I have already mentioned that some are recruited from among Komsomol workers and others from state security organs, but I believe that the majority are drawn from neither of these two sources. Most censors have some experience of literary work, of editing and perhaps even of printing and publishing, and are from the Party's point of view sufficiently reliable to be entrusted with censorship work. I know for a fact that there is a faculty for editing and publishing at the Moscow Polygraphic Institute from which censors are recruited each year. Graduates are interviewed and, if satisfactory, taken straight into *Glavlit* to learn the business.

For six years, from 1960 to 1966, I was in close daily contact with censors, and I can tell you that an exceptionally strong process of renewal is in progress. The censorship cadres are getting younger; in 1960 many censors were quite elderly, but by 1966 there were far more younger ones. Glazatov is no more than 40, for example, and perhaps by now he has even risen to be deputy head of *Glavlit.*

Of course, one should not think of censors as devils with horns. They are ordinary Soviet people. I cannot recollect one ever having spouted propaganda clichés at me—saying that in publishing our journal we must educate the builders of communism, and so on. They tend to be business-like people. Some are quite sceptical about their work, while others even openly complain about it. One told me he was fed up with his job and terribly ashamed of it. He subsequently resigned. This shows that censors are human and just normal people doing what is widely regarded as a normal job. Their work is unusual only in that it is highly paid. A junior female censor at the "Nauka" publishing house—she had the very appropriate name of Ideya Vasilyevna[98]—once told me that she earned 280 rubles a month, which is an exceptionally good salary when you consider that a department head earns 215 and a junior editor 115 rubles a month. Most Soviet people wear rather shabby clothes at work, but censors are always very well dressed. The average chief editor makes about 400 rubles a month,

---

[98] Ideya = idea. Ideyny = having or containing officially approved ideas.

but it varies according to the publication. The post of chief editor is also a Party appointment, and carries a much higher salary than that of deputy chief editor. I never succeeded in finding out the salary of a senior censor, but it must be very high.

Censors' salaries are apparently paid by the State Committee for the Press, of which *Glavlit* is a part. But this Committee was set up only in 1963,[99] and the censorship existed before this. So who controlled and paid the censors then? Perhaps it was the Ministry of Culture. As for the actual number of censors in the Soviet Union, it is my own rough estimate that there are some 70,000, but this may well be inaccurate. I arrived at it by taking the number of oblasts in the Soviet Union, calculating the average number of towns, then assuming one censor for a rayon centre and several for larger towns where there is probably a *Gorlit* (department of *Glavlit* at urban level) and adding the central apparatus. Considering the size of the country, I am inclined to regard 70,000 as a conservative estimate. There are, in addition, quite a number of other, special, censorship bodies, though even the largest of them—the military—has a staff of no more than fifty.[100]

---

[99] On the functions of the *Soyuzno-respublikansky [Gosudarstvenny] Komitet po pechati pri Sovete Ministrov SSSR* see pp. 424–426 of *Administrativnoye pravo*, ed. A. Lunev, Yuridicheskaya literatura, Moscow, 1967. Footnote 2 on p. 425 mentions that the *Glavnoye upravleniye po okhrane gosudarstvennykh i voennykh tayn v pechati Komiteta po pechati pri Sovete Ministrov SSSR* was abolished and replaced in August 1966 by the *Glavnoye upravleniye po okhrane gosudarstvennykh tayn v pechati pri Sovete Ministrov SSSR*. This suggests that the censorship was then separated from the Committee for the Press and brought directly under the Council of Ministers. The abbreviation *Glavlit* is used by the speakers at this symposium for the sake of convenience. B. Stukalin replaced N. Mikhaylov as chairman of the State Committee for the Press in 1970. Mikhaylov's predecessor was P. K. Roma-nov, who spent about two years away from (or combining this job with) his post as head of *Glavlit* when the State Committee for the Press was set up in August 1963 (see *Vedomosti Verkhovnogo Soveta RSFSR*, No. 32 [254], August 15, 1963, p. 673). Four years previously the Main Directorate for Publishing Houses, Polygraphy and the Book Trade had been established as part of the Ministry of Culture; on its functions see the Central Committee resolution (*postanovleniye*) of May 11, 1959 (in *Voprosy ideologicheskoy raboty*, Moscow, Gosudarstvennoye izdatelstvo politicheskoy literatury, 1961, pp. 271–272). All its functions were presumably transferred to the State Committee for the Press in 1963. In 1972 the State Committee for the Press was reorganized and renamed the Union-Republican State Committee of the USSR Council of Ministers for Publishing Houses, Polygraphy, and the Book Trade. Stukalin remained chairman. See *Pravda*, August 2, 1972, p. 6.

[100] The Military Censorship of the General Staff of the USSR Armed Forces is located at 19, Kropotkinskaya ulitsa, but materials sent for examination have to be addressed to the First Building of the USSR Defence Ministry, 19, ulitsa Frunze. The military censors work efficiently and liberally, but their stamp of authorization is insufficient by itself and has to be confirmed by the Glavlit organs. [L.F.]

Victor Frank:

What is the formal relationship between *Glavlit* and the State Committee for the Press on the one hand, and *Glavlit* and the KGB on the other?

Leonid Finkelstein:

Although *Glavlit* salaries appear to be paid by, or rather via, the State Press Committee accounts department, *Glavlit* comes in fact directly under the Central Committee and has some connection with the KGB, although not directly subordinated to it, because all questions directly relating to censorship are decided in the Central Committee Propaganda Department. Complaints about censorship should be addressed to Vladimir Stepakov,[101] or, if you wish to go even higher up the ladder, to Pyotr Demichev.[102] Naturally, it helps if you have connections. Let me quote a well-known example: I worked for the journal *Semya i shkola* (Family and School) from 1958 to 1960. The deputy chief editor was Boris Igritsky, a former comrade of Mikhail Suslov in the First Revolutionary Regiment in 1918, and a devoted communist. I was in the room with him when he learned that the censorship was holding up one of his articles. Very annoyed at this, he dialled a number, shielding the telephone from me, and said: "Misha, this is Boris. Misha, you must help me. *Glavlit* is holding up material which I think ought to be let through. I'll send it to you, all right?" He sent it immediately with a messenger, and one and a half hours later *Glavlit* rang up saying that the material had been approved. This is not usual with *Glavlit*, believe me!

Victor Frank:

You talked about the recruitment of censors and their educational background. I would like to know what sort of person censored Bulgakov's novel *Master i Margarita* (The Master and Margarita).[103] It must have been someone both educated and sensitive.

---

[101] After five years as head of the Propaganda Department V. I. Stepakov lost his job in the first half of 1970 and is now the Soviet ambassador in Belgrade. The name of the new propaganda chief has not yet (March 1973) been made known. The first deputy head is A. N. Yakovlev (see his article in *Literaturnaya gazeta*, No. 46, 1972, pp. 4-5), who is on the editorial board of *Kommunist*. See *Zhurnalist*, No. 2, 1971, p. 74.

[102] An alternate member of the Politburo and a secretary of the CPSU Central Committee.

[103] The Posev edition of this work (Frankfurt, 1969) prints in italics the passages that were censored in the Soviet published version.

Leonid Finkelstein:

It was Diana Tevekelyan, a most charming lady who edited a story of mine for *Moskva* at about the same time.[104] She is not a censor but an editor, and a brilliant one. However, her political intuition is just as well developed as that of any censor. She tried hard to push through Katayev's *Svyatoy kolodets* (The Sacred Well) which was rejected by *Moskva* but later published by *Novy mir*.[105] She also did her best for Aksyonov's *Pobeda* (Victory).[106]

Albert Todd:

Does the same system of censorship operate at *Pravda*? I assume that the chief editor is a high official and a Central Committee member?

Leonid Finkelstein:

He is indeed. And the system is the same. But *Pravda's* editor, M. V. Zimyanin, is a high-ranking and very busy official who has little time for checking everything with the "Talmud." *Pravda* contains a lot of "errors," in spite of the censorship; I could find one for you in every issue. But the *Pravda* people are not journalists, they are clerks who sit in their offices doing some kind of indefinable job. I had several articles published in *Pravda*, yet it is still a mystery to me how they passed the censorship. At *Pravda* they certainly badly need the censor, who checks articles according to the "Talmud" and saves the staff a lot of unpleasantness. Material with an ideological content is checked by the chief editor, however, and the *Pravda* censor scarcely needs to make any corrections.[107]

David Anin:

The dispatches filed by TASS correspondents have presumably been censored before they reach the newspaper offices. Are they then subjected to a second censorship?

---

[104] L. Vladimirov, "Do pensii sorok let," *Moskva*, No. 3, 1965. In English in *Soviet Literature*, Moscow, No. 10, 1965. *Master i Margarita* was printed in *Moskva*, No. 11, 1966 and No. 1, 1967.

[105] No. 5, 1966. On the censorship of this work see Alayne P. Reilly, *America in Contemporary Soviet Literature*, New York-London, N. Y. University Press-University of London Press Ltd., 1971, especially pp. 133 and 168.

[106] Published in *Yunost*, No. 6, 1965.

[107] For an example of Central Committee criticism of *Pravda* see the resolution (*postanovleniye*) of September 15, 1959 (in *Voprosy ideologicheskoy raboty*, Moscow, Gosudarstvennoye izdatelstvo politicheskoy literatury, 1961, pp. 287–288).

Leonid Finkelstein:

No. All the responsibility rests with the TASS censors, who work twenty-four hours a day, seven days a week, like TASS itself. They take all the material, screen it and sort it out into ordinary and white-folder TASS reports, red-folder TASS, and "special bulletins," etc. If an article passes the general TASS censorship it is classified as lilac-folder material and carries no special instructions. The responsible secretary at the newspaper is then allowed to abridge the article. He may cut out only complete paragraphs—it is categorically forbidden to change anything within a paragraph. The newspaper censor never checks TASS material; if the responsible secretary has altered anything and it comes to light, he alone is held responsible, not the censor.

David Anin:

How about Soviet foreign correspondents? A censor cannot be informed on everything, let's say reports from Italy or Japan, where all kinds of left-wing groups exist.

Leonid Finkelstein:

He can. He has to attend all those special seminars. Nobody is hacked about as much as foreign correspondents, by the way. Five newspapers have their own foreign news departments, which are considered to be the most important, and they all have their own censors.

Wasyl Miniajlo:

There was an article in an issue of *Literaturnaya gazeta* entitled "The Intrigues of 'Madam Rumour,'"[108] dealing with information leaks, the speed with which rumours spread and their impact on the general public. I would like to know how well-founded rumours come into circulation in the first place. How does information leak out of the Kremlin? At the time of Kirov's murder, in 1934, I was a student in Kharkov. Leningrad, where Kirov was murdered, is a long way from Kharkov, yet within two weeks rumours were circulating among us students that there was something "fishy" about his death, that the official explanation was false and that he had, in fact, been disposed of by the secret police on Stalin's instructions. If this was possible even under Stalin's strict censorship, does it not happen much more easily today? Perhaps you could also give us some idea of how well-informed the Soviet citizen is about what happens at home and

---

[108] December 3, 1969, p. 11.

abroad? What does he know, say, about the attempt on the lives of the astronauts who were travelling with Brezhnev—or it may have been an attempt to kill Brezhnev himself—which was reported in only a few lines in the press?[109] What about information from abroad? How does he picture the capitalist world?

Leonid Finkelstein:

It is difficult to say with certainty how rumours arise, but one source was related to us by Anatoly Kuznetsov when he arrived in the West. After the Soviet-led invasion of Czechoslovakia high-ranking Party officials called a restricted meeting of the most reliable Party activists and announced:

> Comrades! We were forced to invade Czechoslovakia. You all know that we said we did this at the request of the Czechoslovak leaders, but it is no secret that there was no such request from them. It is an unpleasant business, of course, but we were forced to take this step and want to tell you the reason why. We forestalled the West Germans by a few days, maybe even a few hours, otherwise their tanks would have been in Prague. But keep this to yourselves!

This is the surest way to start a rumour in the Soviet Union, in this case one planted deliberately for political reasons. It was a *canard*, but other information from such a source may be wholly or partly true. It is not surprising that well-founded rumours can start circulating when you consider that three days after the trial of Sinyavsky and Daniel I had a typewritten copy of their last pleas in my hands, and a week later the record of the whole proceedings. Meetings are arranged, resolutions are passed, information leaks out. Meetings held to brief Party activists are also attended by chief editors, because Party or government decisions are frequently preceded by a press campaign, and the editors need to be in the picture. There is obviously scope for rumours here. More often than not, rumours about price increases are well-founded because the new price-lists are sent to the shops before the prices are put up. No matter how well the secret is kept, an inventory has to be compiled and this takes at least one night—time enough for people to pass on the word. This is the second type of rumours, the well-founded ones.

False rumours, the product of somebody's fantasy rather than of a deliberate lie, can result from an interrupted telephone call, a garbled report, etc., and constitute a third group. And last but not least there is a fourth category consisting of objective information passed on by word of mouth and mainly based on radio broadcasts from abroad. In April 1966, for example, I attended a restricted lecture delivered by Konstantin Zarodov (then deputy chief editor of *Pravda*, and former chief editor of *Sovetskaya*

---

[109] See *Pravda*, January 24, 1969, p. 3, *Soobshcheniye*.

Rossiya [Soviet Russia]) to an audience of about one hundred people. The lecture, which was given behind locked doors without a microphone and in a highly confidential atmosphere, was entitled "The Twenty-third Congress of the CPSU and the Tasks of Moscow Journalists." The main burden of Zarodov's lecture was that there are chinks in the iron curtain which are harmful to the Soviet Union, the main "chink" being Western radio broadcasts, followed by tourism and foreign communist newspapers. (You can buy *Humanité, Drapeau Rouge, Morning Star* and *Unità* in Moscow, but only, of course, if they do not carry, say, a speech by Louis Aragon condemning the Soviet invasion of Czechoslovakia.)

Wasyl Miniajlo:

How much more "permeable" are the Kremlin walls now, compared with in Stalin's day?

Leonid Finkelstein:

They are still walls all right, but there is immeasurably more information available nowadays than there used to be. The average Soviet citizen disposes of a hundred times more information than he used to in Stalin's day, and a journalist, through the sort of confidential briefings I have just mentioned, or his chief editor returning from a meeting in the Kremlin, or conversations with colleagues on other publications, knows almost everything that is going on.

Albert Todd:

Do people get into hot water if an article they wrote or recommended is suddenly regarded as objectionable at a late stage in the process of publication?

Leonid Finkelstein:

Yes, they do. Such a calamity befell our first issue of *Znaniye — sila* for 1961. An article on supersonic airliners in the issue had been officially and personally approved by the Deputy Minister of the Aircraft Industry, Belyansky. He had authorized the printing, but later something in the article was found not to be in accordance with the "Talmud," so the article was withdrawn and Belyansky reprimanded by the Central Committee. If the "Talmud" is violated, a censor who is senior to the first censor intervenes and stops publication. In our case "Supercontrol" spotted the slip, but it was already too late, and most of the first edition, including the cover, which mentioned the article, had already been printed, and had to be scrapped.

Albert Todd:

And where are copies of periodicals and books kept if they have already been printed but then banned at the last moment from sale? Who keeps an eye on them? Or are they all simply burnt?

Leonid Finkelstein:

Well, there is the famous case of the book by Sinyavsky and Golomshtok on Picasso.[110] It was printed by the "Znaniye" publishing house, but immediately afterwards there arose a dispute between the chief editor, Rodionov, and *Glavlit* that was carried on even at Central Committee level. Rodionov was forbidden to put the book on the market, and the whole edition was banished to the basement. But a basement is not an armoury, and stolen copies started to circulate. It was then decided to distribute a thousand copies to Westerners—a unique decision in Soviet literature[111]—and to burn the remainder. On another occasion, Somerset Maugham's *The Summing Up* had just reached the bookshops when it was suddenly banned. Telex messages were sent out at once, but the bookshops had been open for half an hour and nobody could prove how many copies had already been sold. The bookshop managers are no fools: they returned one or two copies and kept the remaining 150 or so, selling them for three times the price to trusted customers.

Anthony Adamovich:

I would like to draw a few parallels between censorship in my time, that is, in the late 1920s, and today. At that time everything was much simpler; our literary organization in Belorussia was completely non-Party, which is impossible nowadays. We didn't have a single Party member, just two members of the Komsomol, yet we managed to publish a journal because we succeeded in securing a subsidy from the chairman of the *Sovnarkom*. We had no staff and received no salaries, and only free-lance contributors were paid. I was in charge of taking material to the *Glavlit* censorship (there was only *Glavlit* in those days). We had no premises of our own, but one of us, the late Belorussian writer Kuzma Chorny, was on the regular staff of the rural newspaper *Belaruskaya vyoska* (Belorussian Village), and its editor, who was well-disposed towards us, gave us permission to use their offices. I was able to watch the newspaper at work at close quarters and got to know the jargon, and also the celebrated

---

[110] I. N. Golomshtok and A. D. Sinyavsky, *Pikasso*, Moscow, 1960, in an edition of 100,000 copies.

[111] Although something similar happens with Bibles and other officially printed religious literature which is very hard for most Soviet citizens to acquire.

misprints of those days, both accidental and deliberate. I well remember one "error" ridiculing a popular slogan—"Our 'five-cent' star radiates over the world"[112]—which cost the editor his job. What happened to the censor and the editorial secretary I do not know, but the senior type-setter was dismissed and sent to Siberia, partly because it turned out that he was a former member of the [extremely reactionary and anti-semitic] Union of the Russian People.

In our day *Glavlit* was located on the premises of *Narkompros* (The People's Commissariat for Enlightenment), but its staff wore the OGPU uniform. They were also paid by the OGPU, via *Narkompros*. I knew three censors in turn; the first was not very literate, but at least he did not cause any delays. The other two became writers later on, and are now leading lights in Belorussian literature. Both wore the OGPU uniform, and one of them, Ilya Hursky, was very strict and a real fault-finder. He once delayed an article of mine for a whole year because it was about a pre-revolutionary writer who was considered a rightist, despite the fact that he had been deported from Poland for being a leftist. We had to appeal to the Central Committee press department, which eventually approved its publication. The other censor was quite easy-going. He used to give us articles of his own and we would publish them in our journal, although they were not really in our line. He was an Arabist, and the articles were rather highly specialized, dealing with Belorussian elements in Tatar manuscripts written in Arabic script in the seventeenth century. Still, we printed his articles and he rewarded us by returning our material the day after we had given it to him.

In one respect our censorship was stricter—the stamp had to appear on every page, not just on each printer's sheet. On the other hand the second approval, for publication, was a mere formality. We used to have our material printed in the provinces, because it was cheaper there than in Minsk, and we had to take all the articles to the local *Glavlit* representative. It appears that everything is much more complicated nowadays.[113] Incidentally, in my book on Belorussian literature I devoted a whole chapter[114] to

---

[112] This was a Russian, not Belorussian, misprint: *Pyatikopeyechny* instead of *Pyatikonechny* (five-kopeck instead of five-pointed).

[113] On the censorship of newspapers and periodicals in the Ukraine at the time of which Mr. Adamovich is speaking see pp. 9–14 of A. Kotlyar, *Newspapers in the USSR. Recollections and Observations of a Soviet Journalist*, Research Program on the USSR (Mimeographed Series No. 71), New York, 1955. On censorship in the Ukraine more recently see John Kolasky, *Two Years in Soviet Ukraine*, Toronto, Peter Martin Associates Ltd., 1970, especially chapter 13.

[114] See chapter I, "Ciphers and Deciphers," of his *Opposition to Sovietization in Belorussian Literature (1917–1957)*, Munich and New York, 1958.

the ways we used then to beat the censor, and even in the 1920s we had a *samizdat*, albeit on a very small scale. We used what we called the "disguise," i.e., we would write about Polish persecution of Western Belorussia, but we really meant the Soviet régime in our part of Belorussia. We also used to smuggle out manuscripts.

Aleksey Yakushev:

I would like to make a few remarks concerning the relationship between censorship and science. This is an extensive field, since it covers all the natural and exact sciences, not to mention the social sciences, to which a completely different set of rules applies. One must also take into account the informal censorship, which is much more important than the formal variety.

For a number of years I worked for a publishing house concerned mainly with publishing translations of a wide range of foreign scientific literature—the natural and exact sciences, social and political science, philosophy, etc. It was, in fact, the only publishing house in the Soviet Union to have been founded at Stalin's explicit request,[115] and it had no proper formal censorship. It did not handle classified material—military and industrial secrets and the like—so if the item in question was, say, a translation of a work on mathematics, only such things as the preface and the footnotes, written by Soviet authors, were subjected to formal censorship. Editors and censors were on friendly terms, but everything was settled by telephone and messengers carried the material to and fro. I myself have never set eyes on a censor.

I worked at this publishing house from 1954 to 1962, and I am also familiar with the practice before this period, but I have never heard of a censor rejecting anything. If an editor objected to any of the censor's queries, the latter was quite prepared to give way and leave the responsibility to the editor. This flexibility was less daring than it might appear, because in the course of its preparation the manuscript was subjected to quite a number of processes, the editor being expected to act largely as his own censor. As well as being editor he was also censor, in practice if not in name, and he bore a corresponding degree of responsibility. If I tell you that I was hauled over the coals eight times, on two occasions by the Central Committee secretaries Shkiryatov and Suslov, you will understand

---

[115] In 1946. On the Izdatelstvo inostrannoy literatury see pp. 155–158 of B. Gorokhoff's *Publishing in the USSR*, Indiana University Publications, 1959. On June 4 of that year this publishing house was criticized in a resolution (*postanovleniye*) of the Central Committee: see pp. 274–277 of *Voprosy ideologicheskoy raboty*, Moscow, Gosudarstvennoye izdatelstvo politicheskoy literatury, 1961.

what I mean. Some of my colleagues and I received a severe reprimand from Suslov for a book which we entitled *Kibernetika i obshchestvo* (Cybernetics and Society) by Norbert Wiener. Later I had the opportunity to have a long conversation with Wiener, and he expressed his astonishment that his book had been read by the Politbureau, the pinnacle of the Party hierarchy, adding that he could not imagine President Eisenhower reading a book of that kind.

As I said, the actual censorship was carried out by the editor, or rather the whole editorial staff, because everybody was involved in the process. In the Soviet Union the views expressed in a book are not necessarily those of its author. The editors, the publishing house as a whole, various consultants, an entire network of persons are also responsible for it, and sometimes least blame of all is attached to the author if something is found wanting. Now, in science a formal censorship is of only limited use, because it takes an expert to understand the material, so the system of formal censorship gradually evolved into a more informal one as editors were entrusted with the job. Only once did the censors interfere with my work. I had been asked to act as consultant for the translated version of a book by the French mathematician H. L. Lebesgue. The introduction had been written by the noted Soviet mathematician A. N. Kolmogorov, and I was required to check its philosophical content. The censors suspected that some of the concepts expressed in the introduction were at variance with, and even challenged, current Soviet ideology. This was not the case, but Kolmogorov agreed to a few minor changes because the substance was left intact.

Where editors act as their own censors, as in the case of translated scientific literature, there is always the opportunity to smuggle in important information by making standard Soviet terminology a vehicle for other ideas. The problem of "revisionism" or some such heresy does not suddenly appear out of the blue in the Soviet Union; it arises because certain new ideas have already appeared in print in the guise of orthodox scientific terminology. This is one way of undermining the official ideology, and it is happening constantly. Natural and social scientists often deal with overlapping questions, and they act in collusion to circumvent the censorship.

Finally, a few words about official and unofficial censors. Here we have another two groups which overlap as a result of the close cooperation existing between them, and it is not easy to draw a clear distinction. How do official censors set about checking translations of, let us say, Western scientists? They first investigate the author. Who is he? Has he ever said anything against the Soviet Union? All this despite the fact that his book has nothing to do with politics. The following is a typical example: a book on the ionization of gases by Lyman Spitzer was prepared for print, but it was rumoured that at one time he had said something unflattering about the Soviet Union. The book was badly needed—scientists and research centres kept requesting it and everybody recommended it—so it was decided to publish it as a special, limited edition not for public sale. The book was duly published and distributed according to a special list. Then, all of a sudden, the official censors were prevailed on to admit that the rumour was false. The ban was lifted and a large second edition published.

What I must emphasize is that information from abroad does exist in the Soviet Union but is administered in doses. Certain books are published in very small editions, sometimes consisting of only one copy! Our publishing house had a large "special editions" department with its own printing section and a "hot line" to the Central Committee—the CPSU leadership used to make direct recommendations about various publications. And yet, despite all precautions, a certain number of copies of these restricted editions would disappear somewhere. This special editions department even had a translating section of its own. If there was a query they called me in and I might have to read the book, ask for further details, and so on. When this happens with a number of people, news spreads. In the Soviet Union information has always managed to leak out, and will do so even more in the future, however much the censorship tries to prevent this.

The Unofficial Censorship

Natalia Belinkova:

When I think about censorship in the Soviet Union I never equate it with *Glavlit*. Some of the participants in this symposium are interested in learning how many censors there are, how they lay their hands on a manuscript, what they write on it and how the work of the censor fits in with that of the editor and the author, etc. Well, these facts and figures are of the utmost interest, but they can all be summarized quite briefly.

Censorship in the Soviet Union is actually something far more extensive than *Glavlit*. Although some of the recent arrivals from the Soviet Union who have already spoken here might seem to have strayed from the subject, what they said is, in fact, extremely relevant. The censorship is not a single institution; it is made up of many people and is something all-pervading, a state of mind. For the same reason, I believe that the few hundred censors in Czechoslovakia, or even two or three times that number, could not of themselves turn that seething land into the mute country it has now become.[116]

The habit of self-censorship and compliance is so deeply ingrained that even when the relatives of a deceased author and the director of a publishing house, plus a few writers, form a committee to prepare his posthumous works for publication, they may acquiesce in changes and omissions which distort his real intentions. The diaries of Kazakevich, a writer who in his lifetime was regarded as oppositional, were "treated" in this way,[117] and Mark Shcheglov[118] has now been appropriated by the apologists for Stalinism. I knew Shcheglov very well. He was an amazing person—highly critical and with a fine sense of irony, yet his diaries, as published,[119] show him as a loyal and obedient Soviet citizen.

---

[116] On censorship in Czechoslovakia see D. Hamšík, *Writers Against Rulers*, London, 1971, and for examples of what was censored under Novotný see J. Procházka, *Politika pro každého*, Prague, 1969, in which the passages originally censored are printed in different type. On banned authors and books since the invasion see "Není nutno ...," *Listy*, Rome, No. 2, 1971, pp. 21–24 and No. 3, 1972, pp. 29–30.

[117] See *Voprosy literatury*, No. 6, 1963.

[118] 1926–1956.

[119] See M. Shcheglov, *Literaturno-kriticheskiye stati. Iz dnevnikov i pisem*, Moscow, 1965.

The list of those who edit or otherwise interfere with a publication before it appears in print includes the director of the publishing house, the editorial board, the learned council, the editorial council, the department or section heads, the senior editor, and even the proof-reader. But it is possible to outwit this phalanx of censors, and on one occasion I quite unexpectedly became an ally of Korney Chukovsky in helping him to have an article published in the form in which he had actually written it. At the time I was a senior literary editor on the journal *Moskva*, a journal which in my eyes differed from *Znamya* only in that the latter printed what had been rejected by *Novy mir*, and *Moskva* what had been refused by *Oktyabr*. (I do not want to insult *Novy mir* by bracketing it with *Oktyabr*, but a remark by Anna Akhmatova does spring to mind. When asked how she, of all people, could have published one of her poems in *Oktyabr*, she replied: "My dear fellow, they all have 'Workers of the world, unite!' printed on the cover.")

My immediate superior on *Moskva* was a woman called Ivanova, a zealous Party activist who was constantly trying to persuade me, her only subordinate, of the need to organize a literary purge. Our relationship was a very strained one, and I longed to get away but could not. She never trusted me with a long article, but even these staunch pillars of the régime have to go on holiday, and so it came to pass that Ivanova was granted a free holiday in the south and had to leave in my hands Chukovsky's article containing his reminiscences of Zoshchenko. Before she left she told me that the article was too long and must be abridged, and that in particular all references to the Serapion Brethren[120] must be eliminated. I assured her we would do this, but after she had left I began to worry about what I should say to Korney Chukovsky, who was a very good friend of mine. I visited him, explained the situation, and asked him to abridge the article himself. He crossed out a couple of things, but left in everything about the Serapion Brethren. We sent the article to the censorship and three days later they telephoned the journal's responsible secretary and recommended that five or six corrections be made in the references to the Serapion Brethren. What did we do? In one place we simply crossed out "Serapion Brethren" and inserted "brothers-in-arms," so that the sentence read: "At that time none of these youngsters suspected that they were destined to become brothers-in-arms."[121] In another place we left the name in, but added a quotation from Gorky—part of a letter in which he speaks well of the

---

[120] A writers' "fraternity" founded in 1921 and naming itself after E. T. A. Hoffmann's hermit, Serapion. It was the first literary group in the Soviet Union which, while not opposing the régime, made every effort to remain independent.

[121] *Moskva*, No. 6, 1965, p. 191.

Serapion Brethren.[122] In this context it couldn't fail to pass the censor. Take a look at issue No. 6 of *Moskva* for 1965 and you will see that everything about the Serapion Brethren remained in the article, in spite of the censors' suggestions. The censors like to force you to make alterations, but once you have made them they automatically assume that it is an improvement and trust you more the second time.

However, the mutilation of manuscripts accounts for only a fraction of the crimes that can be laid at the door of the Soviet censorship, and by censorship I don't mean just *Glavlit*, but the activity of the Party and the influence of the whole social climate as well. Not only are works of art distorted, writers are also destroyed mentally and physically. I do not need to remind you of the tragic fates of Mandelshtam, Babel, Pasternak, and those who are now in prison camps. Then there are those who have been driven to emigrate, further impoverishing Soviet literature. The Soviet censorship has upset the balance between universal, eternal values and contemporary life and its problems. Solzhenitsyn expressed this graphically during a discussion of *Cancer Ward* at the Union of Soviet Writers, when all sorts of people were offering him "good advice." He stood up, extended his arms, and with his large, beautiful hands imitating a pair of scales he said: "You know, sometimes I ask myself how I should go about it. Supposing I put in more eternal values, then less will be left for current problems." He lowered one arm and lifted the other: "If I put in more topical problems, there will be less space for eternity." And he lowered the other arm.

This balance between eternal and topical values is disturbed in Soviet literature by the abnormal prevailing conditions. Everything is maimed by the pressures to which both major and minor writers are subjected. One of the best and most interesting illustrations of these pressures is Solzhenitsyn's play *Olen i shalashovka* (The Tenderfoot and the Camp Prostitute), which was secretly rehearsed at the *Sovremennik* (Contemporary) theatre in 1963 but never performed in public. Nobody talked about it, but something leaked out about the stage setting: while the audience were finding their places, fiddling with their hair, opening out their programmes, and still not paying too much attention, they were to become dimly aware of a row of barbed wire stretched across the front of the stage. After they had settled more comfortably into their seats and were able to concentrate more fully on the stage, they would notice a second row of barbed wire beyond the first. The curtain would then be raised to reveal yet a third row of barbed wire. It was also intended that during the interval after the first act the

---

[122] *Ibid.*

public would not be able to leave the auditorium because of an armed guard standing at every exit and pointing a rifle at the audience. I believe this was meant to symbolize the oppressive conditions under which Soviet literature has to operate. It is hemmed in on all sides, and this was represented by the barbed wire fences.[123]

I would like to say something about those books which, thanks to the censorship, or, more accurately, to the ramifications of the dictatorship, never see the light of day. The *samizdat* system tries to salvage the situation somewhat and circulates works written in the 1920s by such writers and poets as Bulgakov, Platonov and Mandelshtam, which are read just as eagerly as the most contemporary works. Among the censorship's victims is a book called *Chukokkala*, based on notebooks which Korney Chukovsky filled with the remarks and *bons mots* of his literary contemporaries from the beginning of his career. The genre is astonishing—its prototype could have been the sort of album kept by young ladies in Pushkin's time. But Chukovsky is not a young lady from a small provincial town in nineteenth-century Russia, and his albums are full not of hussars, but of his own great contemporaries, including Blok, Pasternak, Mandelshtam and Akhmatova, and illustrated by great artists, beginning with Repin. Chukovsky kept these "albums" throughout his life and decided to publish them in 1965. But he had delayed too long and they disappeared into the limbo of the "Iskusstvo" publishing house. Although *Glavlit* was not directly involved, the book was nonetheless blocked.[124] Chukovsky wrote an extensive and indispensable commentary to this work, which is a collection of skits and parodies, and thus essentially something light-hearted and facetious, yet at the same time poignantly tragic, because every one of those who contributed to it came to grief. The book contains things that would never pass the censor; it is a vivid chronicle showing how Russian literature and thought have been degraded.

I worked on Chukovsky's book for a year, helping him to write the commentary. He had a remarkable memory, but there were some situations that even he could not reconstruct, and then I would have to do an incredible amount of research to establish the identity of a given person.

---

[123] Mrs. Belinkova went on to mention briefly the interference by the authorities (especially Tolstikov in Leningrad) with a play by Leonid Zorin, *Rimskaya komediya* (A Roman Comedy). This play (also known as *Dion*) concerns the relations between rulers and writers; the Leningrad production by Tovstonogov featured a gigantic statue of an emperor, the Moscow presentation (at the Vakhtangov theatre) drew attention to the mute slaves. On theatre censorship see p. 131, footnote 209.

[124] For further details see N. Belinkova, "Chukovsky i Chukokkala," *Mosty*, Munich-New York, No. 15.

For example, in *Chukokkala* there is a portrait of a man called Gnesin; not Mikhail, but one Nikolay Gnesin. Who was this Nikolay Gnesin? I checked without success in literary and musical encyclopedias, but nobody knew, not even the literary historians. At last, with great difficulty, I managed to get in contact with Yelena Gnesina herself,[125] by then an old woman and very ill. Since I could not visit her in her home I had to speak to her on the telephone, and it was quite an odd conversation. Her voice was thick and old, and sounded as though it came from the bottom of a well or the depths of time. I explained that I was helping Korney Chukovsky and she asked: "Chukovsky? Which Chukovsky?" Then she recalled the Chukovsky of 1916, but, although I felt she knew something, she seemed frightened and I learned nothing during this telephone call. This fear still makes it difficult to gather even the most innocuous facts about people. I later discovered that Nikolay was a brother of Mikhail Gnesin and had studied at the chemistry faculty of Moscow University. During the disorders at the Moscow Conservatoire in 1905 the famous Gnesin and his friends asked this brother to make them some smoke bombs. He agreed and was then expelled from the university for doing so. He left Russia and went to Italy, where he organized an itinerant musical theatre, returning to Russia sometime in the 1920s to become head of a department in the section for children's music at the Leningrad radio station. He was arrested in 1937, and his family heard nothing more until in 1956 they received a sum of money equal to two months' salary and a certificate to say that he had been rehabilitated. He was just one victim of the system, and the notes to Chukovsky's book referred to many similar cases. Naturally it could not be published—at any rate in full.

I would like now to explain how the censorship influences the layout of a book. An interesting and by no means stereotyped work published recently in the Soviet Union was called *Deti pishut stikhi* (Children Write Verse) by a talented author named Vladimir Glotser. The book, which has a very good foreword by Chukovsky, refutes the ideas on the creative activity of children put forward by the latter in his book *Ot dvukh do pyati* (From Two to Five). Glotser's work was illustrated with drawings by a young and extremely gifted artist whom, for want of a better word, I shall call a primitivist in style. He fully understood the spirit of this book and drew manikins, an elongated steamship, and so on, rather in the manner that children draw them. But it is not thought good for a Soviet artist to draw in this strange, childish manner—indeed, certain people say it is

---

[125] Yelena Gnesina, her sisters and brother Mikhail played an important part in Russian musical life from the end of the nineteenth century. A Moscow music school is now named after them.

harmful. So, although the drawings were excellent and appropriate to the subject, the censors deliberated and finally hit upon the bright idea of taking some real children's drawings and mixing them in with those of this talented young artist. His name is given in the book, but which are his original drawings and which are those done by children it is impossible to distinguish.[126] This was *Glavlit's* work, and I can give you another example of this sort of interference. The third edition of my husband's book *Yury Tynyanov* was illustrated with drawings of various literary figures, and the artists tried very hard to match their drawings to the text. In one case they depicted Pushkin in profile and, because he was not the central figure in this chapter, partly shaded. This illustration did not get through. To portray Pushkin with his face in semi-darkness—impossible!

The quaint antics of the censorship can be quite unpredictable. In 1961 a collection of Pasternak's poems was published (Moscow, Goslitizdat, 1961, 376 pp.) and about a year later *Novy mir* commissioned Sinyavsky to write a short review.[127] I strongly recommend *Novy mir* readers to pay attention to the inconspicuous pages where these reviews are to be found, because, although the more controversial material is usually located in other sections, one sometimes finds something of interest in these short reviews. This was the case with the one by Sinyavsky, for example, which was simply entitled "A Collection of Boris Pasternak's Poems" and was the first posthumous article on Pasternak; it was also the first since the sad affair over the award of the Nobel Prize. Sinyavsky obviously wanted to show Pasternak in the best possible light, but his inner censor warned him that he would have to say something derogatory about *Doctor Zhivago* as a sop to the censorship. He wrote a very good article on Pasternak, but began with a paragraph regretting that the writer had made a mistake with *Doctor Zhivago* and including a few other critical observations on the novel. Everyone read the review, including Tvardovsky, and all agreed that the correct balance had been struck between a positive and negative assessment of Pasternak, although it was almost entirely positive, apart from the criticism of *Doctor Zhivago*, which they realized was uttered through clenched teeth. But when they took the article to the censorship they were told that there could be no mention of *Doctor Zhivago* at all. How could they criticize the novel if they were not allowed to mention it by name? Sinyavsky thought of a compromise. He removed the first paragraph and inserted a neutral phrase to the effect that "in recent years, among wide

---

[126] V. I. Glotser, *Deti pishut stikhi*, Moscow, "Prosveshcheniye," 1964. The artist was M. Klyachko, whose name is given on page four, together with a list of ten children whose drawings are reproduced in the text of the book.

[127] No. 3, 1962.

circles of readers, the name of the author has conjured up impressions of a negative nature..." The censors were satisfied and Sinyavsky, with their unwitting assistance, was able to be fairer to Pasternak than he had originally hoped.

Finally, I would like to tell you how we once beat the censors at their own game and with their own weapons. While I was still an editor on the journal *Moskva*, a critic by the name of Olga Voytinskaya—a typical syco-phant who once endorsed Stalin's ideological policy, later enthused about Khrushchev's, and now heartily supports the ideological policy of Brezhnev and Kosygin—brought me a review of Aleksey Malenky's (this is a pseudo-nym) *Pokoriteli tundry* (Conquerors of the Tundra), a novel published in 1962 by the "Sovetsky pisatel" publishing house. It was a thick book of 716 pages describing in heroic terms how Komsomol members and Party workers had constructed a railway in the tundra. The truth of the matter is that the railway had been built by prisoners, including Malenky himself, at great cost in human life. In other words, history, as described in Nekrasov's famous poem *Zheleznaya doroga* (The Railway)[128] had repeated itself. The manuscript had somehow come to light and, because this was a period when Voytinskaya was assiduously condemning Stalin's crimes and sympathizing with his victims, she also sympathized with Aleksey Malenky. Neither Voytinskaya nor Malenky had a word to say about the way in which this railway was really constructed, yet here was Voytinskaya expressing hypocritical compassion for the hapless people who had suffered in Stalin's concentration camps. She had written a lengthy introduction about Malenky's tragic fate, and I felt I could not permit her to present the readers with a false picture of this man, making him appear to glorify a system which had caused such great suffering, and to which he had later fallen victim himself.[129] So I struck out this touching, sentimental introduction to her review. Voytinskaya was terribly displeased. She complained about me to the Central Committee, which resulted in a call to the editor to say it was quite in order to mention people who had been rehabilitated and to tell their stories. So I decided on a slight change of tactics. I still threw out the original introduction but, together with Voytinskaya, I concocted a new one. We described the prison camp horrors as being simply the result of "unusual circumstances." Then we said that the book was a testimony to the power of socialist ideas to transform life. We wrote that the author's sympathies clearly lay with people who are morally strong and who are

---

[128] 1864.

[129] Malenky (real name Popov) died at the age of 42 in 1947, three days before he was due for release. See the *Kratkaya literaturnaya entsiklopediya*, Vol. 4, col. 541.

faithful to the ideas of Lenin. We also added that the book had been written by a communist who was convinced that the moral principles of socialism would prevail, together with several other phrases thought up by Voytinskaya. She was appeased and a compromise had been reached. But in the introduction we had turned Malenky into such a paragon of communist virtue that any discerning reader would recognize the book as just one more stereotyped propaganda tract and conclude that it would be pointless to waste time ploughing through its 716 pages. As this had been my main aim from the outset, I considered that I had won that particular battle. As you see, there is often a struggle between personalities, between two editors, for example, or between an editor and a writer or critic, rather than a direct confrontation between author and censor.

Herman Achminov:

Where, in the final analysis, does the conflict between the system and the creative intelligentsia really take place? I find it difficult to believe that the censors can be included among the creative intelligentsia, that they can be numbered among those who help to pierce the system.

Natalia Belinkova:

It's the other way round. The majority of the creative intelligentsia can be classified as censors!

Herman Achminov:

That is tantamount to an assertion that the creative intelligentsia is on the side of the régime.

Natalia Belinkova:

The main point I wish to make is that the censorship is not the only instrument or institution that exercises punitive and educative functions on behalf of the Soviet régime. *Glavlit* itself, as an appendix of the Central Committee, is in no way at loggerheads with the editorial offices of journals. People in these editorial offices, on editorial boards, in publishing houses, newspapers, etc., have been appropriately drilled for years to implement official policy. It is not simply a case of a boil on a healthy body, but of a whole body putrefying and covered with ulcers. Only a very few healthy parts try to resist, and herein lies the heroism and greatness of those people who protest and are put into prison. If they had the support of the people, if they had the backing of other writers, they would not be the heroes that they are. They constitute a social phenomenon, notwithstanding the small number of people involved. Herzen was alone when he went abroad and founded *Kolokol* (The Bell), but what he did made him a social phenomenon. And Herzen was cursed by the same majority that damned Sinyavsky and Daniel as double-dealers.

Herman Achminov:

Where do you draw the line between these heroes and the rest of this vast system?

Natalia Belinkova:

The boundary varies according to the periodic changes in policy of the Party Central Committee, but part of the nucleus of the "opposition" is always to be found in the prison camps.

Yuri Demin:

And the rising generation constitutes another element. But we are talking about censorship, and the censor is a policeman. When a policeman hounds you from one street corner to the next, it is not so much his fault as that of the system which put him there. We are basing our discussion on the wrong premise. We have seized upon this policeman and are basing our whole argument upon him. We should put our priorities in the right order, which means that the first thing to bear in mind is the Soviet régime. The Soviet people in general are not really on the side of the censorship, but the crux of the matter is, what do we mean by "the people in general?" In the Soviet Union, as in any other society, the majority are philistines who just want to live their own lives, who adapt themselves to circumstances and mind their own business.

Albert Parry:

The silent majority!

Max Hayward:

We are becoming too wrapped up in political theory. I think that the essence of a totalitarian régime, as opposed to a simple dictatorship, is that the totalitarian régime forces the majority of the population to assist in running the machine. And this, if I understood her correctly, is what Mrs. Belinkova wanted to say.

Natalia Belinkova:

Exactly.

Herman Achminov:

But where do these impulses of coercion and opposition originate? If we regard the censor as a policeman, where do his orders come from?

Yuri Demin:

From the Party Central Committee.

Natalia Belinkova:

Let me illustrate what I mean with a joke. During the build-up for the fiftieth anniversary of the October Revolution two fashion-conscious Moscow girls meet on the street. One asks: "Good heavens, why are you wearing such a crumpled dress?" And the reply comes: "I'm afraid to switch on the iron!" Radio and television dealt with the fiftieth anniversary *ad nauseam*, just as happened with the hundredth anniversary of the birth of Lenin, and people were so sick to death of it [that according to this joke they didn't want to turn anything on at all. *Ed.*]. Propaganda is everywhere, poured out by the government through its own ideological, literary, and other organs. When dictators take power they immediately seize the telegraph offices, radio stations and printing presses, and these are then made to serve the new régime. Only people with suitable ideological qualifications are allowed access to the mass media, while those who do not share this ideology are kicked out if they are lucky or, if unlucky, they are packed off to prison. And that is where the boundary runs between the heroes and the system.

Max Hayward:

Perhaps Anatoly Kuznetsov would like to comment on Mrs. Belinkova's contribution. She has described how things look from behind the editorial desk, and I'm sure many of us would be interested to hear a first-hand account of how things appear to the author who takes his manuscript into the editorial office.

Anatoly Kuznetsov:

Personally, I never met any creative writer who did not complain about censorship, not even the most orthodox, reactionary, stupid and untalented Soviet authors. They all complain, even those who have completely sold themselves, such as Kochetov. He even complained to me once that they had cut out something that was too obviously anti-semitic! No doubt they were justified in this instance, but it would be better if they gave Kochetov a free rein, so long as they give everyone else a free rein too. But there is a reverse side to this coin—the censorship is a convenient means of concealing one's sterility. Kochetov, for example, published some wretched book and then came along and hinted that it had been ruined by the censorship. In this way many people preserve the illusion that they have talent, but when you dig deeper into the matter you find that the fault lies with them, not with the censorship.[130]

One must pay due respect to the ability of the people working in the censorship. You bring along your manuscript and the first censor you encounter is one of the editors of the journal. For example, when I brought *Babi Yar* to *Yunost*, the first person to censor it was Mary Ozerova, wife of the critic Vitaly Ozerov. In conversation with you she is an extremely kind and understanding person with progressive ideas, and she gave my manuscript a sympathetic reading. And here I should pay tribute to the industry of the editors-*cum*-censors: they take all this work home, and day and night they pore over these manuscripts. What heroism! Ozerova reads with only one thought in mind—to pass or to censor? After this she shows me her notes and tells me what is unacceptable and must be excised, and I agree. She performs the preliminary censorship, pointing out certain passages which we pore over and then, regretfully, strike out or recast.

Then everything goes from Ozerova up the chain. The bosses of the journal read the manuscript: Polevoy reads it, his first deputy, Preobrazhensky, reads it, the responsible secretary Zheleznov reads it, and so does somebody else from the editorial board, usually Prilezhayeva. This is terrible, because she is an awful woman who understands nothing but is very sure of herself. All these people censor the manuscript still further; they do not read what Ozerova and I struck out together, but they find other things. This ascending ladder of censorship is very interesting. As early as the first stage I am nervous and think: all right, I'll sacrifice this and that. But at the second stage the cutting starts with a vengeance: Boris Polevoy immediately scores out whole pages in green pencil and writes in the margin the letters "MZ" or the number "22." This is just his brand of humour—"22" is a reference to the card game *vingt-et-un*, in which you must not score more than 21 points. In other words he means you have overplayed your hand and gone too far with your liberal ideas. And "MZ", if you'll pardon the expression, stands for *mladozasranets* ["young shit"]! And then he roars at me: "You, you young shits, I'm not having this! No!" And so on. I dreamt about this "MZ" at night, and still do. Now, restoring the text of *Babi Yar*, I derive enormous satisfaction from

130 On this see A. Sinyavsky's story *Grafomany* (The Graphomaniacs).

saying, ah, he put "MZ" here, and "MZ" there—and I reinstate the original version.

At other times the editors are convinced that something will not be allowed, that although they themselves are in favour of it, it just won't get through higher up. And this was where I began to see red. Not one of my novels has been published without preliminary hysterical scenes, without the sheer fury that gripped me when I had to argue about and justify almost every phrase. I wrote about the Germans entering Kiev. They had horses with golden manes, massive creatures, gigantic in comparison with the wretched Russian nags on which the Red Army retreated.[131] "Stop! Why are the German horses better than the Soviet ones?" This business with the horses really upset me. At the end of my novel[132] there is a sentence describing how the Germans retreat on Russian horses, worn-out things, with not a golden draught-horse in sight. I pointed out that the first reference balanced the other, only to be told that this was not the case, because by the time the reader had finished the book he would only remember that the Germans had better horses than we did.

When this consortium of gods sat in the office and mutilated my work step by step I could have howled. Instead, I said: "Give me my manuscript. I don't want to publish it; it can lie in the drawer. I shan't publish it with all these crazy corrections!" "Oh, no!" they replied. "We shan't give you back the manuscript and you will publish it!" To which I screamed: "It's my manuscript and I don't want to publish it, and that's that. I'm going to tear up my contract with you." "No you're not," they said. "You'll do just what we want." How cynical can you get? The scene was ludicrous. I rushed to the desk and tried to grab my manuscript. Sheets of paper flew in all directions and a scuffle began, with me shouting: "I'll go to the militia! This is my own paper and I typed it on my own typewriter. You have no right to keep it." I managed to snatch up the manuscript and dash out of the building. Then I ran like a maniac along the street, tearing the paper to shreds and stuffing it into the litter bins all the way to the Arbat. I rammed it into various bins, so that it would be impossible to gather it up and piece it together again, and then started to curse the day that I took up literature.

But later it turned out that I had left a second copy of the manuscript in the editorial offices. I had left them thinking that everything was all right—there would be no *Babi Yar*. But then suddenly they telephoned me: "We've done everything for you and, guess what, the opinion we got

---

[131] Posev edition, p. 30; Floyd translation p. 28.

[132] *Yunost*, No. 10, 1966, p. 49; Posev edition p. 470; Floyd translation p. 463.

from there is very positive!" *"From there"* means from the Central Committee, the next stage up. *Yunost* has an influential contact in the Central Committee in the person of Igor Chernoutsan, a great friend of Vitaly Ozerov, the husband of Mary Ozerova, and so it can occasionally allow itself the luxury of "barking." Chernoutsan is a man who keeps completely out of the limelight and who is something of a mystery to me. I have had many long conversations with him, and he is very kind, open-minded and interesting. He is a cripple, without hands, very cultured in conversation, by no means a conservative pachyderm like so many Party functionaries. When you speak to him you have the impression that he understands things and would make a fair decision on an issue. *Yunost* gives anything controversial to him to read, and he passes it on. He knows how to get round Yury Melentyev (one of the most influential people of all in these matters), who has the ear of some of the bigwigs. Melentyev slipped extracts from *Babi Yar* to Suslov, who found nothing to complain about in them. Someone told me this confidentially.

Well, then the next stage arrives. By this time I have lost heart and capitulated. I have even calmed down and my hysterics have subsided; I simply wait dully for what will happen next. They will merely show me what they have chopped out; no need to work and ruin one's nerves. They will do all that is necessary. The typist prepares a new copy at the journal's expense. But then I get an even shorter text. A really strange one. Everything is reversed, everything is upside-down. Where I described how the Kiev Lavra is blown up by the NKVD I now find that it was done by the Germans.[133] Where I described how a person saved at Babi Yar by a miracle is then betrayed by the local inhabitants it turns out that the Germans caught her themselves.[134]

After this comes the final, formal stage when the manuscript is passed to the official censor. By this time I am completely subdued and resigned. All right, I thought, nearly everything has gone, but this remnant is still left, a few worthwhile fragments will get through. But then I was told that even they must be thrown out. "Why?" I asked. "You had already approved it." The answer: "Well, you see, they..." "Who are *they*?" I screamed. "Show them to me. I'll prove to them that this passage is good." But of course I never once succeeded in finding out who "they" were and I was never allowed to see "them." This, then, is the final stage. I counted seven or eight of these stages through which the manuscript of my novel

---

[133] For the full account see the Posev edition, pp. 197–202 (Floyd translation pp. 197–202).

[134] Contrast *Yunost*, No. 8, 1966, p. 27 with Posev edition, p. 114, and Floyd translation p. 115.

passed, and each one resulted in cuts and abridgements, and each time I had to back down. The situation is even worse in the film world.[135] I myself made two films, and I counted eighteen different levels at which cuts and alterations were made.

When a new work is published I read it and know that it is just a pathetic shadow of the author's original. I always asked writers I knew to let me see the original manuscript. It is impossible to read Aksyonov in print, for example; one must read his manuscripts. When we read Soviet literature as published, we have to bear this in mind and make enormous allowances for what the censorship has done. People engaged in censoring would be happy not to be doing it; I never met anyone who relished the work! They excuse themselves by saying things like, "It has to be done." If you start to investigate the situation you find that Ivan fears Pyotr, Pyotr fears Semyon, Semyon fears Yemelyan, and so on up the scale; it is rather like a pyramid with Brezhnev or someone, I do not really know who, at the apex. Yet the strange thing about this system, in which everyone is scared of everyone else, is that basically you don't know what they are afraid of. Ultimately everyone is being intimidated by something abstract, and the entire machine runs on this abstraction. I, too, subscribe to the opinion that the formal censorship is the policeman at the crossroads directing the traffic. The whole tragedy is that one is caught up in this strange, incomprehensible system—from time to time something goes wrong, there is a trial, someone is convicted, but for what reason no one knows.

Peter Reddaway:

Arthur Miller wrote[136] that on her desk Furtseva, the USSR Minister of Culture, has a pile of manuscripts and that she also takes them home. Is this, perhaps, one of the stages to which Anatoly Kuznetsov referred? I would like to ask how the censorship affects right-wingers such as Kochetov, to what extent they are censored. Around 1957–58 Kochetov wrote a work about the Chinese which was published in *Zvezda* (Star)[137] but not reprinted, as his works usually are, in book form in hundreds of thousands of copies.[138] My third question concerns the attitude of Soviet authors to the publication of their works in the West. What do they think about the considerable delay that sometimes precedes publication of their works here, and do they think that this delay may sometimes be due to a sort of voluntary censorship in the West?

---

[135] Film censorship is discussed in more detail on pp. 107—120.

[136] See *Harper's Magazine*, September 1969, pp. 43–47.

[137] No. 10, 1959.

[138] It came out under the title *Ruki naroda* in Moscow, 1961, in only 10,000 copies.

Natalia Belinkova:

Furtseva represents one level of censorship, although she is not employed as a censor in your understanding of the term. Thanks to Furtseva, many of Shakespeare's plays have not been presented on the Soviet stage. In preparation for the fiftieth anniversary of the Soviet régime, for example, many Soviet theatres wanted to cut out the propaganda and present something more reputable and of higher artistic quality, such as classical works from the international repertoire. They chose works that they felt would be above suspicion and began to prepare productions of Shakespeare. But Furtseva heard about this, called together the chief producers of the various theatres and said: "Do you think we don't realize why you have chosen plays by Shakespeare? We know it's because they are all about rulers and the struggle for power!" And that was the end of several productions of Shakespeare's plays.[139]

Anatoly Kuznetsov:

I never met a single person who would not be happy to have his work published in the West, and it is always a cause for secret pride and secret joy for an artist when this happens. If there is a scandal he may protest officially (as in my own case),[140] but in his heart of hearts he will be proud, because it signifies international recognition of his work. There can be unpleasant repercussions for him, of course, but if his book is published here he is prepared to endure them. This is the honest truth, so they should be published without asking for permission, because tacit permission exists.

Natalia Belinkova:

The very fact that a manuscript reaches the West is in itself tantamount to permission.

Anatoly Kuznetsov:

When I made fifteen copies of the original version of *Babi Yar* on cigarette paper and sent them to fifteen people whom I respect, beginning with Solzhenitsyn, Tvardovsky, etc., I secretly entertained the sinful thought that one of them might pass it on to someone else, who would make a copy, and that in this way it would somehow be smuggled abroad.

---

[139] Mrs. Belinkova was thinking in particular of *Richard the Third*. For an interpretation of this play see V. P. Komarova, "'Richard III' Shekspira kak politicheskaya tragediya," *Filologicheskiye nauki*, No. 5, 1971, pp. 40–53.

[140] See on this the report by D. Floyd in *The Daily Telegraph*, August 7, 1969.

But they were all too honest, the manuscript did not end up anywhere here. Really one should go up to someone from the West, thrust it boldly into his hand and say: "Print this!" But that is very risky—anyone of these middlemen could be a KGB agent; there are such types. I know that young writers, friends of mine, would be happy to have their work published abroad. They would be delighted if things that have been lying on their desks for ages were to be published here, but they themselves don't make a move in this direction.[141]

I would like to add that the censorship also bans some of Kochetov's work, because the censorship operates against "right" and "left." The mention of Stalin's name is strictly rationed now, for example.

May I emphasize again that censors and editors can be very difficult to understand. Their psychology is very complex; they suffer and torment themselves, and there are unseen victims. A certain Georgy Marchik, for example. No one knows what he went through. He was editor of *Selskaya molodyozh* (Rural Youth),[142] usually an odious and insignificant rag, but he decided to use it as a vehicle for better things, so he began to publish translations of interesting articles from the West. He invited Fazil Iskander and myself to join the editorial board, and I became a member. We began to print some rather daring pieces. We published an excellent selection of Okudzhava's poems, including his famous *Pesenka pro Chernogo Kota* (Song About a Black Cat.)[143] But Nemesis was swift—Marchik was sacked and I was dismissed from the editorial board, but hardly anyone knows because it was not given any publicity.

Take the case of my novel *Prodolzheniye legendy* (Continuation of a Legend) which *Yunost* had published in mutilated form.[144] Another magazine reprinted it,[145] and here I resorted to a trick. Instead of taking the *Yunost* version I gave them a manuscript in which I had risked reinstating some, though not all that much, of what *Yunost* had thrown out. The editor was a young girl, a university graduate, who realized that I wanted to push through what had been cut out of the original, and she did not say a word. She was very diplomatic. She passed on the manuscript as the *Yunost* text and it was published. Then someone discovered the discrepancy and she was sacked. One could quote many such cases.

---

[141] This problem is discussed in more detail on pp. 140—148.

[142] See, for instance, the first two issues for 1966.

[143] See No. 1, 1966, p. 33. This very interesting issue also contains Bulgakov's *Moskva krasnokamennaya* and *Pokhozhdeniya Chichikova*.

[144] *Yunost*, No. 7, 1957.

[145] *Roman-gazeta*, No. 2, 1958. A comparison of the two versions is most illuminating.

Leonid Finkelstein:

I suppose something similar takes place at *Novy mir*?

Anatoly Kuznetsov:

I published my novel *U sebya doma* (At Home) in *Novy mir*.[146] After I had submitted it, Tvardovsky asked me to come round the next day, congratulated me, said that he had sat up all night reading the manuscript and that it would be the next success after *Ivan Denisovich*. He proposed one or two slight improvements—for "knout" we should substitute "cudgel," he said, and he pointed out that manure smells good, not nasty, as I had written. Then he gave the manuscript to Gerasimov and Berzer, just for the final touches. I was happy; I was walking on air. But then Gerasimov said to me: "The novel begins with a train crash, a disaster, and the censor won't accept that, not even in a work of fiction. We'll have to take it out." I began the novel with a dramatic scene—the train smash—now it had to be expunged, and I would have to think up another beginning. Yet I had no choice but to agree. This was only the start. I went home to Tula, and Gerasimov began to telephone me practically every other day to discuss alterations; so often, in fact, that I kept the manuscript ready by the telephone. One thing had to go and then another. Why? For what reason? Because "they" would never allow it. This went on for weeks; it was one long nightmare, but I trusted *Novy mir* and thought that if they said something was impossible it really must be so. After a month of this treatment only about half the novel was left. The best, the most important part, the central reason why I had written it, had been thrown out. Stage by stage everything of any importance was eliminated, and all that was left was just one more novel constructed around an agricultural theme, and a miserable, banal novel at that! Originally it was an unusual work written on two separate planes, rather like E. T. A. Hoffmann's *Lebensansichten des Katers Murr* (The Life and Opinions of Kater Murr). The pages in my work were interwoven, with the cat and the musician speaking in turns, so to speak, and what "they" did, in effect, was to throw out the musician and keep the cat. On the surface the novel was about a dairy maid who obtained 4,000 litres of milk from each cow, for which she was presented with a pennant and a watch. "They" retained all this, which was intended to be ironic, and threw out the real theme running parallel with it. Such was my experience with *Novy mir*.

I decided not to publish the work in this state, and so it simply lay about for a year. Then I took the manuscript to *Yunost*, where they were

---

[146] It eventually appeared in No. 1, 1964.

quite frank, saying that they could not publish it either, and that the cuts made by *Novy mir* were justified; but if I were to brighten up my descriptions of Soviet village life they would print it. I picked up my manuscript and took it along to *Molodaya gvardiya* (Young Guard), a journal at the opposite pole from *Yunost*. With Jesuitical cunning I said that *Yunost* had rejected it, which for them was a serious reason to read it carefully. And, to give them their due, they did read it carefully, shook me by the hand and congratulated me before telling me that nobody would print it. They returned my manuscript without even censoring it. At least they were honest!

Friends suggested that I take the manuscript to Kochetov in *Oktyabr* and simply say that *Novy mir* had rejected it. He spent a long, long time reading it, and then he phoned and asked me rather coldly to come and see him. "I don't know what they are worried about," he said. "I don't know what displeased Tvardovsky. I think everything is in order and ideologically correct! You say it is bold. What do you mean? I send them more daring things myself." We had a wonderful talk, he was very kind, very pleasant, but then he said, "We can't print it either. Not that there is anything wrong with it really, but it's the countryside, you see.[147] I'm astonished that you could have a lapse like this. It's simply devoid of talent. You have written far better things than this. Forgive me, but I'm speaking frankly as a friend."

I left him, clutching my manuscript under my arm. It lay around for a few more months until one day Gerasimov rang and said that if certain chapters were omitted they could see their way to print it. At this point, as so often happens, the money factor came into play. I had been sitting around up to my neck in debt because of the advance payments I had had, and now it was a matter of either repaying them or letting *Novy mir* go ahead and print the novel. I decided on the latter course, but asked them to change my name to "A. Kovalev." No, they said, in that case we won't print it, because the name is important for us. I insisted and they finally agreed, but when they brought me the galley proofs there stood "A. Kuznetsov." I pointed out for a start that my works always bear my full name—Anatoly Kuznetsov—and received the reply: "We've come half way to meet you. 'A. Kuznetsov,' nobody will know who it is; there are plenty of Kuznetsovs!" This was yet another black day in my life.

I have had four major works published, and the day each of them appeared was a black one in my life. I experienced no pleasure or joy, not the slightest, when they came out. I read what had been published and felt sick, because it was all so awful. At *Novy mir* it was always the same story.

---

[147] I.e., it shows how backward Soviet rural conditions can be.

They never said something had been cut out, simply that it would not be allowed by "them." One magazine is just like all the rest in this respect.

Leonid Finkelstein:

And was it like this with *Artist mimansa* (The Extra)?[148]

Anatoly Kuznetsov:

Because *Artist mimansa* was a short work there were fewer cuts. But even here they sometimes chopped off a head and left the tail. There is one passage, for example, where my hero, an old man called Ilya Ilich, wakes up and goes to work. And the next section begins: "Arriving at work, Ilya Ilich found the theatre whole and intact."[149] But why should he particularly notice that it was whole and intact? Because he had dreamt that it had collapsed in ruins under the weight of his terrible crime, etc. The description of the nightmare was nearly all thrown out, but the stress on the fact that the theatre stood there safe and sound remained; the censor just left the tail, although only a very careful reading revealed this. Let me give you another example of loose ends left by the censors: when they carved up *Babi Yar* at *Yunost* there was a chapter headed "Profession—Fire-Raisers" describing how, during the retreat, Vlasov's men set the houses on fire and turned Kiev into a scorched earth zone. It has me lying in a hayloft reading Pushkin's "You Appeared to Me in Dreams." And then, as I wrote it, the Vlasov men turn up with cans of petrol and start to burn the whole place down. "What's this! You can't mention Vlasov's men,"[150] they said at *Yunost*. So Boris Polevoy himself crossed out all the Vlasovites, and all that was left was a tiny, truncated fragment where I am reading Pushkin. But through an oversight the title "Profession—Fire-Raisers" remained, though if you look it up in *Yunost*[151] you won't find any trace of the word "fire-raiser" in the whole chapter. I was horrified, and when the foreign translations were being done and the translators enquired, "Why does the chapter have this title, Mr. Kuznetsov?" I replied: "Call it 'I Read Pushkin.'" If you look at the first English translation that is what you will find.[152]

---

148 *Novy mir*, No. 4, 1968.
149 *Ibid.*, p. 65.
150 Members of a Soviet force recruited by the Germans to fight on their side during the Nazi-Soviet war, 1941–1945.
151 No. 10, 1966, p. 37.
152 Pages 337–339 of *Babi Yar*, translated by Jacob Guralsky, London, Macgibbon and Kee, 1967.

Edward Crowley:

The censoring of poetry is a very tricky business because the changes there are even more obvious. What do you know, for instance, about the censoring of Yevtushenko's *Bratskaya GES* (The Bratsk Power Station)[153] and how he revised it?

Natalia Belinkova:

I know only that an article by Valery Dementyev, then a member of the *Oktyabr* editorial board, pointing out all the things in the poem that were negative from the régime's point of view, was to have appeared in *Moskva*, but the Central Committee vetoed it because Yevtushenko was already beginning to be of real use to the Soviet authorities. For them he was no longer the spokesman of the opposition to the established order; on the contrary, from their point of view he was doing a useful job, and these "failings" of his were also necessary because they helped to make him appear to be a genuine liberal by preserving something of his original appeal, although in fact they were merely the remnants of his earlier oppositional feelings. This is what I had in mind when I mentioned the review of Pasternak by Sinyavsky[154] as an example of the positive influence that the censorship can have on literature. Anatoly Kuznetsov has told us about the censor restraining Kochetov's anti-semitism,[155] which is another example of the beneficial side of censorship.

---

[153] *Yunost*, No. 4, 1965. For an amusing description of the editorial censorship of a poem see "Uvazhayte trud khudozhnikov," pp. 91–96 of Z. Paperny, *17 1/2 felyetonov*, Moscow, 1966.
[154] See pp. 81–82.
[155] See p. 85.

Censorship of Music

Martin Dewhirst:

We shall next talk about music and the cinema. I would like to invite Michael Goldstein to discuss the official censorship of music in the Soviet Union.

Michael Goldstein:

I must warn you that I can only recount my personal experiences in this particular sphere. From what I have heard at this symposium, however, I realize that the Union of Composers and the Union of Writers have much in common. "Two shoes make a pair," as they say, and these are two shoes which pinch badly, so far as creative artists are concerned. I would like to add that I am a violinist, composer and musicologist all rolled into one, and more recently I became a teacher as well. As I wrote a great deal for the journal *Sovetskaya muzyka* (Soviet Music) I may be able to shed some light on the censorship of articles about music, in addition to the censorship of actual compositions and the control over what is performed.[156]

Music has, of course, close affinities with other forms of creative activity such as literature, but it also displays distinctive features of its own. The literary censorship might authorize publication of a piece of poetry and, whether it is good or indifferent, it still remains verse. Furthermore, a wide variety of genres are tolerated. But the Party recognizes only two types of music—the "relevant" (*aktualny*) and the "irrelevant" (*neaktualny*). Irrelevant, or non-topical, music includes music without any accompanying text. Nobody bans it outright, but nobody promotes it either, and it is difficult to have it performed. On the other hand, music accompanied by a text explaining what it is trying to express is considered by the Party to be relevant, topical and important.[157]

---

[156] See also chapter 13 of Mr. Goldstein's book *Zapiski muzykanta*, Posev, Frankfurt, 1970, and his contribution (pp. 168-180) to *Novy kolokol. Literaturno-publitsisticbesky sbornik*, ed. N. Belinkova, London, 1972.

[157] Except, of course, for settings of religious texts. In his open letter to the Soviet Minister of Culture the conductor Igor Markevich writes that a performance he was due to give in Moscow of Haydn's *Creation* was suddenly cancelled on the grounds that not long before he had conducted Stravinsky's *Symphony of Psalms*. For the Russian text of this letter see *Russkaya mysl*, February 25, 1971, p. 2. Sometimes "outdated" words are dropped or altered, which may require changes in the music. Thus, a cantata by Prokofyev was reported by Reuter (*The Guardian*, April 9, 1966) to have had two of its ten movements cut out in

The censorship interferes with the creative work of composers in the following way. An "irrelevant" work, for instance a sonata or a symphony of considerable professional excellence, has been written and obviously deserves to be performed. It is given a sympathetic hearing at the Union of Composers and permission to perform it is granted, but then all manner of obstacles crop up: it is difficult to have it included in the concert repertoire of the philharmonic societies, performers fight shy of it because it has not been specifically recommended to them, or something of that sort. But performances of "topical" works are organized with lightning speed. Nikolay Chaplygin, artistic director of the All-Union Radio, makes every effort to have the work rehearsed as soon as possible and broadcast. It is then added to the concert repertoire after the minimum of preparation. In short, a composer who wants to see his music performed must tailor it to Party requirements. Nor is he left in the dark as to what these requirements are. For instance, at a joint plenary session of the artistic unions a few years ago, musicians, writers, poets and painters were addressed by Tikhon Khrennikov, who has been First Secretary of the USSR Union of Composers since 1948 and who saw fit to berate such outstanding composers as Shostakovich and Prokofyev while Stalin was still alive. During Khrushchev's reign he had to draw in his horns somewhat, but he retained his post and now, in the present process of re-Stalinization, he is once again firmly ensconced in the saddle. In his speech to the assembled artists[158]

---

order to eliminate favourable references to Stalin; for the same reason the Soviet national anthem is now played but never sung (the words are by Sergey Mikhalkov and El-Registan). Alterations may be made merely to the title of a work (e.g., Rimsky-Korsakov's Easter Overture [*Voskresnaya uvertyura*] is now called Radiant Holiday [*Svetly prazdnik*]), or to the text of an opera (the poet Sergey Gorodetsky turned Glinka's *Zhizn za tsarya* [A Life for the Tsar] into *Ivan Susanin*); or the music itself may be altered, as in Chaykovsky's 1812 Overture, in which the Tsarist national anthem is replaced in Soviet performances by an arrangement of the final chorus from *Ivan Susanin* (i.e., A Life for the Tsar). When this version was played in London by the Moscow Philharmonic Orchestra in 1963 it was said to have caused the greatest surprise among any audience since H. and C. Marx slipped "Take Me Out to the Ball Game" into the orchestral parts of "Il Trovatore" (see "Taken for a Musical Ride," *The Sunday Telegraph*, October 6, 1963). Mstislav Rostropovich mentions the censorship of music in his open letter to four Soviet newspapers (text in *Posev*, No. 12, 1970, pp. 2–3). On the censorship of ballets see Nataliya Makarova in *The Sunday Telegraph*, September 13 and October 4, 1970. Numerous other examples of political interference with music are given in F. K. Prieberg, *Musik in der Sowjetunion*, Cologne, Verlag Wissenschaft und Politik, 1965. On the renaming of musical works before the revolution see pp. 250–252 of P. Blaramberg's article "Tsenzura v muzyke" in *V zashchitu slova*, *Sbornik*, St. Petersburg, Klobukov, 1905. (MG, MD)

[158] See *Sovetskaya kultura*, December 11, 1969.

Khrennikov attacked what he called "unhealthy trends" in the works of some young Soviet composers. They were, he charged, neglecting vital contemporary themes of crucial social importance and displaying an exaggerated interest in technical experimentation. There is a certain amount of truth in this statement, the reason being that many young composers prefer to risk a possibly barren preoccupation with the technical problems of composition rather than kow-tow to the dictates of socialist realism.

On the other hand, there are powerful inducements to toe the Party line in music. A composer must earn a living, and if he wants to secure a commission from the State he must be prepared to set approved libretti, however banal, to music. Perhaps he would also like to be allocated a flat in the new house for composers which is being built in Moscow. He can borrow the money from *Muzfond* and then repay it in the form of musical compositions which must be written in accordance with prescribed themes. This is another means of exerting indirect pressure on composers.

Censorship in music arrived later than censorship in literature. It came into being when the officials of RAPM (Russian Association of Proletarian Musicians), chiefly the composers Davidenko, Bely and Koval, and the musical experts Lebedinsky and Keldysh, had firmly entrenched themselves in positions of power. RAPM was eliminated in 1932 and replaced by the Union of Composers, but by some chance the members of RAPM survived unscathed: for a long time Yury Keldysh was an editor of *Sovetskaya muzyka* and Marian Koval its chief editor, while V. A. Bely is still the chief editor of the journal *Muzykalnaya zhizn* (Musical Life). When I submitted articles to *Sovetskaya muzyka* the editor, without reading them, immediately sent them off to be reviewed. I have no idea who actually performed this work because it was cloaked in secrecy, but I do know that every editorial office in the musical press and musical publishing houses has its own critics, who are sufficiently well-informed to know what is permissible and what is not. They tip off the editor, who then warns you that your article will not get past the censor. When you ask him for a more detailed explanation it becomes quite obvious that he has not read the article himself, only somebody else's comment on it.

What sort of things does this anonymous critic object to? Well, he is less interested in technical aspects, such as tonality, modulation or structure than in seeing that the author of the article brings out the programmatic nature of the work in question and its political message. Once, after playing a sonata by Boris Lyatoshinsky, I had to write a review of it. This I duly did, analysing the work from the technical angle, but when the comment on my article arrived it said that I had not explained what the composer wished to express, nor mentioned that the work was part of the general development of Soviet music. Later I chanced to meet Lyatoshinsky himself in Moscow and told him the story. "My dear fellow," he replied, "I don't even know what this message is myself. I don't know myself what I wanted to say. I simply wrote the music as I felt it; there's no need to concoct a programme for it." Even so, I had to use a bit of cunning and reveal some political significance in the music. After I had done this my article was considered to be "interesting" and fit to print.

It seems to me that the function of the censorship with regard to music publishing and musical periodicals is to hinder the propagation of works considered superfluous because they fail to fulfil any basic propagandistic purpose. Yet I also believe that the choice of the terms "relevant" and "irrelevant" shows how much official interest there is in the development of music. They can talk about traditional boundaries which must not be overstepped, yet at the same time they cannot entirely ignore the importance of creative progress, without which Soviet music would become moribund. It is for this reason that Shostakovich, Khachaturyan and Kabalevsky are still allowed a measure of creative freedom.

Soviet composers, like their literary colleagues, also write for the "desk drawer," playing these compositions only in the presence of close friends. Sometimes these friends make tape recordings of such works or mimeograph them (*izdayutsya steklografom*), and sometimes thirty or forty copies are even mimeographed in Moscow at the Union of Composers to be shown to or studied by performers. They have been granted a form of conditional recognition, but if they are not circulated outside the Union of Composers they will be neither published nor performed in public and will remain in a sort of limbo.

Even works of unimpeachable sycophancy can fail to be performed—but for a totally different reason. The Lenin centenary, for example, prompted a spate of songs eulogising Lenin and the Party, works which the authors were sure would be accepted and for which they would be extremely well paid. Because of the resulting overproduction, however, many of these songs will rarely if ever be performed, but the Party is content because the main objective of stimulating (or simulating?) interest in an event of great political importance has been achieved.

The censorship is omnipresent in the Soviet music world, and even a musician of Oystrakh's stature has to fight hard for permission to play a work like Stravinsky's violin concerto. It is also the music censor's job to see that works stay in the right groove, or that they point in the right direction, so to speak. But what is to be done with those which excite interest and comment but which are not in the "right groove?" A few years ago a musical encyclopedia edited by Nicolas Slonimsky was published in America.[159] Slonimsky, an outstanding expert on contemporary music, included a number of young Soviet composers who do not appear in Soviet encyclopedias and who are almost unknown in the Soviet Union. Among them are Edison Denisov, Andrey Volkonsky, Sergey Slonimsky, the Ukrainian composer Miroslav Skorik, and a whole string of young avant-garde composers who are not recognized by Khrennikov. At the Fourth Congress of the Union of Composers, in 1969, Khrennikov attacked an interview in *Yunost*[160] in which one could read some extremely cogent and logical reasons why music must be allowed to develop freely. *Yunost* did not challenge the arguments—very wisely, because they are entirely just, but thanks to Khrennikov and others the restraint on the activity of young composers is very real. To know their works one must have attended the international festivals in West Berlin, Switzerland or America, where they are performed to impress the West.

On a visit to Moscow the conductor Pierre Boulez was handed a number of works by young Soviet composers. Examining them at home he discovered that they were talented works, and they have subsequently been performed here with great success. Unfortunately such incidents are rare, and a glance at concert programmes in England, France, Germany and America reveals that contemporary Soviet music has disappeared almost completely from the repertoire. During its recent appearance in Paris the Bolshoy Theatre presented a season consisting solely of pre-Soviet works—those which Dyagilev took with him and presented there many decades ago. This is a good indication of the stagnation prevailing in the world of Soviet music.

Albert Parry:

You imply that many good works are written but that there is no opportunity to perform them. I take this to mean that these works are not banned; performances are permitted, but there are simply no takers. Does this not illustrate the great difference between music and other art forms?

Michael Goldstein:

Music comes alive only when it is performed, and in order to be performed it must pass through a lengthy procedure to establish its credentials. A work which ends up abroad avoids these controls and stands a reasonable chance of being performed there. But this is not the case within the Soviet

---

[159] *The International Cyclopedia of Music and Musicians*. See also his *Music Since 1900*, London, Cassell, 1972.

[160] See the interview conducted by Natalya Gorbanevskaya with Valentin Silvestrov, *Yunost*, No. 9, 1967, pp. 100–101.

Union. Think of Shostakovich's *Thirteenth Symphony*. If you look in the catalogue of the "Melodiya" (Melody) record company, which is of course a state monopoly, you will find all Shostakovich's symphonies, with the exception of the *Thirteenth*. The reason is that this symphony is dedicated to Babi Yar—it includes a part for male choir singing Yevtushenko's words. It caused considerable displeasure in its day,[161] and it was very difficult to obtain permission to perform it. It was recorded, rather fortuitously, in the Great Hall of the Conservatoire and this recording came out abroad. The Moscow Philharmonic performed it while on tour in the United States, but the *Thirteenth Symphony* is never heard nowadays in the Soviet Union.

Sometimes a censor says, "Well, we don't forbid this, do as you wish, but we don't recommend it." Yekaterina Furtseva, the USSR Minister of Culture, often has to deal with censorship matters, but naturally she does not delve into the intricacies of atomic physics and other sciences; she has enough on her hands already—opera librettos, plays and variety productions—and she sometimes has the last word on what shall be included in concert programmes.[162] *Glavrepertkom*[163] or *Glavlit* might decline to sanction the performance of a particular work, and the artist, perhaps a prominent People's Artist of the Soviet Union, may refuse to accept this decision meekly, so the question is referred to Furtseva. She may have a talk with the artist personally, and say: "I'm sure you'll play it very well, but I advise you not to perform this work too frequently. It isn't necessary!" This does not mean that Furtseva settles all these problems herself; in the Ministry of Culture there is an involved system for supervising concert programmes which begins with the reviewers, who are Furtseva's deputies, and ends, as a rule, with the various departmental heads. The staff of the Ministry of Culture are especially hard-pressed when the programme for a

---

[161] First performed on December 18, 1962. On the rewriting of this work see p. 309 of F. K. Prieberg's *Musik in der Sowjetunion*, Cologne, 1965.

[162] See Arthur Miller's report of his talk with Furtseva, *Harper's Magazine*, September 1969, pp. 43–47.

[163] *Glavrepertkom* (*Glavny Komitet po kontrolyu za zrelishchami i repertuarom*) is that part of the censorship apparatus which decides what will be and what will not be performed in theatres, cinemas, concert halls, etc. (Works may be passed for publication but not for performance in some or all parts of the country.) For a detailed summary of the functions of *Glavrepertkom* under Stalin (it was then attached to the People's Commissariat of Enlightenment) see pp. 121–126 of L. Fogelevich, *Osnovnyye direktivy i zakonodatelstvo o pechati*, 5th ed., Moscow, OGIZ, 1935. This may be compared with the situation in the 1920s when *Glavrepertkom* was attached to *Glavlit*: see pp. 43–51 of L. Fogelevich, *Deystvuyushcheye zakonodatelstvo o pechati*, Moscow, Yuridicheskoye izdatelstvo NKYu RSFSR, 1927. See vol. 36 of the second edition of the *Bolshaya sovetskaya entsiklopediya*, p. 396, "Repertuarny Komitet."

Government-sponsored concert is being compiled. These concerts, presented in the Kremlin Palace of Congresses, the Kremlin Theatre, the Bolshoy Theatre or the Hall of Columns of the House of the Unions, usually have a fairly predictable programme—the singer Magomayev, the Aleksandrov Ensemble, and similar court favourites—and it is not at all easy for a comparatively little-known artist to perform on such an occasion.

Every Soviet performer has a document called his "Artist's Certificate" (*attestat artista*), to which is affixed a list of the works he is entitled to perform (*repertuarny list*). Whether he is a cellist, a trumpeter, a pianist or a singer, this list contains his repertoire and a stamp authorizing him to perform these works up to a specified date. Sometimes he is told that a particular work is to be removed from the list or is not to be recommended, and in this way he knows what to include in his programmes.[164] When Soviet artists perform abroad they have a wider choice, because the foreign concert agencies have some say in compiling the programmes and express preferences for certain works.

Alec Nove:

I understand why Shostakovich's *Thirteenth Symphony* is forbidden, but why Stravinsky's violin concerto, in which there are no words? Is this not simply a manifestation of an old-fashioned, conservative attitude towards art in general? What connection can a violin concerto possibly have with ideology, power and communism?

Michael Goldstein:

Stravinsky's concerto is too "advanced;" it was not composed in accordance with *Glavlit* prescriptions. Neither was Chaykovsky's *Fifth Symphony*, of course, but that is part of the classical heritage. You see, Stalin's tastes still dominate absolutely; his successors' tastes are just like his. In the Soviet Union the authorities are frightened of allowing creative minds freedom of expression. Western composers are not cramped in this way; they write as they feel, they write what they want to, but that is impermissible in the Soviet Union. Certain tags are pinned on people. The words "avant-gardist" or "modernist," for example, are terms of abuse. So is the label "formalist," but if you ask me what a formalist is in music I couldn't tell you to save my life.

J. René Beermann:

What about performances of works by contemporary foreign composers in general?

---

[164] See also M. Rostropovich's "Open Letter" to four Soviet newspapers, *Posev*, No. 12, 1970, pp. 2–3.

Michael Goldstein:

It depends on their political outlook. If they are communists or members of a society for friendship with the Soviet Union, or if they arrive as delegates to plenary sessions of the USSR Union of Composers, their works are usually recommended and performed. Benjamin Britten, who is very friendly with Soviet musicians, is a case in point, and Alan Bush, a communist, is quite widely performed in the Soviet Union. But if a composer leaves the Communist Party, as the Austrian Marcel Rubin did, he becomes a bad composer overnight.

I should point out that it is practically impossible for two reasons to isolate Soviet composers from what is being done in music abroad. First, music can be heard on the radio, and many people in the Soviet Union speak foreign languages and follow broadcasts in English and German. Volkonsky, for example, has an excellent command of French and also knows German. Then there is the composer Lev Knipper, who wrote the music of the popular song *Polyushko-pole* (The Field, The Little Field). He is of German descent and is highly proficient in the language. These people listen to foreign broadcasts and tape-record what they hear. Secondly, Soviet composers and performers come into contact with foreign musicians visiting the Soviet Union. Stravinsky was in Moscow and Leningrad in 1962, for example.[165] It is true, of course, that visiting musicians are sometimes asked to perform certain works and not others, just as Soviet musicians on tour abroad can be told that certain Soviet works are uninteresting and "not required." Pierre Boulez, for example, has never once performed his works in the Soviet Union, because he writes ultra-modern music and Soviet people must not, if possible, be given the opportunity to listen to it, in case they say: "Look what sort of music they are writing there. It's not bad at all. But in our country it isn't allowed. Why?"

David Anin:

Do you find that stagnation in music is greater than in other forms of art, such as literature?

Michael Goldstein:

Far greater, because the censorship of music is even more ruthless. There are people in the censorship who can analyse music; they have graduated from conservatoires and many of them can sit down and play

---

[165] For an account of this visit see R. Craft, "Stravinsky's Return," in *Encounter*, June 1963.

any composition. But they are two-faced, like Boris Yarustovsky, who spent a long time in the department for music at the Party Central Committee. He gave a favourable review of German Zhukovsky's opera *With All One's Heart*,[166] but then Stalin saw the opera and did not like it, so Yarustovsky proceeded to write the very opposite.

There have been attempts to cause "incorrect" appraisals of works to be revised, and under Khrushchev there were even occasions when the Party Central Committee issued instructions to this effect. Konstantin Dankevich, a good friend of Khrushchev, was able to have "mistakes" in the evaluation of his opera *Bogdan Khmelnitsky* rectified, and Muradeli managed to have his opera *The Great Friendship* rehabilitated. But, these were just isolated cases and are unlikely to be repeated.[167] On the contrary, the authorities will tighten the screws even more and say that apolitical works are not topical and of no benefit to anybody, or claim that they have no more funds available to purchase them. Yet if some politically useful cantata or oratorio is written, the necessary funds will materialise as if by magic. In such a case a composition can first be sold to the USSR Ministry of Culture, then to the RSFSR Ministry of Culture, the Radio Committee, the Philharmonic and to various other organizations, all of whom pay for it, unlike literary works where a certain sum is paid for the first edition and thereafter decreasing sums for subsequent editions. Musical works are paid for according to a set scale laying down the maximum and minimum fees, and considerable sums of money are available to buy the right sort of compositions.

Victor Frank:

Are Soviet musicians capable of playing contemporary Western music, or are they too accustomed to the classics?

Michael Goldstein:

Soviet conservatoires do not train musicians to be receptive to contemporary music. I know pianists in Moscow who are simply incapable of understanding even the compositions of Skryabin's later period.[168] (When people say that Arnold Schönberg was the father of atonal music I object,

---

[166] See the unsigned article (thought to be by Yarustovsky) in *Pravda*, April 19, 1951, and Andrey Olkhovsky, *Music under the Soviets*, London, 1955, p. 175. For a survey of the immediately preceding period, as it affected music, see Alexander Werth's *Musical Uproar in Moscow*, London, 1949.

[167] See the Central Committee decision of May 28, 1958 and the article "Put sovetskoy muzyki — put narodnosti i realizma" in *Pravda*, June 8, 1958.

[168] Skryabin died in 1915.

because atonal music appeared in Russia much earlier. It appeared in the work of Rebikov, who for some reason is rather neglected. It also appeared in the work of Skryabin, whose later works are hardly studied.) In order to gain a true picture of Skryabin you have to know the whole of his creative life. You can't judge a major composer by his early pieces alone; you must be familiar with his mature works, but not many Soviet musicians are. The majority of them are not trained to perform works by contemporary composers at all; they are not familiar with new means of expression, which they often find strange and unnatural. Musical tastes differ, of course, but one ought to be able to understand a modern piece of music. A great deal depends on the degree to which an artist has been trained to appreciate a work, and I believe there are many Soviet musicians, virtuosi in their own right, who can interpret the classics brilliantly but are utterly incapable of understanding the work of modern composers.

Yuri Demin:

Is this Stalin's fault?

Michael Goldstein:

It happened even before Stalin finished consolidating his power. The trend towards modern music developed in the 1920s with the Association of Contemporary Music, which Shostakovich (who did not hesitate to express his admiration for the operas of Krenek and Alban Berg and works by other modern composers) also joined. RAPM, which considered that songs were the sort of musical fare to give the masses, was largely responsible for the end of experimentation. I began my studies at the Moscow Conservatoire in 1930, and that was the hey-day of the RAPM group.

There is one aspect of the censorship which I have not mentioned so far—the censorship of lectures on music. These lectures are very popular in the Soviet Union; I used to deliver them when I was an active member of the All-Union Society for the Propagation of Political and Scientific Knowledge, now known as the "Znaniye" [Knowledge] Society. Well, what does it mean to give lectures on music in the Soviet Union? Take a lecture on Chaykovsky, Glinka or Beethoven. You might imagine you simply go along and talk about what you know. Not a bit of it! First of all you must write out the *complete* text, which is then passed to the (again anonymous) critics for their opinions. After they have written their report you are told what has to be inserted or left out, so you have to reshape the lecture to fit the required purpose. In a lecture on Chaykovsky, for example, it is imperative to refer to the fact that when Lenin was in London he heard a performance of this composer's *Sixth Symphony*, the "Pathétique." Actually, all Lenin did was to mention in a letter to his mother that he had been to a concert and heard and liked this symphony.[169]

"Music in the Life of Lenin" is a popular bread-and-butter theme for many music lecturers. Lenin was in many ways a typical Russian intellectual who had his musical preferences like anyone else, quite independent of whether a symphony or an opera had a greater or lesser degree of political significance. Indeed, it he were alive to hear one of these lecturers, he would probably think the speaker had taken leave of his senses. Lenin was, in fact, fond of Skryabin, and even suggested that a statue of him be erected.

Anyway, after my lectures had been approved I was able to deliver them, but even then they were frequently attended by representatives of the local *Raylit* or *Gorlit*.[170] There is also a censor in every concert organization, known as the "literary editor" or the "music editor." If, for instance, a concert has been arranged for a particular Saturday, then ten days beforehand the censors summon the artists and ask what they will perform and whether they have permission to perform it. It is these editors who are responsible for seeing that the concert has the correct ideological bias, although the concert managers also have a say in deciding what shall be on the programme. As you see, the number of censors is by no means restricted to those who strictly speaking are members of that profession, and if the anonymous critics or advisers are included the number is even higher. In addition to these there are other secret critics who come to a concert simply to listen to what is said in the talk which precedes the music. The concert or recital itself hardly interests them, because what they want to ascertain is whether the text the lecturer reads out corresponds to the one that was approved beforehand.

---

[169] Letter to M. A. Ulyanova of February 4, 1903 (see fourth edition of V. I. Lenin, *Sochineniya*, Vol. 37, p. 278).

[170] I.e., district or city branches of *Glavlit*.

Censorship in the Soviet Cinema

Igor Yeltsov:

I think the censorship of literature will be of more interest to this conference than censorship and control in the cinema. The latter is mainly of concern to those directly involved in film-making, although in principle there are few differences between the two systems.[171] It seems to me that film producers have more to do with the unofficial censorship, which exists on more levels than in literature. Some previous speakers have suggested, however, that the censor plays no direct part in the writer's creative life. He is simply a formal figure who puts his stamp on a book or manuscript and clears it for publication. In the cinema things are more complicated and devious. Everything starts with the script. Actually, it begins even before this with the work schedules, the "creative plans" drawn up by each script department long before the authors, script-writers and dramatists are engaged and given the themes (which no film studio can ignore) they are to write on. These themes include various anniversaries and celebrations, the Soviet village and countryside, Soviet industry, Lenin and, in his day, Stalin, etc. From this moment on you have the so-called "unofficial censor," the studio director, who bears full responsibility for the plans, together with the head of the script-writing department. It is they who take the first step and, guided by the instinct of an editor-censor, draft the plan for the script.

The prophylactic censorship, if one can refer to the process as such, is actually carried out by the chief of the script-writing department, together with the editorial council, the artistic council, and officials from the State Committee for Cinematography. It is now that the destructive process really starts. We used to crack the following joke: "What is a telegraph pole? A telegraph pole is an edited pine-tree." In other words, the script

---

[171] For a reliable account of the origins of Soviet film censorship see Hugh Lunghi's article in *Censorship*, No. 2, London, 1965. Note also pp. 189–195 of Yury Krotkov's *The Angry Exile*, London, Heinemann, 1967, and pp. 49–53 of *The Politics of Ideas in the USSR*, ed. Robert Conquest, London, The Bodley Head, 1967 (this section also deals with theatre censorship, a subject discussed only briefly at this symposium). Lenin's appeals in early 1922 for cinema censorship are printed on pp. 360–361 and 579 of his *Polnoye sobraniye sochineny*, 5th ed., Vol. 44, Moscow, Izdatelstvo politicheskoy literatury, 1964.

is the pine-tree and the film is the telegraph pole.[172] One writer I could name was invited to the studio and prepared several alternative scripts, but it was not long before he vowed that he would never work in films again and left in a huff, full of mistrust towards directors, editors and film-making in general.[173] He called it a complex machine set up to humiliate the writer and make him look a fool. Yet nobody wants to humiliate the writer. Everyone, especially the directors, start out with the best intentions and genuinely want to secure interesting and unusual material, something that is at least fresh and new. This is what everyone dreams about, but as soon as the practical work gets under way the old fogeys in the studio offices set to work on the script, and the upshot is usually that the writer disowns it and offers to return his fee. It is a very rare occurrence when a script manages to pass through the various controls (of which there are some seventeen to twenty) more or less intact. The worst of these stages is the Central Committee, to which the working copy of the script has to be submitted for scrutiny by the USSR State Committee for Cinematography.[174] This latter committee has a huge editorial council and board. In my time a certain Madame Kokareva was there, and she tried to satisfy both sides. She often decided the fate of a script; it depended on her whether it was passed or not. When approving my last script, "The Viennese Postage Stamp," she told me that if I promised to cut out all the "sharp corners" during filming, she would not insist that Aleksandr Dymshits, then the chief editor of the State Committee, read the script. She enumerated point by point what had to be changed and how it was to be done so that the script would contain no sort of critical ideological slant. What they fear most of all is to offend against the current ideological line, and the Committee for Cinematography is particularly sensitive to the prevailing political mood. These die-hard conservatives keep a weather eye on the Central Committee's cinema section, which was, and possibly still is, run by Sazonov and a certain Comrade Orekhova, who is the Party Central

---

[172] For some light-hearted allusions to film censorship see L. Likhodeyev, *Iskusstvo—eto iskusstvo*, Moscow, Iskusstvo, 1970, especially pp. 80–82.

[173] See also Ye. Dorosh, "Pochemu ya ne pishu dlya kino," *Iskusstvo kino*, No. 4, 1962, pp. 76–80.

[174] This committee was established in March 1963 (a few months earlier than the State Committee for the Press) and was headed from the start by Aleksey Vladimirovich Romanov (not to be confused with Pavel Konstantinovich Romanov, the first chairman of the State Committee for the Press). See the *Vedomosti Verkhovnogo Soveta SSSR*, No. 14 (1153), April 3, 1963, articles 163–164. On the recent reorganization of the Committee for Cinematography see *Pravda*, August 5, 1972, p. 6, and August 22, 1972, p. 1. A. V. Romanov was then replaced by Filip Yermash, according to *Pravda*, August 22, 1972, p. 6.

Committee representative at the State Committee for Cinematography. Its chairman, A. V. Romanov, has no say in the matter if Orekhova has any doubts about a film or about certain scenes in it, and if she vetoes a film it is stored in the Committee's film library at the back of the building on Bolshoy Gnezdnikovsky pereulok. The next stage is that one evening a car picks up the film and takes it to a private showing to which the director of the film is seldom invited. They may later phone him in his hotel or at home and tell him that everything is in order and that he can come the following day to collect the certificate of authorization, together with all the other signatures, including the magic stamps from the civil[175] and the military censors. After that the number of copies of the film and the areas of the country where it is to be shown are decided. The number of copies is fixed by the hiring agency, usually in collaboration with the Committee.

The military censor is very important, especially where documentary films are concerned. I have made many of these and must say that I have always found the military censorship to be more agreeable than the civilian variety. I used to invite the military censor, a colonel, to drop in and look at the rough montage, so that there would be no disagreement later when they began cutting the negative. He would ask where you had been filming and then have a look at the results. He had his "Talmud" with him and would say: "Hm. Well, you can't show any military personnel in this town," which meant that if I had accidentally shown even one soldier or sailor in a street scene filmed in, say, a Baltic city, he would tell us to cut this scene out. Then he might say: "Haven't you got some offshore shots of Tallinn there? Let me have a look at them." You'd show them to him and hear: "Impossible! Can't you see? That television aerial and the church tower are military orientation points; they could be used to gauge the range." I would make a note of it, and we would carry on. They even gave us some sample photographs and sketches so that we knew in advance what to avoid.

You have to be very careful where you point a camera in the Soviet Union. I was involved in an incident in Naryan-Mar in 1966,[176] before I left for England. I had met a well-known cinema projectionist from Leningrad Newsreel while they were filming a special feature for export abroad about deer and the Nentsy, a Northern tribe numbering about twenty-five thousand. We decided to take a few snapshots on an airfield which consisted merely of some sort of shed and nothing more. The

---

[175] *Glavlit* checks in particular that there are no discrepancies between the shooting script it has already authorized and what is actually said on the soundtrack.

[176] In the Far North of Russia, near the mouth of the Pechora River.

director of the Leningrad unit took a photograph of us all and gave me the camera so that I could take one of him with the others. Suddenly someone clapped me on the shoulder and said: "Well, citizen, what are you doing?" I replied that we were taking photographs of each other, realizing at once, however, that it must be forbidden, although there was nothing of interest in sight. Then it struck me that there was a military settlement near Naryan-Mar and, in the neighbouring Amderma, a plant for the manufacture of heavy water. This was supposed to be a closely-guarded secret, although everyone knew about it. He checked my papers, and said: "Oho! So you work in films and yet you don't know that it is forbidden to take photographs here." I replied that I could not see anything apart from a few pine-trees, whereupon he rejoined: "And do you know what there is behind those pine-trees?" "Well, you tell me what the big secret is," I answered. "Don't tell me my job," came the reply. "Give me the film." He opened the camera, exposed the film and snapped: "Now try and develop that!"[177] When it comes to the military censor you cannot argue, as you sometimes can with the civilian censors, because they are very strict about films, knowing that there is always the chance that some military secret will be disclosed inadvertently.

There is one curious thing that still puzzles me: in feature films you are not allowed to show a calendar with the proper date. I once inadvertently included a shot of such a calendar while making a film based on a novel called *V odnom dome* (In One House) by Hans Leberecht.[178] We had no qualified film cutter for the montage and it was not possible to cut out this frame. They would not pass it. *Glavlit* was the first to notice it, and although I managed to convince them that a calendar was really a trivial thing, the man at *Glavlit* said: "Well, that may be...but I have my instructions." However, as there was nothing obviously seditious in it, it was passed. Then the Central Committee inspected the film and refused to approve it, and to this day I do not know what the fuss was about.

It is even trickier where portraits are involved. After the exposure and condemnation of the Stalin personality cult, a long list arrived from the

---

[177] For security reasons atlases are subject to exceptionally strict censorship in the Soviet Union, with some places marked "many kilometres" away from their real situation. "Not only have towns mysteriously shifted but rivers, railways and similar features have started wandering around..." H. Jackson, "Cartographers Keeping Russia on the Move," *The Guardian*, January 20, 1970. On the special instructions for preparing and publishing maps in the 1920s and 1930s see pp. 42–43 of L. Fogelevich, *Deystvuyushcheye zakonodatelstvo o pechati*, Moscow, 1927, and pp. 114–115 of L. Fogelevich, *Osnovnyye direktivy i zakonoda-telstvo o pechati*, Moscow, 1935.

[178] An Estonian writer (1910–1960).

official censorship containing all the films that were to be taken out of circulation immediately. Wherever a portrait of Stalin appeared the sequence had to be cut out, and if this proved impossible a portrait of Lenin would be superimposed on the picture of Stalin by some technical means. In many films these insertions were not technically perfect; you can see at once by the way it flickers at the edges that a film has been withdrawn and that, by a very complicated and expensive method, Stalin's portrait was replaced by that of Lenin so that the film would not have to be discarded completely.[179] This was, of course, at the behest of the Central Committee.

What can I tell you from personal experience about the KGB censorship? I made my first major full-length film from a script by Genrikh Borovik, now an APN correspondent in New York, and the late Andrey Novikov, a friend of Sofronov.[180] It was a documentary film about a group of three American, West German or British spies who were landed on the Baltic coast and later caught; I was never told which country they were from. Anyway, a script was written, based on this incident. First of all a story entitled "The Leaves are Falling" appeared in *Ogonyok*[181] (under fictitious names, not those of Borovik and Novikov. There were evidently reasons for this). For the film the title was changed to "Uninvited Guests" (*Nezvannyye gosti*). The interesting thing is that in the story some of the names were real, and when they began to turn the story into a film script they kept these names at first, but then instructions arrived to replace them with others. They were no longer documentary characters but literary characters tailored to suit the propaganda purpose of the film.

Then I was introduced to a Colonel Uglov, a KGB officer from Moscow. He had two surnames—Uglov and Uzlov—and he was the man who had the final say regarding technical details. His chief concern was to see that the main character, a *chekist*, was presented in a positive and sympathetic light and that the *chekisty* were not made to look stupid. Apart from this, he ensured that all the original props—an American radio transmitter, pistols and even the clothing the spies had worn—were put at our disposal for the filming. My curiosity aroused, I said that as director it would be useful for me to see these foreign agents in the flesh. After considerable deliberation I was allowed to meet one of the spies in a hotel. He was a very nervous, trembling man, who had, in my opinion, been badly beaten up and who kept repeating: "I don't remember, it's all

---

[179] E.g., in another film based on a work by Leberecht, *Svet v Koordi* (Light in Koordi).

[180] Anatoly Sofronov, poet, dramatist and chief editor of *Ogonyok* (Little Fire).

[181] G. Grishin and A. Normet, "Listya padayut," *Ogonyok*, Nos. 12–16, 1957.

a blank, I don't remember that." And quite obviously, after the inter-
rogations, he could not remember anything at all. For some reason or
other they did not show me the other two.

After this they placed another adviser above the colonel as head consultant and censor. This was General Oleg Gribanov, whom I discovered
to be head of the USSR counter-intelligence service and in charge of the
entire intelligence service abroad. He is a very clever man, by no means
the typical *chekist* gorilla. Three times he came personally to look at the
film and was also mainly interested in seeing that the *chekisty* were not
made to appear stupid. He looked at the silent version, without the soundtrack; then he saw the completed film. He was empowered to decide
everything, and I soon realized that there could be no question of artistry
and creativity. I was really boxed in, but because it was the first film with
which they had entrusted me, I thought I had better cooperate, otherwise it
would probably be my first and last commission.

KGB censorship of literature is also quite thorough. I realized that this
same Uglov (or Uzlov) had read many manuscripts. They bring him novels
and stories on military themes and about the secret police from the Writers'
Union, and he recommends what should be cut out or altered. Take the
novel "The Bronze Button" in *Ogonyok*,[182] for example. I know that the
KGB checked it from start to finish before it went to press with their
blessing.[183] They usually send along an adviser, who is sometimes in effect
the co-author.

A few words about the delivery of your film. You take the finished
product to the committee and show it to the editorial council. "Very well,"
they say, "we'll discuss it tomorrow after lunch." The following day after
lunch, however, they say "the day after tomorrow." This means that
certain doubts have cropped up. Gloom descends upon you and while
waiting for further news you remember the saying that it is easier to make
a film than to have it accepted for distribution.

With "Uninvited Guests" the final decision was taken by a KGB board
consisting of three of Shelepin's deputies.[184] While they were viewing
the film—in the Lubyanka—I sat outside the projection room in a large
armchair thinking that if it displeased them I would probably never leave the

---

[182] L. Ovalov, "Mednaya pugovitsa," *Ogonyok*, Nos. 20–36, 1958.

[183] However, a Central Committee resolution (*postanovleniye*) of September 9,
1958, declared that this work had no aesthetic or educational value (see *Voprosy
ideologicheskoy raboty*, Moscow, Gosudarstvennoye izdatelstvo politicheskoy
literatury, 1961, p. 259).

[184] Shelepin was head of the KGB from 1958 to 1961.

building. One of Shelepin's consultants came up to me while I was waiting, and said: "I suppose you know, Comrade Yeltsov, that Lavrenty Pavlovich Beriya was very fond of sitting in that armchair." They like to have their little jokes. After the KGB board had seen the film there was a telephone call from the Lubyanka to Nikolay Mikhaylov, then the USSR Minister of Culture. When I arrived at the Committee for Cinematography the next day to show them the film, Igor Rachuk (a close friend of Yury Krotkov who was later dismissed because the latter defected in England)[185] asked: "What do you mean by it? Comrade Mikhaylov has telephoned me to say that someone has already seen the film and that the maximum number of copies should be made, but we haven't seen it yet." I explained that I had acted on Gribanov's instructions and that everything had already been decided after the film had been viewed at the KGB. He quieted down at once, and said: "All right, all right, it doesn't matter then. But have you the permit to show it? Give it to me and I'll sign it." And without having seen the film he signed the certificate, which proved that he had no real say in the matter.

I'd like to touch briefly on those films which, on various grounds, are shelved for six months or a year and sometimes never released at all. You may have read in the press about "Andrey Rublyov," which they began to film in about 1966 and which has been shown in the Paris cinemas, and even at Cannes. It has not yet been on general display for Soviet audiences, and everybody knows the reason why: it failed to conjure up the positive associations for which the authorities had hoped. It is considered to be too depressing.[186]

I was once at a seminar in Bolshevo[187] when Mikhail Romm arrived after showing his film *Obyknovenny fashizm* (Ordinary Fascism)[188] to members of the government and the Central Committee. He told us that Brezhnev, Kosygin and other bigwigs had been present, and after the film had ended there was a stony silence. Suslov stood up to ask: "Well, comrades, are there any questions for the director?" Nobody spoke, so he continued:

---

[185] Mr. Krotkov's stories and plays now appear regularly in the émigré Russian press; he is also the author of a fascinating manuscript about the KGB.

[186] The script, by A. Konchalovsky and the producer, A. Tarkovsky, is published in *Iskusstvo kino*, Nos. 4–5, 1964. The film was shown to a selected audience in Moscow in February, 1969 (see *The Guardian*, February 20, 1969), and then put on more general release at the end of 1971 (see *The Times*, December 21, 1971).

[187] Where there is a "house of creativity" for people working in the cinema industry.

[188] This film is discussed in *Iskusstvo kino*, No. 1, 1966, pp. 16–24.

"Why is it that you have such a dislike for us, Mikhail Ilich?"[189] Romm realized what Suslov was getting at, but replied: "Well really, comrades! You can see for yourselves what I dislike...I made this anti-Fascist film, a film against Fascist dictatorship." But they all grasped the real point, and so did the public. The film was divided into sections on science, art, society, etc., and before each section a quotation was flashed onto the screen. The section on art, for example, was preceded by a quotation which went approximately as follows: " 'From time to time it is necessary to wag an admonitory finger at writers and artists'—Adolf Hitler." When the film was shown at Bolshevo the whole hall broke into laughter, because this was obviously a dig at Khrushchev and his well-known fondness for laying down the law about how films should be made, music written, pictures painted, and so on. The whole film was built around delicate hints of this sort, but they could not ban it as anti-Soviet, because on the surface it was an anti-Fascist film. It enjoyed a great success even abroad.

Then there is the case of Alov and Naumov's film based on Dostoyevsky's *Skverny anekdot* (A Nasty Story). No censor now would dare to ban such a script, because Dostoyevsky is a writer of world stature, although publication of his works was forbidden under Stalin and his name mentioned only in histories of literature. When the film "A Nasty Story" was completed, and it is a remarkable film, I realized for the first time that you can screen Dostoyevsky; hitherto I had seen nothing like it. The picture was shown to Romanov, who felt there might be certain political implications which he couldn't quite put his finger on, so he sent a consultant named Mikhail Bleyman to Bolshevo to inspect the film. Bleyman was one of those secret censors, a sort of personal assistant to Romanov, but not a bad dramatist in his own right. He was unable to allay official suspicions, however, because Ivan Pyryev, then the secretary of the Union of Cinematographers, had claimed that the characters in the film—Russians, of course—were "walking mummies, without heart or soul." The Central Committee used Pyryev's statement as an excuse to put the film into cold storage, where it still remains. It may be released one day, like the second part of "Ivan the Terrible," which Eisenstein never saw screened during his lifetime.

I could quote dozens of similar examples. Look at Marlen Khutsiyev's *Zastava Ilyicha* (Outpost of Ilich).[190] It turned out that Khrushchev himself had never seen this film, although he claimed he had, even attacking it in

---

[189] But see footnote 195, p. 116.

[190] Later rewritten, remade, and retitled *Nam dvadtsat let* (We are Twenty Years Old). See *Iskusstvo kino*, No. 4, 1965, pp. 27–46.

a speech.[191] One of his advisers did see it and sent in a report listing certain points which Khrushchev then took up in his speech—it maligned our fathers, exaggerated the conflict between the younger and the older generations, etc. For a whole year they suggested one "improvement" after another to Khutsiyev. He went to the Committee for Cinematography for consultations, re-wrote whole scenes and begged them not to spoil the film. Finally, when they had ground him down and the film had been spoiled anyway, they released a dull and insipid version of it.

I must also mention "33" by Georgy Daneliya, possibly the only satire on the Party ever to reach the cinemas. It ridicules the Party's habit of taking quite ordinary people—leading workers, milkmaids and so on—and building them up into national heroes. The hero of this film is a worker in a lemonade factory who is given the full treatment, although he does not have aninkling why. There is a press conference, he is dragged hither and thither, and the Academy of Sciences and the Institute of Language and Literature become interested in him. Just before he is dispatched to another planet, after having been driven to the launching-pad in a large limousine with a motorcycle escort, an Academician rushes up and beseeches him: "Tell us, what is the correct way to write the word '*hare*?' Is it '*zayats*' or '*zayets*?'" All this happens because he is discovered to have thirty-three teeth—he is a freak. The film is also a dig at the adulation surrounding Soviet cosmonauts, several of whom saw the film and lodged a protest, but for some obscure reason it was not taken out of circulation and was a huge success with the public. *Pokhozhdeniya zubnogo vracha* (Adventures of a Dentist) was another satirical film very similar in style, although it did not get any public showings.[192]

Films like these could be made a few years ago, but now, just as since Kuznetsov's flight to the West all writers are checked three times before they are allowed to travel abroad, so after films like "33" were shown every script is scrutinized three times as thoroughly as before at every stage.

When a film has been approved by the State Committee for Cinematography it is submitted to Central Committee officials for final clearance.

---

[191] On March 8, 1963 (see *Pravda*, March 10, 1963). For a useful annotated English translation see *Khrushchev on Culture*, *Encounter* Pamphlet No. 9, especially pp. 9–12. For numerous examples of direct and indirect censorship at this time see *Khrushchev and the Arts. The Politics of Soviet Culture, 1962–1964*, ed. Priscilla Johnson and Leopold Labedz, Cambridge, Massachusetts, 1965. On banned films see also *Khronika tekushchikh sobyty*, No. 19, 1971.

[192] Scenario (by A. Volodin) published in *Iskusstvo kino*, No. 9, 1964. It was directed by E. Klimov and completed in 1967. The film is also known as *Istoriya zubnogo vracha* (Story of a Dentist).

Since "33" they are particularly sensitive about any scenes smacking of satire. They removed an episode about the Stakhanovite movement from Mikhail Kalik's "Goodbye, Boys!"[193] because it showed workers on a construction site in the south in the 1930s trotting around with wheelbarrows to light, rhythmic music. This was considered to be undignified—"It looks as though they are simply larking about!" Romanov said: "This ridicules our five-year plans and our fathers. I shall not allow it!" Kalik refused to make the recommended cuts, so he was sacked by *Mosfilm* and went to the Riga studios to work as a consultant. A year later I saw the film and the controversial scene was missing. When I next met Kalik he confirmed that he had not given his permission for the cuts, adding: "To hell with it! I'm sick of it." And he certainly appeared to be fed up with the whole business, because during the Arab-Israeli Six-Day War in 1967 he pinned on a Star of David and went to Moscow. People asked him if he had taken leave of his senses, and he answered: "Why? My homeland is at war, and I am on its side."

Leonid Finkelstein:

The otherwise improbable remark attributed to Suslov and recounted by Mr. Yeltsov—"Why is it that you have such a dislike for us?"—would seem to be corroborated by the fact that Kochetov's novel *Chego zhe ty khochesh?* (What is it You Want?) contains the first open attack on the film "Ordinary Fascism," to which Suslov was referring. At one point,[194] a character says that he recently saw a Soviet film supposedly about fascism, but in fact it was "about us.... There was laughter in the hall, of course. The public are not idiots, they understand these tricks. And what do you think, they even gave a prize to the man who knocked this film together!"[195]

There is an even more striking scene in the film: the doors to an exhibition open and the audience sees a parody of Fyodor Shurpin's picture "The Morning of Our Homeland." But instead of Stalin posed against a background of the wide expanses of Russia there stands Hitler with a cloak thrown over his arm; so unmistakable is the resemblance that the audience begins to roar with laughter and applaud.[196]

---

[193] Based on Boris Balter's novel *Do svidaniya, malchiki*, Moscow, 1963. According to the *International Herald Tribune* of May 7, 1971, Kalik was expelled from the Union of Cinematographers "for wishing to leave for Israel, which is incompatible with membership." He was later allowed to go there.

[194] *Oktyabr*, No. 9, 1969, p. 114.

[195] The samizdat journal *Politichesky dnevnik*, No. 33, 1967, claims that Suslov liked this film (see the section *"Iz literaturnoy zhizni.* Kinofilmy").

[196] *Utro nashey rodiny* dates from 1948 and was awarded a Stalin Prize the following year. Shurpin subsequently apologized for "varnishing" reality in some of his paintings, *Ogonyok*, No. 43, 1966, pp. 16–17.

Arkady Belinkov:

Fascism has become a very dangerous theme to play around with, and is subjected to strict censorship in literature as well as in the cinema. There was a direct reference to this in an article by N. Razgovorov in *Literaturnaya gazeta* after the publication of the issue of *Inostrannaya literatura* (Foreign Literature) which contained Ionesco's "Rhinocéros." If you are talking about fascism, he said, then don't forget to specify which sort of fascism.[197]

Anatoly Kuznetsov:

I wrote the scripts for two films, and these were two Golgothas in the real sense of the word; I still shudder when I think about them. After the second film I vowed I would never work for the Soviet cinema again. (I had extricated myself from a similar situation earlier by refusing to revise the script; I duly returned the advance payment and tore up the contract.) One film was called *My—dvoye muzhchin* (We Two Men), a film about ordinary human problems and daily life, absolutely non-political. The director liked the script and went off with his team to shoot some country scenes. But when he brought back the material and showed it to the studio bosses there was an air of stunned surprise. They had never seen anything like this at the Dovzhenko Studio in Kiev; they were so embarrassed they did not know what to do. "Well, piece it together," they said, "and we'll see what happens." The film was made up, but the studio didn't know what to do with it, because it showed the unvarnished truth; the director had filmed the countryside as it really is, not as it appears in the usual idealised tracts. An influential critic by the name of Lyudmila Pogozheva came to the studio to view the film and was quite impressed with it. She wrote a complimentary article about it in *Pravda*,[198] and suddenly everyone began to say that new standards had been set, that at last the Ukraine had been depicted realistically, and that this was the way the Kiev studio would go about film-making in the future.

But then the censors reached for their scissors. They cut out a great deal of what had been shot and left only what was utterly inoffensive. A dirty road could not be shown, for example; if there was a scene showing puddles in a road, then out it came. A sequence where the hero meditates about life and death and the pointlessness of existence was also thrown out—Soviet people are too positive to dwell upon death! Thanks to the

---

[197] See *Inostrannaya literatura*, No. 9, 1965, and *Literaturnaya gazeta*, December 30, 1965.
[198] February 25, 1963.

article in *Pravda*, however, it was decided to show the film at the Moscow Film Festival, the same one at which "$8^1/_2$" received a prize.[199] I was a member of our delegation to this festival, for which there were two Soviet entries—*Znakomtes, Baluyev* (Let's Get Acquainted, Baluyev)[200] and "We Two Men." The audience received the first of these in complete silence, which was a disgrace for the Soviet film industry; even the East German and Vietnam entries were applauded, and here was a Soviet film being greeted with deathly silence. After this fiasco the only Soviet hope was "We Two Men." But suddenly, two days before our film was due to be shown, notices were posted on the doors of the Kremlin Palace of Congresses saying that "We Two Men" was being replaced by *Porozhny reys* (Trip Without Cargo). Why? Nobody knows. No matter whom I asked, I was given the same answer: "That is the decision." They entered "Trip Without Cargo," which is adapted from a story by Sergey Antonov,[201] and my film was shown "outside the competition," in the *Rossiya* cinema theatre. Since then I have not seen it again; some people told me that it went the rounds of various clubs for a short time and then disappeared. In any case, only twenty-five percent of my original plot reached the screen and fifty percent of the material shot by the director was destroyed.

I also wrote the script for *U sebya doma* (At Home). Two young directors in Moscow started shooting, and when they had about eighty percent of the material they took it along and showed it to the board of directors. We all sat down together beforehand and sorted out what we had: we will show this, but we will not show that, because it is too risky and will only cause trouble. We will not risk this, and we will put that into the final version, etc. In this way we made the film quite inoffensive. Then Surin, the head of *Mosfilm*, had a look at it. Afterwards he thundered on for a full forty minutes—he bawled, stamped his feet, and shouted: "I won't allow you to show filthy foot-rags on the screen...," and so on. It was a film about village life, without any real political targets, simply portraying people's sorrows and their small joys. Surin insisted that the film be radically revised and the script rewritten accordingly. It was a depressing spectacle. The director was crushed; everybody just sat there mutely because they were all subordinate to Surin and did not dare to raise any objections. I was not directly under him, however, so I rose to my feet and tackled him on every point. My basic argument was that all this had already appeared in

---

[199] 1963. Western films are periodically banned after running for some time in the Soviet Union: see the Reuter report and the leading article in *The Guardian*, October 14, 1968.

[200] Based on a novel by Vadim Kozhevnikov (*Znamya*, Nos. 4–5, 1960).

[201] *Yunost*, No. 10, 1960.

print. Surin shrieked: "Published where? In *Novy mir*? What difference does that make anyway? Thousands read what's published, but millions see a film; the impact of the cinema is far greater. If you write that he is dressed in filthy foot-rags, that's one thing, but when you show them on the screen in all their glory it's a different matter. So get going and work it over again, otherwise I'll send the lot of you packing." I said that we would not revise it. It was a case of diamond cut diamond, and we parted enemies. They stopped the film and refused to finance the project further until I had agreed to alter the script. I refused for a whole year and was prepared to let the whole thing drop. But the directors and actors who had already put so much into it were upset. Among them was Tamara Degtyaryova, a wonderful actress who had played her part very well. They all came to Tula several times to see me, pleading that this was an unprecedented situation because, in effect, the whole team had been dismissed and nobody was getting paid. They were all hanging around and waiting in the hope that filming would begin again because they had become so fond of the project. "Look here," they said, "you don't have to alter much, just rework a bit here and there to satisfy them and we'll film it in such a way that the alterations won't show. They only want the houses and collective farms to be clean and everyone dolled up like members of the Russian national choir. So they object because everyone looks miserable? All right, we'll put a smile on their faces then!" "But this will be awful...," I protested. Finally they persuaded me, and I gave way: "Very well. I won't revise it. You do what you want and I'll have a look at it. If it's no good at all I'll withdraw my name from it." They started work again and reshot about fifty percent of the film, showing well-kept houses, modern collective farms, laughing peasants—it was almost like another version of *Kubanskiye kazaki* (The Kuban Cossacks).[202] When it was finished they invited me to the showing, but none of them turned up. I sat alone in the small room, and the technicians ran the film through just for me. When I left I felt utterly sickened: it was hopeless, the whole struggle had been in vain. You cannot get the better of people like Surin and Polevoy, you cannot fool them; they are old hands at this sort of thing. The others had not stayed away for nothing. They were ashamed, and if they saw me in the distance in a corridor after this they would dart quickly into the nearest office to avoid meeting me. The film was released in this form in June 1969, but although I found it revolting I could not bring myself to withdraw my name from it, because that seemed puerile. As I was driving to Moscow airport on what I knew would be a one-way trip to London I saw the posters advertising

---

[202] A very bad film directed by Ivan Pyryev in 1950. It was later criticized for its "varnishing" of Soviet reality.

"At Home," and thought with malicious satisfaction: "Never mind, in a few days time you will be taking those posters down again."

Michael Goldstein:

Composers who write film music often told me that they put the finishing touches to the score after the film had passed through all the stages of the censorship. Initially they would be told that, say, one minute and six seconds of music, or a song, was required in a certain place. This they would write, but later they might be asked to extend it to, say, two minutes, seven seconds. Does this not provide them with an opportunity to slip in something which would not normally get past the censor?

Igor Yeltsov:

Composers are often such sensitive people that they do not wish to provoke anyone in this way. I myself never used music to put over things that you might consider "seditious." There were plenty of other ways of working in something unauthorized without resorting to composers. The music for many films made in Stalin's time was written by Nikolay Kryukov, who later committed suicide, possibly because he was forced to write pompous, pretentious music alien to his creative urges. Incidentally, the only director in the Soviet Union during Stalin's life-time whose scripts were never questioned was Mikhail Chiaureli. When an artistic council was appointed to discuss the script of his *Klyatva* (The Vow), for example, Chiaureli turned up at the meeting and asked if anyone had any comments on the script. At first there was silence, then Aleksandr Dovzhenko apparently made a remark displeasing to Chiaureli, who stood up and said: "Well, here is another copy of the script, by the way, and Comrade Stalin found time to add a few comments on it." After this, of course, there was no questioning the script. Yuly Kun, a fairly well known film director, who was present at the meeting, described to me how Chiaureli got his revenge on Dovzhenko. The latter was showing one of his films in which there was no mention of Stalin whatever. After the showing Chiaureli got up with the words: "Sashko, Sashko, couldn't you have spared ten metres of film for the leader?" Afterwards the film was altered and "the leader" made an appearance in it.

Censorship and Science

Max Hayward:

Aleksey Yakushev will now speak about censorship and science, after which we shall turn to the struggle with the censorship and techniques for outwitting it. Then we shall examine the question of how foreign writers and journalists are influenced by the Soviet censorship and discuss in particular how they should react to the Aesopian allusions in the works of Soviet writers.

Aleksey Yakushev:

Some of those present have complained that we have received a contradictory impression of the Soviet censorship. On the one hand—and I believe this has been particularly well brought out—the censorship permeates all spheres of Soviet life, yet on the other it appears that censors are really quite decent people. Actually, there is no contradiction involved here, because there are good people and bad everywhere. Unfortunately, a situation has arisen in the Soviet Union in which ordinarily decent people do nasty things. There is a dichotomy: people must knuckle under and conform to certain rules and official guidelines because this is the only way they can earn their daily bread. Yet these same people believe only half-heartedly in the official ideology of the Soviet régime. Theirs is not a fanatical belief. We have said repeatedly and quite correctly that the censors, both official and unofficial, cause authors much anguish. They mutilate books, they violate ideas. This is an interesting fact in itself, but for me the cardinal question is why there is such an abundance of material that must be dealt with so severely. By all the laws of logic it should not even exist, but the fact that it does gives me grounds for optimism.

Intellectual life, not least in the sciences, is in a state of flux. People are beginning to question the official ideology, some more radically, some less so. The official ideology itself is becoming less and less dynamic and attractive; the process started many years ago and has been progressing steadily since. The men in power know about it, and this is why they panic from time to time. They grow nervous and feel insecure. In Stalin's day, ideology was a kind of rule-book laying down a code of behaviour, and no one ever asked whether there was any truth, justice or conviction behind it. Social science consisted solely of a set of functional principles;

it presupposed a blind faith and had no use for any argument or proof, and it was the best formula for the preservation of the Soviet system. But this edifice is crumbling; now a process of ideological decay is taking place which, strange though it may sound, embraces not only the creative intelligentsia but also sections of the ruling caste. Once there was a stable system, a system that operated according to a set of rigid principles in response to a mechanism of its own. But now the system is no longer stable: it is searching at all levels for paths along which to develop, and no one quite knows what these paths should be. The ideological system is beginning to come apart at the seams, various alternatives are emerging, and I believe that this process is deeply reflected in the censorship.

Formerly it was simply claimed that the social sciences issue from Marxist-Leninist doctrine, thus making them a mere appendage to ideology. But when people begin to open their eyes and become aware of a complex and contradictory conglomeration of facts which do not all fit in with the dogma, it is necessary to provide some sort of more sophisticated explanation, if not strictly honest then at least plausible, of the course of events. Mikoyan identified the dilemma when he said on one occasion in private:

> Look here, I sign all sorts of papers concerning trade, but I'm in the dark. I don't know whether something is correct or not. I don't know what I sign; I have no idea how prices are fixed in the Soviet Union. It's all a haze, it's all mysticism.

What we are now witnessing is, in a narrow, restricted sense, a relative independence of the social sciences from pure ideology. People are beginning to recognise that in the social sciences one must have facts, that there must be concrete methods of research. The right to some degree of freedom from ideology, won by the natural sciences much earlier, is now beginning to extend to the social sciences. This process is still in its infancy and moves by fits and starts, but its existence is a fact. It is reflected in the censorship, which is being taken out of the hands of officials and entrusted to various influential groups among specialists who are perhaps themselves sociologists. This is definitely progress.

How did real Soviet sociology begin? It began with the rejection of Stalinist sociology, with its Fedoseyevs, its Mitins, etc., asking what Marxist sociology is and deciding that it is historical materialism, everything else being simply bourgeois padding. A new group then emerged and established itself, not without difficulty, exclaiming: We are blind! Give us some real information, not for the general public, heaven forbid, but for us, so that we know what is happening in this country. It is impossible to go on any longer like this! Some sort of decisions must be taken, and we are blind... And so gradually the pressure from below increases. There is a simple human logic, apparently, that mischievous human thoughts and actions always prefer to be rooted in some sort of convictions. These can be mistaken, fanatical convictions as long as they are convictions. Where there are no convictions it is difficult to act. A gradual and halting erosion of ideology is taking place, a new content is being imparted to the old terminology. Observers in the West frequently do not notice this, yet it is there, and as a result new control groups supervising whole areas of research, groups wishing to appear scientifically educated, are gaining ground. But they still remain *ideological* groups exercising all this supervision.

A specific group has emerged in Soviet sociological circles consisting of people whom we would consider almost enlightened, but they still maintain surveillance over others. I can name some of them: Igor Kon, Andrey Zdravomyslov, Gennady Osipov, and a whole batch of other sociologists. This is the group with authority to decide where to draw the boundaries and which facts and analyses shall or shall not appear in print.

Leonid Finkelstein:

I do not agree. These people only accept decisions. I lived among them, worked with them and published their articles. Up to now they have not been able to force through even the most elementary thing—a genuine public opinion poll in the streets. They beg, they entreat, they squat on doorsteps, they prostrate themselves at people's feet, they write articles and say it is shameful, but they can't even achieve the first step in real sociology—a Gallup poll.

Aleksey Yakushev:

I did not say they have achieved everything. There are gradations of decision-making, and the more critical questions are decided by Central Committee officials and others. But there is another side to this—the men sitting in the Central Committee cannot control sociology because they know nothing about it. So this new group has gained a measure of power in the scientific field. Let me give a concrete example. A detailed sociological investigation was conducted at Kuybyshev into time and motion, labour relations, etc. I took part in the analysis of the material that was gathered, together with Osipov, Aleksey Rumyantsev, who was in charge of the whole project, and others. These were people whom I quite liked and with whom one could on occasion talk quite reasonably. But they quickly began to sift, select and reject certain parts of the findings of our survey.

They knew very well what was forbidden because they themselves set the limits, and that is the whole point. And I regard this as a positive feature: the boundaries of scientific research are being expanded.

Natalia Belinkova:

Sociology has not yet had time in the Soviet Union; it is still nascent. I know from my work in television that Soviet sociologists worked in covert, almost underground groups such as those at Moscow scientific research institutes. Then the powers-that-be decided to flush them out into the open, and the moment they were allowed to practise overtly can be considered the beginning of their demise, because a month to six weeks later a Central Committee decree regulating work on sociology was issued.[203] There is no need at all for the Central Committee to know anything about sociology in order to put an end to it. At one time or another they made a good job of finishing off literature, art, music and a number of sciences, including biology, genetics and cybernetics.

Aleksey Yakushev:

What I meant to say was that the boundaries in the social sciences were pushed further back when it was announced that these are a definite, specific field of study, and when the ideological straight-jacket was somewhat loosened. The authorities no longer do violence to the facts and no longer interfere with the very basis of these sciences. The pressure is coming from below, the leadership is yielding slightly, and shifts are taking place among the groups holding authority. Those who decide what shall constitute the bases of these sciences are becoming rather more tolerant.

If I compare Osipov or Yury Zamoshkin with Mark Mitin and Pyotr Fedoseyev, then the former are almost enlightened, "almost" but not quite, because they are partly working to orders. They have bifurcated souls, they are schizophrenic, but it is a special form of schizophrenia, because they perform special functions. Zamoshkin, for example, told me that he and his colleagues were investigating cases of distress among families in Moscow and had made astonishing progress. I questioned him about his methodology and whether he could ask those interviewed if their troubles were a result of difficult living conditions. He told me that no Soviet sociologist would dare to formulate the question so openly, but that it was possible to put it in a more round-about way. That is the point I want to make. All this is the result of pressure from various forces at different levels and from different sides. Just imagine the immediate

---

[203] See *Kommunist*, No. 13, 1967, pp. 3–13.

postwar years—or the prewar years—when there really was a kind of *homo sovieticus*. If the brakes had been relaxed he would have remained absolutely the same; it would never have entered his head that it was possible to think otherwise. Today it is a very different matter. Anatoly Kuznetsov has told us that practically every writer nowadays complains about being censored and no longer meekly submits a pre-censored text to his editor; his text is already something broader than the authorities would like, something which oversteps the narrow confines of ideology.

Deep stirrings are taking place, and this is a process of liberation of thought. Full intellectual freedom will not arrive overnight; it will come by degrees and involve millions of individuals. The system is strong and people are far from having everything straight and clear in their minds. It is most important to regard the process of liberation not as having ground to a halt, as though some demarcation line had been reached, but as something developing according to its own internal laws, however difficult these may be to define at the present juncture.

Leonid Finkelstein:

I agree that in Soviet sociology there are quite a number of fine people who are enthusiastic about their work, but what Mr. Yakushev omitted to take into account is that as soon as sociologists start to publish "seditious" material they will be joining dissident writers in the prison camps. The authorities are not putting sociologists in camps because there is as yet no sociological *samizdat*, or *tamizdat*—as material smuggled out and published in the West is now called. If such material starts to circulate, the authorities will put sociologists into camps alongside writers. There will be no difference. Sociologists are a nightmare for the Soviet leaders. But sociology without public opinion polls is not sociology, as I hope Professor Nove will agree. It is baptism without the font, or shooting without weapons. If we are not studying society we are not sociologists. And it is forbidden to examine the actual state of society in the Soviet Union and publish your results. You may study the utilization of working time and everyone's opinion about it, and whether people want to open a club or not, but the régime does not permit investigation of *real* social problems.

Alec Nove:

It seems to me that a dual process is taking place: there is pressure from below and uncertainty at the top, and this is particularly evident in economics and the social sciences. The State needs results, not simply ideological constancy. This makes room for inconsistencies, of course. It is not correct to say there are no polls; they do exist. In Novosibirsk, for example, sociologists used polls to try to discover the reasons why people are leaving Siberia to work in Central Asia, the North Caucasus and the Baltic region.[204] Of course, this information was necessary to the government. The same applies to the considerable advances in economic thinking made by mathematical economists. The Central Committee certainly approved the plan of their work, and the Central Committee is also involved in the present criticism of this tendency: some people there say it is necessary, others that it is harmful, but both sides argue their case, and in this way some sort of shift takes place all the same. People with different opinions, many with the best intentions, are taking part in the disputes in and around the Central Committee. The opportunity for discussion has been widened by the publication of thick volumes of statistics that were formerly kept secret. Numerous independent social research projects have become possible. Under Stalin this was not the case.

J. René Beermann:

I believe a certain equilibrium can often be observed here: if pressure is being applied in one field of study the reins are slackened somewhat in another; for instance, when there is a clamp-down on literature there may be a relaxation of controls on the publication of books and articles on legal problems. The sociology of law is now often discussed in Soviet legal journals, and general sociological questions are raised there too.

Natalia Belinkova:

I would like to ask those present to bear one thing in mind: the same "internal editor" who exists in every writer has also long existed in every Soviet citizen, whether he is a reader or the object of a sociological investigation, and I doubt if the answers given by the ordinary Soviet citizen on the street or in his home can be taken very seriously. Attempts to conduct polls were made by television, and when people were asked how they liked a certain programme, the man who the evening before spat and switched off his set would say that the programme was extremely interesting, although there could have been nothing of interest to him in it.

Albert Parry:

On the other hand, newspapers such as *Sovetskaya Rossiya* state that from time to time readers write in to complain about programmes. It is not

---

[204] See for instance the article by L. Yelovikov in No. 1, 1967 and the articles by Ye. Antosenkov, V. Kalmyk and L. Shishkina in No. 11, 1968, of *Izvestiya Sibirskogo otdeleniya AN SSSR*.

clear whether they sign these letters with their real names, but obviously some sort of public opinion is filtering through; as well as letters written to order there are also genuine letters.

Besides polls there is other evidence that things are moving forward in an evolutionary, not revolutionary, way. I am thinking of a report in a Soviet newspaper about a Party meeting in a factory where it was announced that a sociologist was being appointed to the list of Party officials and a voice from the rear asked what, in that case, was the point of having a Party organization!

Anatol Popluiko:

Are scientists subjected to censorship while they are abroad, and is there a censorship for foreign scientific journals?

Aleksey Yakushev:

Scientists travelling abroad are screened, of course—not by *Glavlit*, but through other channels, and some categories of scientists are forbidden to travel abroad at all, or else are closely supervised. Sakharov, for example, once spent two or three days in Paris, but I believe he was accompanied by a whole regiment of security men. Artsimovich travels in the same way, although he is no longer directly concerned with atomic research.[205]

I do not know what the position is in other institutes, but in the publishing house for foreign literature there is a room in the library where you can read most foreign periodicals. You just tell the librarian that you need material for a special project. All the senior employees had access to these periodicals, but you could not take them away with you.

Igor Yeltsov:

In our film studios we received an American technical journal, something like *Cinema, Radio and Television*. I saw it on the chief engineer's desk and noticed that it had been reprinted in Moscow. Everything undesirable, including advertisements, had been removed, and only those technical articles with which the engineer could be trusted were retained. Everything else, even whole pages, was missing. This was done by a photocopying process, but the finished product appeared to be printed.[206]

---

[205] There is much more on this subject in the first part of the book named in footnote 206.

[206] This procedure is employed with other journals as well, e.g., *Science*. See on this chapter 7 of Zhores Medvedev's *Tayna perepiski okhranyayetsya zakonom* (Secrecy of Correspondence is Guaranteed by Law), *The Medvedev Papers*, London, Macmillan, 1971.

I do not know much about the screening of Soviet scientists and other citizens travelling abroad, but when I went to Argentina in 1959 as a member of the Soviet delegation I had to attend a briefing on the third floor of the Central Committee headquarters. A young woman arrived and shouted: "Mongolians to room 31, English to room 65, Finns to room 35." Groups of men and women went off to these rooms for their briefing and then emerged, making such remarks as: "You idiot, why did you say that? You shouldn't have spoken like that," and so on. The same happened to us. We went into a special room where a person named Yelin explained that we were the first group to go to Argentina and must be worthy of the trust of the Soviet people, etc., etc. After this, we were taken to another room furnished with a long table covered with green cloth and lent booklets, rubber-stamped "Top Secret," containing all the rules of behaviour for Soviet citizens abroad. For example, if one was in a train compartment and someone else came in, one had to ask the conductor to find a separate compartment where one could either be alone or with other Soviet citizens.

Then we were given a paper to sign promising to guard faithfully all state, military and God knows what kinds of secrets. I cannot remember exactly what was on it, but I do recall the man next to me, an Armenian journalist, saying he would not sign, and I nudged him, because there might have been a hidden microphone somewhere. I told him there was no choice if he wanted to go abroad. Then we were summoned to Comrade Shcherbakov, who said to me: "Comrade Yeltsov, how are you? I'm so glad that everything is well with you, that everything is all right with your family, that you and your wife are getting on so well..." I said: "Excuse me, I am not married," and he said: "Oh...er, yes, yes. Well now, er...aha, well, were you ever abroad? You were. Where? I see,..." Another person was present, sitting behind a newspaper which he was pretending to read, but he was watching the whole time; he was probably a psychiatrist checking up on my behaviour. I expect it was the final test, a last attempt to trap me just before I was due to leave.[207]

Tourists are advised to say they do not speak any foreign languages if it looks as if they are getting involved in serious conversation, and if they receive private invitations they should excuse themselves by saying they have no time or are not feeling well.[208]

---

[207] Mr. Yeltsov might have been expected not to "remind" his listeners that he was a bachelor, as it is especially difficult for unmarried people to receive permission to visit the West.

[208] For an account of the preliminaries to and instructions for the visit to the West of another cinema worker see pp. 27–46 of Yury Krotkov's *The Angry Exile*, London, Heinemann, 1967.

Anatol Popluiko:

In 1939 I was working in Moscow on the journal *Novosti tekhnicheskoy literatury* (News of Technical Literature), and at that time none of our journals was censored, although when they arrived at the scientific and technical library in Dnepropetrovsk parts of them had been removed. At one time scientists had the right to subscribe to journals personally, but this practice was stopped in 1935. Can one personally subscribe to Western journals now?

Aleksey Yakushev:

Only people who are pretty high up. A small amount of money is allotted for the purchase of books abroad—mainly scientific books, which are also scrutinised by the censorship before they are delivered to the addressee.

Evading the Censor

Max Hayward:

Now let us turn—or return—to ways in which the censorship can be outwitted.

Arkady Belinkov:

I would like to enlarge a little on what I said on the first day of our conference about various tricks with which one can sometimes outwit the censor. I shall be talking mainly about occasions on which it was possible to evade the censor, but I do not want my remarks, which are devoted to one specific aspect that does not play a decisive role in Soviet public life, to be interpreted as proof that the ideological walls are tottering and about to come tumbling down in the near future.

The Soviet censorship has not only prevented information from reaching the reading public but has also had the incidental effect of keeping the people who run the ideological machine in the dark about many important matters. To overcome this problem a means of circumventing the censor was devised, and it was thought up by the censorship itself. Special editions of books on the official index are published in a standard, reddish-coloured cover, bearing the words "Top Secret" in the upper right-hand corner and distributed according to a special list. At first the list was very restricted, but later on it had to be considerably lengthened to include all persons dealing with ideological matters. Thus, anyone living in a House for Writers or having contacts anywhere where "creative rehashing" was undertaken could manage to acquaint himself with such works as Orwell's *Animal Farm*. (There are many Orwellian features of life in the Soviet Union. If a man has committed what the régime considers to be a crime he is first blasted as hard as possible, but after that his name ceases to be mentioned. This can lead to absurd situations. If, for example, you look in all the editions of all Soviet encyclopedias published after 1928 you will find the word *Trotskyism* but not the name *Trotsky*.)

In my book on Olesha I quoted his account of the enthusiastic reception accorded to Khrushchev in Paris during the famous trip which was part of his peace offensive in 1960. Then came the October 1964 plenary session of the Party Central Committee at which Khrushchev was deposed and branded a "voluntarist" and "subjectivist." When my manuscript landed on the desk of the deputy chief editor of the "Iskusstvo" (Art) publishing house, a worthy gentleman called Yuly Shub, he took hold of a red pencil, crossed out every mention of Khrushchev and substituted "voluntarist and subjectivist." Imagine the result: a motorcycle escort and an enormous motor car in which sits the "voluntarist and subjectivist," the French crowds waving their arms and screaming "voluntarist and subjectivist!" This was one of the few occasions when I did not quarrel with the censorship. I decided to let it be broadcast like this in the radio adaptation, and I think it was more interesting for the Soviet audience than Olesha's original version.[209]

I should like to relate an episode which you probably know about already, but there are perhaps certain details less well known in the West. On the last page of the fourth issue of *Novy mir* (New World) for 1926 there is a note to the effect that the next issue would contain a work by Boris Pilnyak entitled *Povest o nepogashennoy lune* (The Tale of the Unextinguished Moon). The fifth issue of *Novy mir* for 1926 duly came out, but it did not contain Pilnyak's story. If you go to the Lenin Library or any other library and ask for this issue you will find Aleksandr Sytin's *Stada Allakha* (The Flocks of Allah) in place of the promised Pilnyak story. The mystery deepens when you turn to the last page of the following issue and find a strange statement by A. Voronsky, editor-in-chief of the journal *Krasnaya nov* (Red Virgin Soil), which begins: "The fifth issue of the journal *Novy mir* carried Boris Pilnyak's 'The Tale of the Unextinguished Moon'... The tale is dedicated to me..." Voronsky goes on to reject this dedication in the strongest terms, saying that it is a great insult to him as a communist and could cast a shadow on his reputation as a Party member. Why was Voronsky protesting about something that apparently did not exist? Well, if you go to the Lenin Library and ask for Pilnyak's "Tale" the librarian may give you a ticket for the *spetskhran* (special store for books not generally available) where you will actually be given a fifth issue of *Novy mir* for 1926 containing "The Tale of the Unextinguished Moon." The answer to the

---

[209] Mr. Belinkov proceeded here to demonstrate how the way in which certain lines were spoken led to the banning of A. Efros's recent production in Moscow of Chekhov's *Tri sestry* (Three Sisters). Because of the intonation, etc., audiences might have felt that Chekhov was not as optimistic about the future as most Soviet critics make him out to have been. See the excellent article on this production, "Yesli by znat," by M. Stroyeva in *Sovetskaya kultura*, January 18, 1968. On theatre censorship see A. Kron, "Zametki pisatelya," *Literaturnaya Moskva*, No. 2, 1956; *The Politics of Ideas in the USSR*, ed. R. Conquest, London, The Bodley Head, 1967, pp. 49–53; and "Drama as a Weapon," pp. 118–157 of G. Counts and N. Lodge, *The Country of the Blind*, Boston, Houghton Mifflin Company, 1949.

mystery is that there were two May issues. After a number of copies had already been mailed to subscribers, the first issue, containing Pilnyak's story, was suddenly withdrawn and replaced by a new May issue containing Sytin's story in place of Pilnyak. The reason why it was deleted is that its plot has a historical parallel—the death of the Red Army Commander Frunze on the operating table in 1925, an event followed by rumours that the operation had been ordered by Stalin as a means of eliminating Frunze.[210]

It is sometimes possible to force the censorship to back down by unleashing a storm of protest at the editorial stage. "Rhinocéros" was due to appear in *Inostrannaya literatura*, but at the last minute it was decided in the Central Committee that Soviet citizens ought not to read a play in which so much doubt is cast on the spirit of collectivism, and all that we could do for the moment was to publish an article about the play in *Novy mir*.[211] There was such a scandal and we kicked up such a fuss that eventually, after a tremendous struggle, Chernoutsan succeeded in forcing it through. His real concern in taking this stand, however, was that the Soviet régime's image should not suffer abroad. I mention this example to indicate that something positive can result if one does not simply throw in the towel at the first setback, but there are also other, subtler, methods that are often much more fruitful.

One should not simply keep quiet when one sees the editor's red pencil mark; one should fight tooth and nail for every word. Persistence can result in a series of small concessions which in the end amount to a considerable advance. Once I wrote:

> When unfavourable circumstances reach the stage of complete victory for autocratic power [what I meant is: When does a writer perish? What degree of deformation can a human being withstand?], art gives up the ghost and in its stead vast numbers of chauvinistic oratorios and chorales of praise are churned out.

All this was crossed right through, and after over a week of protests, quarrels and hysterical scenes all I managed to salvage was "chorales of praise." Two years later, employing the same tactics, I managed to expand this to "...squeals of loyalty, rapturous iambics, choruses of canine devotion, chauvinistic oratorios and chorales of praise," and on a third occasion I managed to introduce "hyenas," "jackals," etc. This does not

---

[210] Pilnyak apologises for his "malicious slander" in *Novy mir*, No. 1, 1927, p. 256. A recent case of two different issues of the same number of a journal is *Yunost*, No. 7, 1969. The first copies sold have A. V. Kuznetsov as a member of the editorial board. Later copies of this issue are identical except that his name is missing, as he had decided to stay in England.

[211] See A. Anikst's article in No. 8, 1965.

mean that the censorship became progressively less stringent, but that it is easier and more profitable to work on ground already won.[212]

It is easier to circumvent the censorship in a book than in an article, because of the sheer volume of the printed matter. Furthermore, the censor is usually a person of average intellect who does not approach a book from the point of trying to understand its structure, its architecture. When he reads a sentence he is not usually interested in tracing its logic. (When you hand over a dog for training in the Soviet Union, you are asked whether you want it to be trained to be good or to be vicious. Censors, naturally, are trained to be vicious.) In the second chapter of the second edition of my book on Tynyanov I wrote: "If the history of a country contains a Frederick the Great there is good reason to suppose that later on a Bismarck will appear."[213] In the next chapter but one I wrote: "If in the past [of a country] there was an Ivan the Terrible, then the appearance of a Paul I can be expected."[214] And in chapter six: "If in the history of a country there was a Paul I, then one can expect a Nicholas I."[215] And in the next chapter I implied that Nicholas's present successors were fools, nonentities and scoundrels.[216] But this last chapter was devoted to Soviet literature, so it was not possible to mention names! When I had to make up an article based on this book for a volume on the history of Russian literature,[217] I gathered all these sentences together on one page. The meaning then became too obvious and the article was stopped, but in a book of 650 pages these allusions may be overlooked.

The Soviet censorship is a bitter fact of life for us, and we suffer at its hands, but we realize that if the censorship deletes something that in its eyes is harmful to the Soviet régime, this is more or less natural, given the nature of this régime. We condemn it, but we cannot regard it as something unnatural. It is doubly bitter, therefore, to find the Soviet censorship receiving help from unexpected quarters. In my book the censors missed the following quote from Pushkin: "Paul's reign proves one thing: that even in enlightened times Caligulas can be born. The Russian defenders of autocracy do not agree with this and take the splendid joke of Mme. de Staël as the basis of our constitution: 'En Russie le gouvernement est un

---

[212] The quoted passage is on p. 368 of Mr. Belinkov's *Yury Tynyanov*, Moscow, 1965. The third edition of this book, which was not released for sale because its author escaped to the West, almost certainly contains a fuller text.

[213] P. 93.

[214] P. 382.

[215] P. 596.

[216] P. 626.

[217] *Istoriya russkoy sovetskoy literatury*, Vol. 2, Moscow, 1967.

despotisme mitigé par la strangulation.'"[218] These are strong words and,
as we realize, by no means apply only to those far-off years of 1796—1801,
yet they nonetheless got past the Soviet censor. But when an Italian journal in Rome printed an extract from my book, this piece was removed.
I asked the editor why he had deleted a paragraph that even the Soviet
censor had passed, and he answered: "Well, why should we annoy them?"
The point is not that some Italian journal edited my work—they have been
known to do this sort of thing on other occasions—but that the tentacles
of the Soviet censorship reach out beyond the country's geographical
boundaries and inhibit foreign publishers and writers.[219] If a sociologist
in Oklahoma lets fly at the Soviet régime, or if a literary historian in Rome
writes something indiscreet about the Soviet system, he must reckon on
being refused a visa to visit the Soviet Union or access to archives and other
documents, or even on being arrested if he does get there. These Wester-

---

[218] Quoted by Belinkov on pp. 383–384.

[219] This is a subject which requires much closer attention. One might mention
Soviet attempts to persuade the BBC not to televise a programme on the trial of
Sinyavsky and Daniel (*The Times*, April 20, July 8 and 10, 1967, *The Sunday
Telegraph*, April 30, 1967, *The Observer*, July 2, 1967, *The Daily Telegraph*, July 10,
1967) or broadcast in Russian Svetlana Alliluyeva's article on Pasternak (*The
Daily Telegraph*, May 26, 27 and 29, 1967, July 14, 1967, *The Times*, May 26,
1967, *The Observer*, May 28, 1967, *The Guardian*, May 29, 1967). The virtual
absence of censorship in Czechoslovakia in the summer of 1968 was one of the
main reasons for the Soviet invasion, and the restoration of censorship was one
of the first demands made of the Czechoslovak leaders at the beginning of the
occupation (see for instance *The Times*, June 12 and August 17, 1968, *The Guardian*,
August 12, 1968, *The Daily Telegraph*, August 30, 1968, *The Sunday Times*, April 27.
1969); this did not prevent Moscow Radio accusing the BBC of "gross interference" in Czechoslovakia's internal affairs (*The Daily Telegraph*, April 8, 1969).
Soviet attempts to control what is printed and broadcast abroad show no signs
of diminishing; see, for example, the complaint of the Soviet ambassador in
Helsinki about the design of a Finnish beer-bottle label, *Der Spiegel*, August 31,
1970, p. 102. It should, however, be stressed that pressure of this sort is effective
in the West only when there is a willingness to submit to it; for Swedish censorship
of Solzhenitsyn, for instance, see *Posev*, No. 1, 1971, pp. 16–21, and No. 4, 1971,
p. 9. It goes without saying that foreign works published in the USSR are
frequently cut and censored without any indication that changes have been made;
on this, see *inter alia*, "Anger at Cuts in Tito Article," *The Times*, October 25,
1967, and (concerning alterations made to Arthur Miller's *A View from the Bridge*)
Harper's Magazine, September 1969, p. 44. Occasionally a Western writer even
approves the publication in the Soviet Union of a censored version of one of his
own works; see pp. 154–59 of *Russia—Hopes and Fears*, Penguin Books, 1969,
where Alexander Werth attempts to justify his authorization of a cut translation
of his *Russia at War, 1941–1945*, London, Barrie and Rockliffe, 1964. For a recent
samizdat article on some of these matters see German Smirnovsky, "S kem vy,
Uilyam Fulbrayt?," Moscow, March 1972.

ners are thus to a considerable degree forced to handle with kid gloves the ideological principles according to which the Soviet régime operates and which stifle the free word in the Soviet Union.

David Anin:

The historical journals *Voprosy istorii* (Questions of History) and *Istoriya SSSR* (History of the USSR) appear to disarm the censor by publishing extensive quotations from the works of foreign sovietologists and historians, complete with sources, which they preface with assertions that their authors are "falsifiers" and their opinions "slanders." I think that they are also to some extent trying to get some new ideas past the censorship. Do you agree?

Arkady Belinkov:

There are open discussions on this score in Moscow.

Leonid Finkelstein:

The late Nikolay Smirnov-Sokolsky[220] expressed it like this: "You write a dirty word on the fence and then invite everyone to come and read it, saying: 'Look, how disgusting!'" That's the technique, and Professor Anikst demonstrated it brilliantly in his article about "Rhinocéros."[221] You put in your quotation and then you add, say, "as that ardent enemy of the Soviet Union, the not unknown so-and-so, writes" or, if it is someone to be taken seriously, you place the word "notorious" before his name.

There is another, widely-used and purely technical method of evading the censor which I once successfully employed shortly before I left. It works like this: you quote something quite seditious, but instead of naming the author you refer to a "great writer" or, even better, to a "great Russian writer." In the twelfth issue of *Znaniye — sila* for 1965 I began an article with the words, "I recently read a story by a very great writer..." and then proceeded to relate Solzhenitsyn's *Utyonok* (The Duckling).[222] I was banking on my chief editor not knowing this story and being too proud to ask which writer I meant. Here we have a story by a "very great writer," and he as chief editor does not know whose story it is—how embarrassing! And the censor does not want to admit his ignorance

---

[220] A leading Soviet bibliophile (1898–1962). See his *Rasskazy o knigakh*, Moscow, Izdatelstvo vsesoyuznoy knizhnoy palaty, 1960.

[221] *Novy mir*, No. 8, 1965.

[222] Published in *Grani*, No. 56, 1964, and *Encounter*, March 1965. Mr. Finkelstein's article "Planeta zemlya — strana khimiya" (signed "L. Vladimirov") begins on the inside front cover of *Znaniye-sila*, No. 12, 1965.

either. Everything went swimmingly, and after three months I heard from
Solzhenitsyn via someone else that he had read my piece and was pleased
with it.

Martin Dewhirst:

Some Soviet critics publish articles in foreign communist journals.
Lev Kopelev, for example, published something in the Viennese journal
Tagebuch in 1968,[223] and Anatoly Aleksandrov's articles about Kharms and
Vvedensky appeared recently in Czechoslovakia.[224] This appears to be
another method of avoiding the Soviet censorship.[225] One could also
mention Amalrik, who says quite frankly that he feels he has the right to
publish his works abroad and receive payment for them, and who for this
reason, apparently, does not circulate his writing through *samizdat*, but
simply sends it straight abroad.

Arkady Belinkov:

It is not a punishable offence under the Soviet Criminal Code to publish
works abroad. There is no article forbidding this, but there is an article
concerning "anti-Soviet agitation," and this agitation is punishable no
matter where it takes place. In the case of Sinyavsky and Daniel it merely
aggravated their guilt, but they could not be convicted simply for publishing
their work abroad. Many Soviet writers publish abroad and nobody puts
them on trial for it. The *Novosti* press agency even earns hard currency by
selling manuscripts which have or have not been published in the Soviet
Union to certain people in the West.[226]

Natalia Belinkova:

In 1965 I met some economists at the Academy of Sciences who told
me that sometimes they publish an analysis which ostensibly relates to one
of the underdeveloped countries, but which is really based on facts and
figures taken from Soviet life. They are thus able to say everything they

---

[223] January-February, 1968.

[224] *Československá rusistika*, No. 5, 1968 and *Svetová literatura*, No. 6, 1968.

[225] Soviet journalists, writers, etc., are of course frequently authorized to
contribute to foreign publications. Such articles as K. Zelinski's "Russian Poetry
Today" (*Survey*, No. 40, January 1962) can be distinguished from works such
as Ye. Yevtushenko's autobiography (Penguin Books, 1965), which was printed
abroad (for the first time in 1963) with the permission of the author but not of the
Soviet authorities.

[226] E.g., Pasternak's *Letters to Georgian Friends*, Secker and Warburg, London,
1968 (the copyright was bought by Giulio Einaudi in 1967).

want about the Soviet economy and everyone understands quite well what they are referring to. So if you are reading an article about the under-developed countries in *Voprosy filosofii* (Questions of Philosophy) or *Voprosy ekonomiki* (Questions of Economics), you in the West should bear in mind that you might really be reading an analysis of the Soviet economy.

Max Hayward:

What about the work of Western writers in and on the Soviet Union? How does the Soviet censorship system affect their work?

David Floyd:

I can tell you how the censorship affects the activities of foreign corres-pondents in Moscow. Not that I consider our work to be in any way artistic—although some reports from Moscow about what goes on in the Kremlin contain an element of creative writing and are not simply journal-ism—but I do see a connection between what we are discussing here and the activity of reporters. The correspondent is also involved in the struggle with the Soviet censorship, even if he merely serves as a post box for today's Soviet intelligentsia. I would say that foreign correspondents, and not only those representing non-communist newspapers, all suffer at the hands of the censorship. I would even say that the censorship harms and hampers their work more seriously than it does that of its own foreign correspondents.

At one time a correspondent had to take his copy direct to the Central Telegraph Office on Gorky Street, where he first of all handed it in to be censored. He did not know who was checking what he had written. He simply sat and waited, sometimes for ten minutes, sometimes for half an hour, and sometimes for days, no matter how important or urgent his reports were, and they always came back heavily censored. I recall one instance of direct interference with my work when I was in Moscow in an unofficial capacity, as a tourist. I wanted to transmit something to London and asked the advice of my colleagues, who said: "Oh, just pick up the telephone in the hotel, ask for your newspaper in London and try your luck." I got through to my editor and said: "Listen, I'm now going to tell you something that I think might be interesting, but they may interrupt me." I had just dictated the place and date when a female voice cut in and said: "Mr. Floyd, if this is just a normal correspondent's conversation, please go ahead, but if it is a report, then apply to the Central Telegraph Office." But when I did this they would have nothing to do with me because I was a tourist. I got the same response at the press department of the Foreign Ministry. This is the sort of game played with foreign correspondents a few years ago.[227]

I would like to add that they do not so much forbid something outright as give you "advice." They are very hard-working in Moscow, establishing contacts with correspondents and even "helping" them by leaking certain information. The whole business is extremely well organized, and they have established almost full control over foreign reporters. It is very difficult to phone or wire information out of Moscow when you are working there on a permanent basis. They realize how important it is to the ordinary correspondent not to be expelled from the country, and for this reason they have a certain hold on him. A man can be sent there knowing very little Russian and poorly informed about Soviet affairs, and this they exploit. In the final analysis this influences what the outside world learns about the Soviet Union.

David Anin:

How do you explain the fact that highly critical dispatches still filter through? I'm thinking, for example, of Michel Tatu's articles when he was the Moscow correspondent of *Le Monde*. They were clearly anti-Soviet, but nonetheless the censorship let them straight through. There was also the case of Voznesensky's 1967 letter,[228] which was transmitted directly by telex from Moscow, apparently with the permission of the authorities. How is this possible? And what about Amalrik?[229]

David Floyd:

Amalrik simply approached our correspondent and asked him to send it. The Soviet leaders want Western reporters in Moscow; they need foreign journalists, and if they are going to exploit them, they must also allow them some rope. Eventually they wanted to get rid of Tatu but, if I am not mistaken, de Gaulle said: "Very well, if you throw him out then all Soviet correspondents will be deported from France." Since 1961 they have switched from direct, formal censorship to enforcing self-censorship. Every correspondent now knows beforehand that if he goes too far he will

---

[227] Direct censorship of outgoing news dispatches by foreign correspondents ended in March 1961. For the restrictions on the exchange of information between East and West in the years leading up to this date see Paul Winterton, *Report on Russia*, London, The Cresset Press, 1945, especially chapters 3 and 4, and Frederick Barghoorn, *The Soviet Cultural Offensive*, Princeton, Princeton University Press, 1960, especially chapter four, "Barriers and Controls."

[228] See *Problems of Communism*, No. 5, 1968, p. 55.

[229] This refers to Amalrik's letter to Kuznetsov, published in full in *Survey*, Nos. 74–75, 1970.

be summoned to the Ministry of Foreign Affairs or expelled from Moscow. From time to time they do this. It happened recently with Shub.[230] A Soviet journalist in America was discovered to be a spy and deported, whereupon the Soviet authorities made Shub leave the country. Officially, there is now no censorship, but if a correspondent oversteps the mark in a report, it can mean the end of his sojourn in the USSR and trouble for his newspaper. They may even punish the newspaper for the correspondent's slip, and the correspondent for the newspaper's. When *Life* magazine did a feature on Lenin, for example, the Soviet authorities expelled the correspondent, although the parts they objected to had been inserted by the editors.[231]

Igor Yeltsov:

A foreign correspondent can arrive in Moscow, and some importunate character, perhaps a Soviet journalist, starts being friendly and frank and offers his help. That is done, isn't it?

David Floyd:

Yes, but they go even further. After one correspondent had been involved in a car accident someone rang him up and told him: "Look here, you are in a difficult spot. This is a very serious accident and things don't look good for you at all. But we can help you if you'll help us." He knew what that meant, so he made some sort of excuse and left the Soviet Union. But he assured me that many Western correspondents are in their hands.[232]

Igor Yeltsov:

Can foreign press representatives correspond with Soviet citizens? If a foreign journalist in Moscow wants to write a personal letter to a Soviet citizen in Kiev, the Far East or Leningrad, is his correspondence intercepted and opened?

---

230 Anatol Shub (of the *Washington Post*) was forced to leave the Soviet Union in May 1969.

231 For other examples of the difficulties experienced by Western correspondents in Moscow see *Survey*, No. 68, July 1968, pp. 118–69, and K. Tidmarsh, "Moscow Officials Set up an Iron Curtain Round Foreign Press," *The Times*, May 1, 1968. See also P. Tempest, "Soviet Security Bars Way to Pressmen," *Morning Star*, January 20, 1968; K. Tidmarsh, "Soviet Police Bar US Reporters," *The Times*, January 20, 1968, and the contributions by D. Bonavia and P. E. Hegge to *Survey*, No. 85, Autumn 1972, pp. 1—29.

232 On this matter see A. Amalrik, "Inostrannyye korrespondenty v Moskve," *Posev*, No. 11, 1970, pp. 42–48. The English version ("News from Moscow," *New York Review of Books*, March 25, 1971) has been censored by the Western editors, who drop the name of one of the journalists concerned (Henry Shapiro).

David Floyd:

There are contacts of this sort between correspondents and Soviet citizens, although they are severely frowned on, if not actually forbidden. Letters are exchanged, but not usually through the post.[233]

Yuri Demin:

What about those correspondents whose revelations harm people in the Soviet Union who are trying to oppose or at least change the system? I remember one case of this sort. When Vladimir Serov was put up for re-election as an official of the Union of Artists, some of the younger, more progressive members began scheming to prevent it. While this was happening an American correspondent prowled around all the painters' studios, gathering information which was later published in *Life* magazine,[234]

[233] On postal censorship in the Soviet Union see Zhores Medvedev, "Secrecy of Correspondence is Guaranteed by Law," pp. 295–471 of Zhores A. Medvedev, *The Medvedev Papers*, London, Macmillan, 1971.

[234] March 28, 1960. See also P. Sjeklocha and I. Mead, *Unofficial Art in the Soviet Union*, Berkeley, 1967; J. Berger, *New Society*, September 8 and 15, 1966, *The Sunday Times Supplement*, November 6, 1966, and his book *Art and Revolution*, London, 1969; the supplement to *L'Espresso* (Rome) of March 16, 1969; and A. Pohribny, *Problems of Communism*, March–April, 1970, for some examples of recent and contemporary Soviet art not considered fit for public display. The ideological tightening up which began shortly after the publication of *Odin den Ivana Denisovicha* became quite clear when Mr. Khrushchev visited an art exhibition on December 1, 1962 — see especially pp. 101–113 of P. Johnson, *Khrushchev and the Arts*, The MIT Press, 1965. Since then public and semi-public art exhibitions have regularly been closed down, or not even allowed to open, by the authorities — see for instance *The Daily Telegraph*, December 31, 1966 (Chagall, Kandinsky), *The Times*, January 23, 1967 (Rabin, Zverev, Plavinsky, Neizvestny), *The Guardian*, February 13, 1967 (Chagall), February 15, 1967 (Lentulov) and April 13, 1968 (Chagall), *The Sunday Times*, September 1, 1968 (Filonov), *The Times*, March 11, 1969 (Rabin, Plavinsky, Sveshnikov, Krapivnitsky, Nemukhin), and May 28, 1970 (Tselkov). The Soviet authorities also try to control what Russian and Soviet art is shown abroad, even going so far as to censor an entire room of an exhibition in London (see *The Times*, February 26, 1971). On the political control of art in the USSR see also *The Guardian*, October 28, 1967 and February 1, 1968, and *The Times*, January 3, 1968. One might recall here that in his novel *Ottepel* (The Thaw) Ehrenburg was concerned with the censorship of art rather than of literature. On the censorship of art exhibitions before 1917 (this involved the removal of "pornographic" and "tendentiously-harmful" pictures and sculptures) see p. 591 of D. V. Valdenberg, *Spravochnaya kniga o pechati vsey Rossii*, St. Petersburg, T-vo Khudozhestvennoy Pechati, 1911. For a Soviet allusion to the censorship of art exhibitions in more recent times see *Iskusstvo*, No. 2, 1968, p. 15. Photographs are also censored and unpersons (e.g., Trotsky) are normally removed before group pictures are reprinted. For some Czechoslovak examples of this see *The Sunday Times Magazine*, April 26, 1970. On the disappearance of a bottle of beer from a photograph of Brezhnev see "No Smoking," *The Guardian*, October 1, 1971.

where he hinted that some of these younger people prefer Western painting and abhor everything Soviet, even mentioning some names and addresses. At the congress of artists an enraged Serov brandished this copy of *Life* and was duly re-elected. Does not any sort of court of honour or moral code exist in your journalistic circles, especially among foreign correspondents? Surely some sort of self-restraint is required?

Max Hayward:

Could we here turn also to the question of how one should react to the use of Aesopian language by Soviet writers?

J. René Beermann:

I think this is a particularly important point, and there is another query that can be added to it. Things that are not possible in the Soviet central publications sometimes manage to slip into the provincial press, and the question is, how advisable is it to draw attention to this in Western periodicals and academic journals? Provincial newspapers frequently become annoyed about certain matters and write on sensitive topics which they are not supposed to touch. If you see that the provincial press has dealt with an issue of this sort, should it be written about in the West? I have often had my doubts. Provincial legal journals often give exact statistics about crime in a given area, about alcoholism and hooliganism, for example, and they even publish graphs.

Yuri Demin:

We have said little about the provinces, and yet this is a very important subject. To put it briefly, I would say that if anyone should be spared it is those who live in the provinces. Provincial writers are doubly oppressed, whereas writers who live in the capital are part of a more varied environment and have more opportunity to defend themselves and to seek advice—they can always ask influential colleagues to use their connections. In the provinces this is by no means the case. In every large provincial town there are perhaps two or three honest writers, and they lead a very lonely existence. They are under pressure from the local Party chiefs, they are surrounded by informers, and if a writer in Novosibirsk publishes a good poem or a frank article and someone abroad writes that at long last a writer has emerged in Novosibirsk who has said the truth, who points out that "the king is naked," then this writer won't last five minutes; he won't even have time to empty his wastepaper basket. In Moscow, on the other hand, you have a chance to save your neck. After the appearance of an article of this sort I would rush round Moscow, phone, or otherwise contact someone, and in the end, with the assistance of friends, we would prove that it was all a misunderstanding. But the provinces must be spared. And if one is thinking about the future, then the point is that Russia can revive, can change for the better, only when the cultural centres properly "infect" the provinces, and though this process is under way it still has a very long distance to go. Already, however, the provinces can occasionally be more active than the centre, because, after all, the Central Committee is mainly concerned with the centre so far as intellectual matters are concerned, and pays less attention to what goes on in the provinces, where everything is left to the *oblast* Party committees. The curious thing is that while it is impossible for a sociologist to publish something of value about the country as a whole, he can write quite easily about his own *oblast*. There is no risk at all in this. It is quite possible for him to say that in his *oblast* there are 300,000 alcoholics. The Central Committee entrusts the supervisory functions to the *oblast* committee and the latter is usually not worried about local "subversives," because if there are two good writers they are isolated individuals and it is quite easy to keep an eye on them. It is because of this that such a writer can lull their suspicions and convince them that he has nothing more in his head than the desire to sit in a restaurant and enjoy himself. It is then that he can write a good poem and sometimes even have it published.

There was a rather illuminating situation in Novosibirsk at the end of the 1950s, by the way. I had written my first verses there, or rather a little farther east, and then I travelled all over the eastern Soviet Union, at first as a poet and afterwards as a journalist. I knew all the towns and everywhere the situation was roughly the same. Suddenly everything changed in Novosibirsk because a lot of scientists arrived. And when Akademgorodok[235] sprang up it disorganized the *oblast* committee from the bottom upwards. The regional Party committee now had to be "intellectual," and, as you know, the main characteristic of an intellectual is that he vacillates all the time. Their talks with the scientists began to send them off the rails, and all at once it became possible to do something good in Novosibirsk. People began to flock there, but then the police intervened and stopped issuing residence permits.

If there is a war going on, and it is going on, writers in the capital are behind the lines and not too badly off. It is the provinces that are in the front line, and one must be more cautious with them. If you "decode" the Aesopian language of a writer in the capital—and now I am appealing to

---

[235] A small town where many scientists live, not far from Novosibirsk.

Western journalists—he may possibly save his neck, possibly not, so it is perhaps best not to decipher it, but rather to leave the matter to history. As far as the writer in the provinces is concerned, he is on his own, every step he makes is known, so leave him absolutely alone. If there is a stool-pigeon in the Moscow House of Writers—and we know all of them—he doesn't have a comfortable time of it. In the provinces the atmosphere is completely different. Spare the provinces particularly—but spare the capital as well.

Anthony Adamovich:

This is a very sensitive topic for me, because of the internal censorship that dwells in me and prevents me from writing many things for fear of harming anyone in the Soviet Union. One could claim that in the Soviet Union there is a war in progress and that in a war casualties are inevitable. But it is extremely difficult to decide who will suffer and who will not suffer; one can try to gauge exactly who might be injured and who might not, but this is very, very difficult.

Aleksey Yakushev:

I do not think there is any hard-and-fast rule. Just as there are many different ways of employing Aesopian language, so there are many ways of defending a man who is suddenly discovered to be employing it. It is hardly possible to come to some sort of blanket and universally applicable decision about this problem. In individual cases, of course, a method can to some extent be constructed by which the person could perhaps defend himself. He could claim, for example, that it was a misunderstanding, that he was being misrepresented or wrongly interpreted.

As far as science, sociology, etc., are concerned it is easy and I believe one may speak out, because there is a more or less specific content that can be interpreted in various ways. But insofar as straightforward political statements are involved, I think one should exercise the greatest care. With philosophy almost no difficulties exist, because philosophical material can be approached from so many angles and interpreted in so many ways.

Anatoly Kuznetsov:

I would like to express a diametrically opposite view. I completely stick to the opinion I expressed earlier,[236] though I don't want to force it on anyone and merely offer it as information. I am simply speaking as a witness—I was also a provincial writer who sometimes lived in the capital

---

[236] See pp. 90–91.

as well. I was only proud when my work was published abroad. It was a source of great satisfaction to me when my book *The Continuation of a Legend* came out in France in an anti-Soviet form and with an anti-Soviet bias. But of course I couldn't tell anyone officially that I was proud. And when they suggested that I sue the publishers of the French translation, I did so, as I described in the press here.[237] It was all part of one's daily existence in that Orwellian Soviet world.

If you were to ask in confidence any of the writers I know and any of my friends among leading writers, they would all unreservedly state, as I do, that they would be proud to have their Aesopian language decoded. I was once utterly shaken to read that some publishers, "in order not to harm Solzhenitsyn," had decided not to bring out one of his novels. In the first place this was ineffective, because the novel was published anyway, and secondly it was a tactical and strategic error. If a poet, say one from the provinces, writes a poem, and if he has managed to express something in it, if it has reached the printing press and is already being sold at the kiosks —what joy! Let me explain the writer's psychology. (There are probably those who for some reason or other might send through a request to be attacked and not praised; one has to take this into account, but I am talking about the typical author's attitude.) I am shaken by your "solicitude." Indeed, why are you concerned about me? Don't care, for God's sake! This "solicitude" only disturbs me. You should write about this Aesopian language instead of hanging a padlock on your lips and applying self-censorship! You have the opportunity to decode all this, but in trying to protect me you are doing me a disservice. This is one aspect, the moral one. There is another side to the coin, which I would call the purely practical. Please do not be naive and think that if you have decoded the poem *Soyuz* (Union)[238] or some admirable poem by a Novosibirsk poet this means you have denounced him in the Soviet Union. You are frightened of harming him, but don't worry, you will not be denouncing him any more than the person who ran to the Novosibirsk KGB the day after the publication of the work in question. You underestimate the amount of informing that goes on in Soviet Russia; people are beside themselves with eagerness to denounce somebody. Imagine the glee with which Natalya Parygina, a writer from Tula, rushed to the *oblast* committee after the publication of Solzhenitsyn's *Matryonin dvor* (Matryona's Home) shouting: "This is a slander on the Soviet village. How did they let it through? How could it be printed?" She shouted this out loud, but there are many who are more

---

237 See *The Daily Telegraph*, August 7, 1969.
238 See note 66 on p. 33.

stealthy and trot around with a copy of the journal under their arm, saying: "Here, look at this! Look what's just come out!" Don't worry, the authorities have already been told a hundred times before your article reaches them. They are already keeping a dossier, they are already shadowing the poet and tapping his telephone.

I did everything that was expected of me in France, and they later quoted me as an example to Solzhenitsyn, trying to make him protest about the publication of his work abroad.[239] But all the same, the KGB kept a close check on me for eight years, although I had done everything according to the book. So no article written about me in the West, no matter how anti-Soviet in tone, could do me any more harm. The poet writes a poem and dreams of reaching the widest possible audience, and if it is international, so much the better.

Leonid Finkelstein:

Each case should be judged in its own context. *Quod licet Jovi non licet bovi*. If the famous writer Kuznetsov allows himself a bit of rope and is informed upon, at first within and then outside the Soviet Union, the Writers' Union says: "Ah, Kuznetsov has had his little joke." And the KGB thinks: "We'll have to keep a closer watch on him, put another microphone in the lavatory or take similar steps." But they still won't grab him by the gills. Imagine, on the other hand, that some correspondent in the West had suddenly spotted my article in issue No. 12 of *Znaniye — sila* for 1965[240] and written: "The Moscow journal *Znaniye — sila* has quoted Solzhenitsyn. They've got some artful dodgers there." This could have cost me my position, to say the least. The moral is, therefore, to judge each case on its individual merits. In some cases one should probably refrain from mentioning certain things, and in others it is possible to draw attention to them because it has already been done in the Soviet Union. But so far as the deciphering of the *podtekst*—the meaning below the surface—is concerned, the Western journalist must not only be familiar with the picture from the outside but also with what is going on internally, below the surface.

Aleksey Yakushev:

I do not want to mention any names, but we were in complete agreement that people sometimes write interestingly even in the larger Soviet newspapers, and sometimes in such a cunning way that it is difficult for a man

---

[239] *Literaturnaya gazeta*, June 26, 1968, p. 5. In English on p. 136 of *Solzhenitsyn. A Documentary Record*, ed. L. Labedz, London, 1970.

[240] See pp. 135–136.

who is not initiated to grasp the point. But as insiders we know these people, and we are aware that they are absolutely anti-Soviet; I fear that if we start spelling out what they really mean it will be tantamount to denouncing them. This danger is always present.

Karel van het Reve:

I have manuscripts lying on my desk in Amsterdam which fall into three categories: first, the manuscripts which authors give to me to be published under their real name so that everyone knows they deliberately entrusted me with their publication. Here, of course, there is no problem. Second, manuscripts which I received from authors or their friends to publish as works of *samizdat* that have come into my hands by chance. This is also a clear-cut case. But there is a third category, and these are the manuscripts that did indeed fall into my hands as *samizdat* works, not from the author or from friends, but simply as literary works, such as, say, memoirs about Ilya Ehrenburg by someone who knew him well. It is not a seditious work, but it is something that will not get through in Moscow. What should I do?

Leonid Finkelstein:

Publish everything, but refrain from commentaries and evaluations.

Nadine Popluiko:

I put the question about the extent to which the mentioning of names and works in the West may help or harm unorthodox writers to my friends in Moscow at the end of May (1969). One of them answered frankly: "Well, I have spent my ten years in prison, they have already expelled me from the Party, they dog my footsteps and they have planted microphones in my flat, so it is absolutely all the same to me what you write and say about me."

I think that here we are not distinguishing two elements quite clearly enough. Let there be as much publicity as possible for those writers and people who are in danger, only do not write that some author or other is well known for his anti-Soviet statements, because this can cause him harm. The more publicity the better, but if you are writing about his works, judge them rather from the purely artistic or scholarly point of view. I feel that the American Academy of Arts and Letters and the National Institute of Arts and Letters took the right approach when they made Solzhenitsyn an honorary member.[241] The Academy stressed that this honorary member-

---

[241] On May 21, 1969.

ship was awarded to Solzhenitsyn purely on the basis of the literary significance of his works.

As for the rather different question of deciphering "Aesopian" statements, I personally believe that there is no single answer and that we should be extremely careful. If we suddenly start to stress the hidden anti-Soviet meaning of the work of some writer or poet who is well known in the Soviet Union but still not identified there as an opponent of the system, I think we may well do him only harm. Western reviewers and critics should try to give a clear interpretation of what the writer wanted to say, and if they depart from purely aesthetic concerns and discuss the historical or possibly sociological and political significance of his work, then, of course, they should be sure they are thoroughly familiar with the circumstances and his situation.

Martin Dewhirst:

In my opinion we should pay much more attention to the so-called "right-wing" journals, which show their official true colours all the time. There is no need to talk so much about *Novy mir*, because in other journals there are also exceedingly illuminating articles about the way things are going. Take *Molodaya gvardiya*, for example; it is a pity to ignore it. It would be better to broaden the range of the journals about which we write.

J. René Beermann:

There is another facet of the problem. As you know, émigrés are seldom of one mind. They usually disagree: there are right-wingers, left-wingers, and even some who support the Soviet Union. Many old émigrés attack interesting young Soviet writers, who for their part support and receive the support of leftists in the West. You get a situation that may favour the Soviet modernists, because the most reactionary émigré clique joins in the attack on them by Soviet dogmatists, and this serves to bolster the modernist trend. This can apply to the national minority groups as well as to Soviet Russian writers. One must take into account that the national minorities, like the provinces, are frequently in a more exposed position than Russians or other people at the centre. It is easier to attack and harass them.

Anthony Adamovich:

My position is quite close to that of Anatoly Kuznetsov. I well remember the great feeling of satisfaction and triumph I experienced when a Western

Belorussian journal wrote about me in 1928. I never regretted this when in 1930 the OGPU took me down into their cellar and I became a "zek" (prisoner) for eight years. Even if I had remained there and were not among you today, I know that I should never have been sorry about it.

But Kuznetsov made the reservation that one must, of course, behave differently in different cases. There is not and cannot be one prescription.

Natalia Belinkova:

Do not forget that in the Soviet Union the minority is struggling against the majority, and you in the West should give us all the help you can.

The Participants

Herman Achminov

Born at Arkhangelsk, Russia. He is a graduate of Leningrad University, where he studied before World War II. In 1959 he studied for a B. Litt. at Oxford University, England. Since 1957 he has been a member of the research staff at the Institute for the Study of the USSR. Writes and lectures frequently on Soviet affairs and is the author of *Die Macht im Hintergrund* (1950), *Die Totengräber des Kommunismus* (1964), *Breschnew und Kossygin: Die neuen Männer im Kreml?* (1964).

Anthony Adamovich

Born in Minsk and graduated from the Pedagogical Faculty of Minsk University. He is author of several publications on Belorussian literature and history.

David Anin

Author of *The 1917 Russian Revolution Through the Eyes of Its Leaders* (published in Russian), and managing-editor of the McGraw Hill *Encyclopedia of Russia and the Soviet Union*. He is a contributor on Soviet affairs to English, American, French and Russian-language publications.

J. René Beermann

A lecturer at the Institute of Soviet and East European Studies, University of Glasgow.

Arkady Viktorovich Belinkov

Born in Moscow. Died in New Haven, Connecticut in 1970. Studied at the Gorky Literary Institute in Moscow and at Moscow University. Arrested in 1944 for his dissident literary activity, in particular for his unpublished *Antisovetsky roman* (An Anti-Soviet Novel) and sentenced to death after an investigation lasting 22 months, during which he was subjected to various forms of torture which seriously undermined his health. He was reprieved, and until 1956 was in prisons and labour camps, where he managed to write two more (unpublished) novels for which he was re-sentenced. After release he was allowed to teach for a short while at the Literary Institute in Moscow. After leaving the Soviet Union in 1968 he lectured at the University of Yale. He made a close study of the works of Pushkin and his contemporaries, and of Blok, Akhmatova, and Russian formalist criticism.

Natalia Aleksandrovna Belinkova

Born in Moscow; studied at Moscow University and the Gorky Literary Institute. Thereafter she worked as a critic, reviewer, and editor for journals such as *Novy mir* and *Moskva*. She has published a number of articles in the western and émigré press since her departure from the USSR in 1968, and has edited an anthology (*Novy kolokol*) consisting mainly of works by Soviet intellectuals who settled in the West during the 1960s.

150

Edward L. Crowley

Formerly deputy director of the Institute for the Study of the USSR and editor (with Max Hayward) of *Soviet Literature in the Sixties*, Frederick A. Praeger, New York, London, 1964.

Yuri Demin

Writer, poet and journalist. Was born in Finland of Russian parents. His father, a Don Cossack, who held senior military and administrative posts under the Soviet régime, died during the Stalin purges of 1937, and in 1942 Demin himself was sentenced to two years in a labour camp for failing to report for factory work. He served in the Red Army and after the war became a journalist. Between 1954 and 1968, when he left the Soviet Union to settle in France, he had four volumes of poems and a prose work published, and contributed numerous articles to Moscow literary journals. He helped to compile Moscow Radio youth programmes, was appointed poetry editor of the magazine *Smena*, and literary adviser to *Literaturnaya gazeta*. In 1959 he was elected a member of the Union of Soviet Writers.

Martin Dewhirst

Lecturer in Russian language and literature, Dept. of Slavonic Languages, Glasgow University.

Robert Farrell

Editor. Formerly, Assistant Director, Munich Center, University of Oklahoma. Editor, with Vladimir G. Treml, of *The Development of the Soviet Economy: Plan and Performance* (1968).

Leonid Finkelstein

Born in the Ukraine in 1924, the son of a professor of mathematics in Leningrad. In 1947, while a student in the senior class at the Moscow Institute of Aviation, he was arrested and spent five and a half years in various labour camps. Released and rehabilitated after Stalin's death in 1953, he completed his studies and graduated as an automobile engineer. He worked three years at a factory and simultaneously wrote articles popularising science for the press. In 1958 he became a full-time journalist, and four of his books on science were published in the Soviet Union, followed by a short story in 1965. In 1960 he was appointed editor of the technology section of the journal *Znaniye-sila*. In June 1966, while on a visit to London with a group of Soviet writers and journalists, he decided to apply for political asylum in Great Britain.

David Floyd

Communist affairs correspondent of the London *Daily Telegraph*.

Victor Frank

A Russian-born British journalist specialising in the study of Russian literature.

Michael Goldstein

A violinist and composer. Born in Odessa, he studied at Moscow Conservatoire from 1930 to 1936, in 1935 coming third (after David Oystrakh and Yelizaveta Gilels) in the All-Union Competition for Soviet violinists. In 1962 he won three prizes at the All-Union Competition for Composers in Moscow. From 1964 to 1967 he lived in East Berlin, working as a teacher, composer and performer. In 1967 he emigrated to Israel where he was appointed to teach the violin at the Rubin Academy of Music in Jerusalem. He now lives in Germany.

Max Hayward

Fellow of St. Antony's College, Oxford, is co-translator of Boris Pasternak's *Doctor Zhivago* (1958), of Aleksandr Solzhenitsyn's *One Day in the Life of Ivan Denisovich* (1963) and *For the Good of the Cause* (1964), and co-editor of *Soviet Literature in the Sixties* (1964). He translated and edited *On Trial: The Soviet State versus "Abram Tertz" and "Nikolai Arzhak"* (1966).

Anatoly Kuznetsóv

Born in Kiev, began writing at the age of 14, recording what he saw of the German occupation. After the war he studied at the Kiev Opera ballet school, later transferring to the Russian Dramatic Theatre. In 1946 he won his first literary competition for a series of short stories. From 1960 he lived in Tula, where he wrote three novels, two film scripts, and several collections of short stories. His books in print in the Soviet Union reached a circulation of about seven million and have been translated into over thirty languages. In 1969, while in London, he defected, and since then has been living and writing in England. He now wishes to be known as "A. Anatoli," in order to show that he has broken with his past as a Soviet writer and renounced the censored Soviet editions of his works.

Leopold Labedz

Editor of *Survey*, a journal of East and West studies, published in Great Britain. He has edited several publications dealing with aspects of Marxism and Communist affairs in general.

Wasyl Miniajlo

Born in the Ukraine and graduated from Kharkov Pedagogical Institute. He subsequently studied at the All-Ukrainian Institute of Journalism, and has since the 1950s been on the editorial staff of the Institute for the Study of the USSR.

Alec Nove

Professor in the Department of International Economic Studies, Glasgow University. He is an authority on Soviet economics and contributes regularly to various journals specialising in Communist affairs.

Albert Parry

Professor of Russian Civilization and Language, and director of Russian Studies at Colgate University, Hamilton, New York. His books include *The New Class Divided : Science and Technology versus Communism*, published in 1966.

Anatol Popluiko

Engineer and journalist. Worked in the Soviet Union as an engineer and economic consultant.

Nadine Popluiko

Associate Professor at George Washington University in Washington, D.C. Has written several articles on Russian and Soviet literature.

Peter B. Reddaway

A graduate of Cambridge University, has engaged in advanced studies at Harvard, Moscow and London Universities and is a senior lecturer in government at the London School of Economics. His articles have appeared in *Survey* and in *Soviet Studies* (Glasgow). He is co-editor (with Leonard B. Schapiro) of *Lenin After Fifty Years*.

Karel van het Reve

Born in Amsterdam, is Professor of Russian Literature at the University of Leyden, Holland. He was for a short time a newspaper correspondent in Moscow. He is secretary of the Alexander Herzen Foundation in Amsterdam.

Albert Todd

A lecturer at Queen's College, New York.

Aleksey Yakushev

Holds a Ph.D. from Moscow University, where he occupied the post of Reader in the Philosophy of Science until 1966, when he was appointed Research Professor at the Institute of Philosophy and Sociology of the Polish Academy of Arts and Sciences, Warsaw. In 1969 he defected to the West, and in 1970 was Research Fellow in the Department of Government of the University of Sydney. At present he is an associate of the Russian Institute at Columbia University, USA.

Igor Yeltsov

Born in Estonia. In 1951 he entered the All-Union State Institute of Cinematography and graduated as a film director in 1956. His first job was with the *Tallinnfilm* studios, as chief editor of the script department. In 1957 he himself wrote the script for his first film *V dome ostayutsya muzhchiny* (The Men Remain at Home). His later films include *Nezvannye gosti* (Uninvited Guests) and *Pod odnoy kryshey* (Under One Roof), apart from a number of documentaries. In 1966 he broke off work on a comedy entitled *Venskaya pochtovaya marka* (The Viennese Postage Stamp) to leave for Great Britain, where he now lives.

A Selective Bibliography of Works on Censorship

CATALOGUES AND BIBLIOGRAPHIES

The most easily available bibliographies on the period up to 1917 are in: BERKOV, P. N. (ed.), *Istoriya russkoy literatury XVIII veka. Bibliograficbesky ukazatel,* Leningrad: Nauka, 1968; MURATOVA, K. D. (ed.), *Istoriya russkoy literatury XIX veka. Bibliograficbesky ukazatel,* Moscow-Leningrad: AN SSSR, 1962; and MURATOVA, K. D. (ed.), *Istoriya russkoy literatury kontsa XIX—nachala XX veka. Bibliograficbesky ukazatel,* Moscow-Leningrad: AN SSSR, 1963. In each case, see both the section entitled "'Tsenzura" and the entry "Tsenzura" in the index. As a rule, works mentioned in these three volumes, as well as studies cited in the footnotes to the text of this book, are not referred to again in this bibliography.

Bibliograficbeskiye materialy. Opis knig, broshyur i statey biblioteki Senatora N. P. Smirnova, St. Petersburg: Porokhovshchikov, 1898, pp. 147—168 (see also pp. 207—225).

RUBAKIN, N. A., *Sredi knig,* Vol. 1, Part 2, Moscow: Nauka, 1911; and Vol. 2, Moscow: Nauka, 1913 (see Vol. 1, Part 2, pp. 12—13 and Vol. 2, p. 490).

NIKOLAYEV, A. S. and OKSMAN, YU. G. (eds.), *Literaturny muzeum,* Petersburg [sic], 1921 (see the introduction [on unnumbered pages] on archival materials concerning censorship).

MASHKOVA, M. V., *Istoriya russkoy bibliografii nachala XX veka (do oktyabrya 1917 goda),* Moscow: Kniga, 1969, pp. 109—130.

LEVINA, S. S., "Vazhnaya otrasl istoricheskoy bibliografii. (Istoriya i sovremennoye sostoyaniye bibliografii nelegalnoy i zapreshchennoy pechati)," *Sovetskaya bibliografiya,* No. 3 (1969), pp. 10—20.

MAKSAKOVA, V. V. (ed.), *Krasny arkhiv. Istoricbesky zhurnal 1922—1941. Annotirovanny ukazatel soderzhaniya,* Moscow: Vsesoyuznaya knizhnaya palata, 1960 (especially pp. 76—87).

See also the entry "Censorship" in the catalogues of the Library of Congress, the Hoover Institution, and the Slavonic Collection of the New York Public Library. For a list of some recent Soviet articles on Tsarist censorship, see: HÜBNER, PETER, "Aspekte der sowjetischen Zensur," *Osteuropa,* No. 1 (1972), pp. 1—24 (in particular footnote 7 on pp. 22—23).

CENSORSHIP IN GENERAL

"Tsenzura" and "Tsenzurnyya vzyskaniya," *Entsiklopedicbesky slovar,* St. Petersburg: Brokgauz-Yefron, 1903, Vol. 37 (74), pp. 948—962 and Vol. 38 (75), pp. 1—8.

"Tsenzura," *Entsiklopedicbesky slovar,* Moscow: Granat, [c. 1928], Vol. 45, Part 3, columns 285—292.

"Tsenzura," *Bolshaya sovetskaya entsiklopediya,* Moscow: OGIZ RSFSR, 1934, Vol. 60, columns 454—474 (see also the second edition, 1957, Vol. 46, pp. 518—519).

ZIMMER, DIETER E. (ed.), *Die Grenzen literarischer Freiheit,* Hamburg: Die Zeit Bücher, 1966.

LAREDO, URSULA, "Bibliography of South African Literature in English 1964—1968," *The Journal of Commonwealth Literature,* No. 9 (July, 1970), pp. 1—9.

DRYUBIN, G., *Knigi, vosstavshiye iz pepla,* Moscow: Kniga, 1966; see the review by A. P. OGURTSOV in *Voprosy filosofii,* No. 4 (1967), pp. 163—166.

154

See also *Index*, a quarterly journal on censorship, the first issue of which was published in London in spring, 1972.

GENERAL WORKS ON TSARIST CENSORSHIP

BOGUCHARSKY, V., "Ocherki iz istorii russkoy zhurnalistiki XIX veka," pp. 281–406 of his *Iz proshlogo russkago obshchestva*, St. Petersburg: Pirozhkov, 1904.

YEVGENYEV-MAKSIMOV, V., *Ocherki po istorii sotsialisticheskoy zhurnalistiki v Rossii XIX veka*, Moscow-Leningrad: Gosizdat, 1927.

ARESHYAN, S. G., *Armyanskaya pechat i tsarskaya tsenzura*, Yerevan: AN Armyanskoy SSR, 1957.

TOMPKINS, S. R., *The Russian Mind*, Norman: University of Oklahoma Press, 1953, pp. 120–142 and 265–266.

See also: (i) the memoirs of such nineteenth-century figures as A. YA. PANAYEVA and N. V. SHELGUNOV; (ii) the entry "Tsenzura" in the index (Part 2, p. 164) to: V. L. BURTSEV, *Za sto let (1800–1896)*. *Sbornik po istorii politicheskikh i obshchestvennykh dvizheny v Rossii*, London, 1897; (iii) *Sbornik materialov k izucheniyu istorii russkoy zhurnalistiki*, No. 1, ed. B. KOZMIN (Moscow, 1952), pp. 111–113 and 179–184; No. 2, ed. B. KOZMIN (Moscow, 1952), pp. 207–210; and No. 3, eds. B. P. KOZMIN and K. A. KOVALEVSKY (Moscow, 1956), pp. 283–286; (iv) footnote 3 to the introduction to this volume (p. ii).

CENSORSHIP IN EIGHTEENTH-CENTURY RUSSIA

PAPMEHL, K. A., *Freedom of Expression in Eighteenth Century Russia*, The Hague: Nijhoff, 1971. This book has a very good bibliography.

ZAPADOV, V. A., "Kratky ocherk istorii russkoy tsenzury 60-90-kh godov XVIII veka," *Uchenyye zapiski Leningradskogo gosudarstvennogo pedagogicheskogo instituta imeni A. I. Gertsena*, Vol. 414 (1971), pp. 94–135.

TYULICHEV, D. V., "Tsenzura izdany Akademii nauk v XVIII v.," pp. 71–114 of *Sbornik statey i materialov po knigovedeniyu*, No. 2, resp. ed. A. MOISEYEVA, Leningrad: Izdatelsky otdel Biblioteki AN SSSR, 1970.

MIYAKOVSKY, V., "K istorii tsenzurnykh goneny na sochineniya A. N. Radishcheva," *Russky Bibliofil*, No. 3 (1914), pp. 49–59.

CENSORSHIP IN RUSSIA, 1800–1860

Zapiski, mneniya i perepiska Admirala A. A. Shishkova, 2 Vols., Berlin-Prague: N. Kiselev and Yu. Samarin, 1870. See especially his 1815 memorandum "Mneniye moyo o razsmatrivanii knig ili tsenzure," pp. 43–53 of Vol. 2.

"Tsenzura meditsinskikh sochineny v 1819 godu," *Russkaya Starina*, Vol. 106 (June, 1901), pp. 587–594.

PYATKOVSKY, A. P., "Tsenzurny Proyekt Magnitskogo. Iz istorii tsenzury v Rossii," in his *Iz istorii nashego literaturnago i obshchestvennago razvitiya* (2nd. ed.), Part 1, St. Petersburg: Transhel, 1889, pp. 237–264. See also his article "Zhurnalny triumvirat. (Iz istorii russkoy zhurnalistiki 30-kh godov)," on pp. 206–235 of Part 2 of this work, St. Petersburg: Dobrodeyev, 1888.

Obshchy alfavitny spisok knigam na frantsuzskom yazyke, zapreshchennym inostrannoyu tsensuroyu bezuslovno i dlya publiki s 1815 po 1853 god vklyuchitelno, St. Petersburg: Eduard Prats, 1855. This work contains 2,879 entries.

SUKHOMLINOV, M. I., "Imperator Nikolay Pavlovich—kritik i tsenzor sochineny Pushkina," pp. 207—246 of Vol. 2 of his *Izsledovaniya i stati po russkoy literature i prosveshcheniyu*, St. Petersburg: A. S. Suvorin, 1889. Pp. 527—538 in Vol. 1 of this work contain the original draft of MAGNITSKY's proposals for a new code of censorship.

FEYNBERG, I. L., *Istoriya odnoy rukopisi*, Moscow: Sovetskaya Rossiya, 1967.

VATSURO, V. E. and GILLELSON, M. I., *Skvoz "umstvennyye plotiny."* *Iz istorii knig i pressy pushkinskoy pory*, Moscow: Kniga, 1972.

YEVGENYEV-MAKSIMOV, V., *"Sovremennik" v 40—50 gg. Ot Belinskogo do Chernyshevskogo*, Leningrad: Izdatelstvo pisateley v Leningrade, [1934].

DANILOV, VL., "K tsenzurnoy istorii sochineny T. G. Shevchenka," *Nachala*, No. 2 (1922), pp. 239—255.

BORODIN, V. S., *T. G. Shevchenko i tsarska tsenzura; doslidzhennya ta dokumenti 1840—1862 roki*, Kiev: Naukova dumka, 1969.

SWOBODA, V., "Shevchenko and Censorship," *The Ukrainian Review*, Vol. 8, No. 1 (1961), and Vol. 9, No. 1—2 (1962), pp. 13—22 and 25—32.

RUUD, CHARLES A., "Censorship and the Peasant Question: The Contingencies of Reform under Alexander II (1855—1859)," *California Slavic Studies*, Vol. 5 (1970), pp. 137—167.

WALDECK, FRIEDRICH MEYER VON, *Unter dem russischen Scepter. Aus den Erinnerungen eines deutschen Publicisten*, Heidelberg: Carl Winter's Universitätsbuchhandlung, 1894. See especially pp. 1—21, "Russische Censur (1852—1861)," and pp. 134—161, "Glückliche Zeiten der russischen Presse (1861—1867)."

"Vospominaniya O. A. Przhetslavskago. Tsensura. 1830—1865," *Russkaya Starina*, Vol. 14 (1875), pp. 131—160.

LAZERSON, B. I., "Ezopovskaya rech v publitsistike Chernyshevskogo," *N. G. Chernyshevsky. Stati, issledovaniya i materialy*, No. 4 (1965), ed. YE. I. POKUSAYEV, pp. 61—82.

CENSORSHIP IN RUSSIA, 1860's

MAZON, A., *Un Maître du roman russe. Ivan Gontcharov 1812—1891*, Paris: Champion, 1914. See especially pp. 189—209, "Gontcharov censeur (1856—1860 et 1863—1867)," and the documents, published in Russian, on pp. 342—421.

RADCHENKO, YE. S. (comp.), *"Kolokol." Izdaniye A. I. Gertsena i N. P. Ogaryova 1857—1867. Sistematizirovannaya rospis statey i zametok*, Moscow: Vsesoyuznaya knizhnaya palata, 1957. See in particular items 1, 403—1, 574, pp. 113—127.

YEVGENYEV-MAKSIMOV, V., *"Sovremennik" pri Chernyshevskom i Dobrolyubove*, Leningrad: Goslitizdat, 1936. See especially pp. 95—110, 225—241, 308—318, 421—434, and 485—518.

CHUMIKOV, A., "Moi tsenzurnyya mytarstva. (Vospominaniya)," *Russkaya Starina*, Vol. 99 (September, 1899), pp. 617—627 and Vol. 100 (December, 1899), pp. 583—600.

DINTSES, L. A., *Neopublikovannyye karikatury "Iskry" i "Gudka." 1861—1862 gody*, Moscow-Leningrad: Iskusstvo, 1939.

YAMPOLSKY, I. G., *Satiricheskaya zhurnalistika 1860-kh godov. Zhurnal revolyutsionnoy satiry "Iskra" (1859—1873)*, Moscow: Khudozhestvennaya literatura, 1964.

"Ultra-tsensurnaya kabala. (Obrashchik psevdo-liberalnykh reform sovremenno-byurokraticheskago kharaktera)," *Svobodnoye Slovo*, Berlin, 1862, pp. 262—271.

CHERNYSHEVSKY, N. G., "Pismo o tsenzure," *Zvenya*, No. 6 (1936), pp. 609—613.

156

————, "Frantsuzskiye zakony po delam knigopechataniya," *Polnoye sobraniye sochineny*, Vol. 10, Moscow: Goslitizdat, 1951, pp. 136—167 and 1020—1022. This was originally published in *Sovremennik* (March, 1862), pp. 141—176.

"Po delu o preobrazovanii tsenzury," *Sovremennik* (March, 1862), pp. 59—64. (Yu. Masanov, *Literaturnoye nasledstvo*, Vol. 53—54, p. 480, gives the author as N. L. Tiblen.)

Zhuravlyov, K. N., "K voprosu ob avtore zapiski redaktsii zhurnala 'Sovremennika' o preobrazovanii tsenzury," *Istoricheskiye zapiski*, No. 37 (1951), pp. 215—251.

Bukhbinder, N. A., "Tsenzura o 'Chto delat?' N. G. Chernyshevskogo," *Katorga i ssylka*, No. 44 (1928), pp. 43—50.

Ruud, Charles A., "A. V. Golovnin and Liberal Russian Censorship, January-June 1862," *The Slavonic and East European Review*, No. 119 (April, 1972), pp. 198—219. This article has some valuable bibliographical references in the footnotes.

————, "The Russian Empire's New Censorship Law of 1865," *Canadian Slavic Studies*, Vol. 3, No. 2 (1969), pp. 235—245.

Balmuth, Daniel, "A Bibliographical Note on the Imperial Russian Censorship under Alexander II," *Canadian Slavic Studies*, Vol. 3, No. 2 (1969), pp. 377—382.

Yevgenyev-Maksimov, V. Ye. and Tizengauzen, G., *Posledniye gody "Sovremennika." 1863—1866*, Leningrad: Goslitizdat, 1939. See also Yevgenyev-Maksimov's "Agoniya 'Sovremennika,' " *Byloye*, No. 20 (1922), pp. 32—64.

Dolinin, A., "K tsenzurnoy istorii pervykh dvukh zhurnalov Dostoyevskogo," pp. 559—577 of *F. M. Dostoyevsky. Stati i materialy. Sbornik vtoroy*, ed. A. S. Dolinin, Leningrad-Moscow: Mysl, 1924.

Yesin, B. I., "Iz tsenzurnoy istorii stati D. I. Pisareva 'Borba za zhizn,' " pp. 217—221 of *Iz istorii russkoy zhurnalistiki*, ed. A. V. Zapadov, Moscow: Izdatelstvo Moskovskogo universiteta, 1959.

"Literatura 60-kh godov po otchetam III otdeleniya," *Krasny arkhiv*, No. 8 (1925), pp. 207—232.

Dzhanshiyev, Gr., *Epokha velikikh reform* (10th ed.), St. Petersburg: Volf, 1907. See chap. 6, "Zakon o pechati 6-go aprelya 1865 goda," and chap. 7, "Pervyye shagi beztsenzurnoy pechati," pp. 337—364 and 365—382.

Aksakov, I. S., *Sochineniya*, Vol. 4, Moscow: Volchaninov, 1886, pp. 361—530.

CENSORSHIP IN RUSSIA, 1870's

Gennadi, G. N., *Russkiya knizhnyya redkosti. Bibliografichesky spisok russkikh redkikh knig*, St. Petersburg: A. Transhel, 1872, pp. 12—13 and 141—144.
This work gives some idea of which Russian books were banned in 1870.

[Polyakov, N. P.], *Svoboda rechi, terpimost i nashi zakony o pechati* (2nd. ed.), St. Petersburg: N. Neklyudov, 1870. (Part 2, pp. 135—197, is entitled "Nashi zakony o pechati.")

The periodical *Ukazatel po delam pechati* provides regular details on both favourable and unfavourable decisions of the censorship during the 1870's.

Papkovsky, B. and Makashin, S., "Nekrasov i literaturnaya politika samoderzhaviya. K istorii zhurnala 'Otechestvennyye zapiski,' " *Literaturnoye nasledstvo*, Vol. 49—50 (1946), pp. 429—532.

Garkavi, A. M., *N. A. Nekrasov v borbe s tsarskoy tsenzuroy*, Kaliningrad: Kaliningradskoye knizhnoye izdatelstvo, 1966. This supersedes most previous works on the subject.

TEPLINSKY, M. V., *"Otechestvennyye zapiski"* 1868—1884, Yuzhno-Sakhalinsk: Dalnevostochnoye knizhnoye izdatelstvo, 1966. See in particular Part 1, chap. 2, "'Otechestvennyye zapiski' i tsenzura," pp. 64—111.

YEVGENYEV-MAKSIMOV, V. YE., *V tiskakh reaktsii. K stoletiyu rozhdeniya M. Ye. Saltykova-Shchedrina*, Moscow-Leningrad: Gosizdat, 1926.

"Tsenzurnyye materialy o Shchedrine," *Literaturnoye nasledstvo*, Vol. 13—14 (1934), pp. 97—170.

YEVGENYEV-MAKSIMOV, V., "Iz istorii odnogo tsenzurnogo auto da fe. (O vnov otkrytoy statye N. K. Mikhaylovskogo)," *Kniga i revolyutsiya*, No. 12 (1921), pp. 6—15.

PAKLINA, L. YA., *Iskusstvo inoskazatelnoy rechi. Ezopovskoye slovo v khudozhestvennoy literature i publitsistike*, Saratov: Izdatelstvo Saratovskogo universiteta, 1971 (on *Otechestvennyye zapiski*). See the section of the present bibliography entitled "Censorship of Materialist Thinkers before 1917" for PAKLINA's article on Lenin's use of Aesopian language, and note also the corresponding chapter in the various editions of K. CHUKOVSKY's book on Nekrasov.

KATKOV, M. N., *O pechati*, Moscow: Snegiryova, 1905. This work contains a collection of articles on freedom of the press, originally published during this period or a little later.

CENSORSHIP IN RUSSIA, 1880—1900

LEMKE, MIKH., "Sozhzhennyye i svarennyye knigi," *Kniga i revolyutsiya*, No. 5 (1920), and No. 7 (1921), pp. 73—76 and 78—81. This contains a list of books banned between 1872 and 1904.

BALUYEV, B. P., *Politicheskaya reaktsiya 80-kh godov XIX veka i russkaya zhurnalistika*, Moscow: Izdatelstvo Moskovskogo universiteta, 1971 (especially chap. 1).

ZAYONCHKOVSKY, P. A., *Rossiyskoye samoderzhaviye v kontse XIX stoletiya (politicheskaya reaktsiya 80-kh — nachala 90-kh godov)*, Moscow: Mysl, 1970. (See chap. 6, "Pressa i administratsiya," pp. 262—308.)

ROZENBERG, VLADIMIR, *Iz istorii russkoy pechati. Organizatsiya obshchestvennogo mneniya v Rossii i nezavisimaya bezpartiynaya gazeta "Russkiya Vedomosti" (1863—1918 g. g.)*, Prague: Plamya, 1924. See in particular pp. 101—171.

NYURENBERG, A. M. (comp.), *Svod zakonov Rossiyskoy Imperii*, Moscow: Levenson, 1910. The 1890 *Ustav o Tsenzure i Pechati* and 1906 supplements are printed in columns 61—96 of Book 4, Vol. 14.

LANIN, E. B., *Russian Traits and Terrors*, Boston, Mass.: Tucker, 1891 (chap. 9, "The Russian Censure," pp. 256—288).

NAGRADOW, W. J., *Moderne Russische Censur und Presse vor und hinter den Coulissen*, Berlin: Siegfried Cronbach, 1894.

Samoderzhaviye i pechat v Rossii (Biblioteka "Svetochka," ed. S. A. VENGEROVA, No. 4, Seriya "Materialy dlya istorii russkago obshchestvennago dvizheniya," No. 1), St. Petersburg: A. E. Vineke, 1906. (Another edition: Berlin: Fridrikh Gotgeyner, 1898.)

Khodataystvo russkikh literatorov ob oblegchenii tsenzury, London: Russian Free Press Fund, 1895. This was addressed to the new tsar.

BONCH-BRUYEVICH, V., "Moyo pervoye izdaniye. Iz vospominany," *Zvenya*, No. 8 (1950), pp. 641—716.

LEMKE, M. K., *Dumy zhurnalista*, St. Petersburg: Pirozhkov, 1903. See pp. 9—24 on the censorship of provincial newspapers at the end of the nineteenth century. On LEMKE see: VANDALKOVSKAYA, M. G., *M. K. Lemke — istorik russkogo revolyutsionnogo dvizheniya*, Moscow: Nauka, 1972.

158

PRITYKIN, YA. M., "Presledovaniye tsarskoy tsenzuroy knigi I. I. Mechnikova 'Etyudy o prirode cheloveka,'" *Yezhegodnik muzeya istorii religii i ateizma*, No. 4 (1960), pp. 286—292.

GIZETTI, A., *Pisatel-podvizhnik Gl. Uspensky*, Petrograd: Nonin, 1922. See pp. 55—59, "Gleb Uspensky i tsenzura. (Iz arkhivnykh materialov)."

BLYUM, A.V., "F.M. Dostoyevsky i 'pedagogicheskaya tsenzura,'" *Sovetskiye arkhivy*, No. 5 (1971), pp. 96—98.

KOVALEV, I. F., "Borba tsarskoy tsenzury s proizvedeniyami L. N. Tolstogo," *Sovetskiye arkhivy*, No. 4 (1970), pp. 94—98.

"Chto takoye iskusstvo? L. N. Tolstogo. Dopolneniya i ispravleniya k russkomu izdaniyu, iskazhennomu tsenzuroy," *Svobodnoye Slovo*, No. 2 (1899), pp. 241—250.

CHERTKOV, V., *Dopolnitelnaya tsenzura dlya Tolstogo*, Moscow: I. D. Sytin, 1914.

CENSORSHIP IN RUSSIA, 1900—1917

PROPPER, S. M. v., *Was nicht in die Zeitung kam. Erinnerungen des Chefredakteurs der "Birschewyja Wedomosti,"* Frankfurt: Frankfurter Societäts-Druckerei, 1929.

Pomogayte volnoy pechati, n. p., Tipografiya Partii Sotsialistov-Revolyutsionerov, 1903. This is a particularly interesting work for the light it sheds on the close link between censorship and what is now called *samizdat*.

GRADOVSKY, A., *O svobode russkoy pechati*, St. Petersburg: Gershunin [1905].

BOTSYANOVSKY, V. and GOLLERBAKH, E., *Russkaya satira pervoy revolyutsii 1905—1906*, Leningrad: Gosudarstvennoye izdatelstvo, 1925.

VATEYSHVILI, D. L., *Iz istorii legalnoy rabochey pechati Zakavkazya*, Tbilisi: Literatura i iskusstvo, 1963. See chap. 3, "Pervyye legalnyye rabochiye izdaniya Zakavkazya i tsarskaya tsenzura."

MINTSLOV, S. R., "14 mesyatsev 'svobody pechati'. 17 Oktyabrya 1905 g. — 1 Yanvarya 1907 g. Zametki bibliografa," *Byloye*, No. 3 (1907), pp. 123—148.

ANISIMOV, S., "Kak sudili za 'Konka-Skakunka,'" *Katorga i ssylka*, No. 6 (91) (1932), pp. 139—156.

YEVSTIGNEYEVA, L., *Zhurnal Satirikon i poety-satirikontsy*, Moscow: Nauka, 1968. See especially pp. 84—121.

VALDENBERG, D. V. (comp.), *Spravochnaya kniga o pechati vsey Rossii*, St. Petersburg: T-vo Khudo-zhestvennoy Pechati, 1911. Part 1, "Zakony o pechati," includes the 1890 *Ustav o tsenzure i pechati*, the 1906 and 1908 supplements to it, and other legislation. Part 2 provides, *inter alia*, the names of the senior censors of the time (pp. 255—258), a list of books and brochures considered banned in January, 1911, including eight works by N. LENIN, three by K. MARX, eight by L. MARTOV, thirty-four by L. TOLSTOY, and four by N. TROTSKY (pp. 259—324), and a definition of the word censorship: tsenzura — razresheniye na vypusk izdaniya v svet ustanovlennymi na sey predmet uchrezhdeniyami i litsami (p. 620).

"Zhandarmy o *Pravde*," *Proletarskaya revolyutsiya*, No. 2 (14) (1923), pp. 454—468.

BASSOW, W., "The Pre-Revolutionary *Pravda* and Tsarist Censorship," *The American Slavic and East European Review*, Vol. 13, No. 1 (February, 1954), pp. 47—65.

ZINOVYEV, G., *Sochineniya*, Vol. 4, Leningrad: Gosizdat, 1926. For his views on press freedom in 1913 and 1914, see pp. 293—296, 494—497, 522—526, and 543—548.

LEMKE, M., *250 dney v tsarskoy stavke (25 sent. 1915—2 iyulya 1916)*, Petersburg [sic]: Gosudarstvennoye Izdatelstvo, 1920, pp. 360—442.

SIDOROV, A., "Iz zapisok Moskovskogo tsenzora (1909—1917)," *Golos minuvshego*, Nos. 1—3 (1918) pp. 93—114.

See also footnote 3 of the introduction to the present volume, p. ii.

CENSORSHIP IN RUSSIA, 1917–1922

BROWDER, ROBERT and KERENSKY, ALEXANDER (eds.), *The Russian Provisional Government 1917*, 3 Vols., Stanford: Stanford University Press, 1961, especially pp. 194–195, 226–234, 977–980, 1436–1437, 1575 (footnote), 1777–1778, and 1789–1790. This work provides information on censorship after the February Revolution.

OKOROKOV, A. Z., *Oktyabr i krakh russkoy burzhuaznoy pressy*, Moscow: Mysl, 1970. This is the most detailed study of the closure of nearly all non-Bolshevik newspapers and journals in the year following the October Revolution. See pp. 343–376 for a list of 170 different bourgeois and 166 different petty-bourgeois newspapers closed down in 1917 and 1918, and pp. 377–397 for some very useful bibliographies.

CHUGAYEV, D. A. (resp. ed.), *Petrogradsky Voyenno-Revolyutsionny Komitet. Dokumenty i materialy*, Moscow: Nauka, 1966. Vols. 1 and 2 contain many indications of how non-Bolshevik newspapers were shut down in the first weeks after Lenin came to power.

STRUVE, G., "The Writers," *Studies on the Soviet Union*, Vol. VII, No. 2 (1967), pp. 166–170 (on *Gazeta-Protest*, November 26, 1917).

KAYROVICH, V. S. (comp.), *Obzor dolyatelnosti Moskovskago Soyuza Rabochikh Pechatnago Truda (s 28 fevralya 1916 g. po 1-oye yanvarya 1918 goda)*, Moscow: Izdaniye Moskovskago Soyuza Rabochikh Pechatnago Truda, 1918.

GORKY, M., *Untimely Thoughts*, London: Garnstone Press, 1970, pp. 86–88, 113–114, and 182–184.

ROZENBERG, VLADIMIR, "Pered gibelyu," *Na chuzhoy storone*, No. 8 (1924), pp. 281–293.

PAQUET, ALFONS, *Im kommunistischen Russland. Briefe aus Moskau*, Jena: Eugen Diederichs, 1919, pp. 169–180.

LUTOKHIN, D., "Sovetskaya tsenzura. (Po lichnym vospominaniyam)," *Arkhiv russkoy revolyutsii*, No. 12 (1923), pp. 157–166.

LUNACHARSKY, A., "Svoboda knigi i revolyutsiya," *Pechat i revolyutsiya*, No. 1 (1921), pp. 3–9.

YERMAKOV, A. F., "A. V. Lunacharsky i politika partii v oblasti iskusstva. 1917–1925 gg.," pp. 340–383 of *Obogashcheniye metoda sotsialisticheskogo realizma i problema mnogoobraziya sovetskogo iskusstva*, ed. M. N. PARKHOMENKO *et al.*, Moscow: Mysl, 1967.

DINERSHTEYN, YE. A. and YAVORKAYA, T. P. (comps.), *Izdatelskoye delo v pervyy gody Sovetskoy vlasty (1917-1922)*, Moscow: Kniga, 1972.

See also the Mezyer bibliographies (items 1731 and 1732 in *Istoriya russkoy literatury XIX veka. Bibliografichesky ukazatel*, ed. K. D. MURATOVA, Moscow-Leningrad: AN SSSR, 1962) and footnotes 4 and 8–11 to the text of the present volume.

CENSORSHIP IN THE SOVIET UNION, 1922–1931

ROZENBERG, VLADIMIR, "Prazdnik pechati," *Na chuzhoy storone*, No. 6 (1924), pp. 269–278.

LUNACHARSKY, A. V., "O khudozhestvennoy politike Narkomprosa," *Literaturnoye nasledstvo*, Vol. 82 (1970), pp. 407–411.

IZRAELIT, M. N., "Iz zakonodatelstva o pechati," pp. 415–430 of *Gazetny i knizhny mir*, ed. M. BRAZ and S. INGULOV, No. 2 (1926). *Tsenzura* is on pp. 424–425.

STALIN, I., "Otvet Bill-Belotserkovskomu," *Sochineniya*, Vol. 11, Moscow: Gosudarstvennoye izdatelstvo politicheskoy literatury, 1949, pp. 326–329.

"Pismo M. Bulgakova sovetskomu pravitelstvu," *Grani*, No. 66 (1967), pp. 155–161.

ZAMYATIN, YEVGENY, "Pismo Stalinu," pp. 277–282 of ZAMYATIN's *Litsa*, New York: Mezhdunarodnoye Literaturnoye Sodruzhestvo, 1967.

JUST, ARTUR W., *Die Presse der Sowjetunion*, Berlin: Carl Duncker, 1931, pp. 46–55 (and pp. 284–304 for a useful bibliography, in particular of Russian works of the 1920's on the Soviet press).

160

MIRKIN-GEZEWITSCH, BORIS, *Das sowjetrussische Presserecht*, Berlin: Georg Stilke, 1931, especially pp. 16—31.

See also footnote 5 of the introduction to this volume, pp. iii-iv, and footnotes 4, 113, and 114 to the text.

CENSORSHIP IN THE SOVIET UNION, 1931—1964

FOGELEVICH, L. G. (comp.), *Deystvuyushcheye zakonodatelstvo o pechati. Sistematichesky sbornik*, Moscow: Sovetskoye zakonodatelstvo, 1931, pp. 44—47, 60—74, 88—89, 98—99, 132—135, 162—163, 170—177, 218—219, 230—231.

YELAGIN, YU., *Ukroshcheniye iskusstv*, New York: Izdatelstvo imeni Chekhova, 1952.

YEVTIKHIYEV, I. and VLASOV, V., *Administrativnoye pravo*, Moscow: Yuridicheskoye izdatelstvo ministerstva yustitsii SSSR, 1946, especially pp. 229—232, 342—343, and 387—388.

ZAVALISHIN, V., "Sovetskiye tsenzory za rabotoy," *Narodnaya pravda*, No. 11—12 (1950), pp. 23—26.

KIPIANI, K., "Sovetskaya tsenzura," *Nashi dni*, No. 6 (1959), pp. 28—38.

The Press in Authoritarian Countries, Zürich: The International Press Institute, 1959, pp. 13—43.

STRUVE, GLEB, "Chekhov in Communist Censorship," *The Slavonic and East European Review*, Vol. 33, No. 81 (June, 1955), pp. 327—341.

GOLDSHTEYN, D., "Peredelka pisem Dostoyevskogo," *Novy zhurnal*, No. 65 (1961), pp. 111—120 (English version: GOLDSTEIN, DAVID I., "Rewriting Dostoevsky's Letters," *The American Slavic and East European Review*, Vol. 20, No. 2 [1961], pp. 279—288).

See also footnotes 5, 6, and 8 of the introduction to the present volume and footnotes 13, 21, 26, 38, 83, 94, 113, 227, and 231 to the text.

CENSORSHIP IN THE SOVIET UNION, 1964—1972

SLAVINSKY, M., "Tsenzura — perezhitok srednevekovya," *Posev*, No. 7 (1968), pp. 47—50.

Anonymous, "Glavlit," *Posev*, No. 7 (1968), pp. 50—53.

RANN, A., "Spravka," *Zarubezhye*, No. 3 (23) (1969), pp. 17—19.

REDDAWAY, PETER (ed.), *Uncensored Russia*, London: Jonathan Cape, 1972, pp. 433—437 (items on censorship from the first eleven issues of the "Chronicle of Current Events").

"Dokumenty vremeni," *Posev*, No. 10 (1971), pp. 59—63 (appeals concerning censorship by V. KAVERIN and V. SOSNORA).

VOLPIN, A. S., "Glasnost sudoproizvodstva," (a *samizdat* manuscript, part of a longer work, *O protsessualnykh garantiyakh prav cheloveka*, apparently written in Moscow in 1970).

"Posvyashchayetsya yubileyu," *Pravda*, June 6, 1972, p. 3. This is a TASS report on the celebration of the fiftieth anniversary of *Glavlit*. For more details see *Literaturnaya gazeta*, No. 23, 1972, p. 3 (the participants elected the Politburo as the honorary presidium of their meeting).

HÜBNER, PETER, "Aspekte der sowjetischen Zensur," *Osteuropa*, No. 1 (1972), pp. 1—24.

KLIMANOVA, L. S. (comp.), *O partiynoy i sovetskoy pechati, radioveshchanii i televidenii*, Moscow: Mysl, 1972. This documents Bolshevik attitudes towards the press, etc., from the end of the last century.

See also footnotes 4-6 of the introduction to the present volume and footnotes 8, 38, 71, and 232 to the text.

CENSORSHIP OF MATERIALIST THINKERS BEFORE 1917

KOVALYOV, I. F., "L. Feyerbakh i tsarskaya tsenzura," *Voprosy istorii religii i ateizma*, No. 12 (1964), pp. 289—296.

"Sochineniya Marksa v russkoy tsenzure," *Dela i dni*, No. 1 (1920), pp. 321—345.

"Karl Marks i tsarskaya tsenzura," *Krasny arkhiv*, No. 1 (56) (1933), pp. 5—32.

V zashchitu slova. Sbornik, St. Petersburg: Klobukov, 1905, p. 179 (for an example of the censorship of the name Marx).

KOVALYOV, I. F., "Dokumentalnyye materialy o presledovanii tsarskoy tsenzuroy proizvedeny K. Marksa i F. Engelsa," *Sovetskiye arkhivy*, No. 6 (1970), pp. 31—36.

"Tsarskaya tsenzura o proizvedeniyakh Fr. Engelsa," *Istorik-marksist*, No. 8—9 (1935), pp. 61—89.

"Doklad tsenzora Matveyeva o sozhzhennom marksistskom sbornike," *Krasny arkhiv*, No.4 (1923), pp. 308—316.

POLYANSKAYA, L., "Arkhivny fond Glavnogo Upravleniya po Delam Pechati," *Literaturnoye nasledstvo*, Vol. 22—24 (1935), pp. 603—634. See section 2, Klassiki marksizma v tsarskoy tsenzure, pp. 611—615.

YAKOVLEV, N., "Lenin v tsenzure," *Krasnaya letopis*, No. 2 (11) (1924), pp. 19—34.

FOYNITSKY, V., "Vopreki tsarskoy tsenzure," *Zvezda*, No. 1 (1970), pp. 181—186. See his first footnote for further references.

PAKLINA, LIDIYA, "'Khudozhestvenno vytochennaya pravda,'" *Volga*, No. 10 (1970), pp. 175—181 (on Lenin's mastery of Aesopian techniques, enabling him to publish about 400 articles in the censored press).

MURATOVA, K. D. (ed.), *Istoriya russkoy literatury kontsa XIX—nachala XX veka. Bibliografichesky ukazatel*, Moscow-Leningrad: AN SSSR, 1963 (p. 47, item 849 for Lenin's references to censorship).

KALEKINA, O. P., *Izdaniye marksistskoy literatury v Rossii kontsa XIX v.*, Moscow: Gospolitizdat, 1957).

CENSORSHIP BY THE CHURCH IN PREREVOLUTIONARY RUSSIA

KOTOVICH, AL., *Dukhovnaya tsenzura v Rossii (1799—1855 gg.)*, St. Petersburg: Rodnik, 1909.

NAGRADOW, W. J., *Moderne Russische Censur und Presse vor und hinter den Coulissen*, Berlin: Siegfried Cronbach, 1894, pp. 298—355.

GREKULOV, YE. F., *Kak rossiyskoye dukhovenstvo dushilo pechat*, Moscow: Ateist, 1930. (See the bibliography on p. 74.)

KARPOV, N., "Dukhovnaya tsenzura—dushitel ateizma v russkoy literature," pp. 265—271 of *Russkaya literatura v borbe s religiyey*, resp. ed. N. STEPANOV, Moscow: AN SSSR, 1963.

KOVALYOV, I. F., "Borba tsarskoy tsenzury protiv ateisticheskoy propagandy v Rossii," *Istorichesky arkhiv*, No. 4 (1955), pp. 212—216.

EYDELMAN, N. YA., "Tserkov v borbe s volnym russkim slovom," *Istorichesky arkhiv*, No. 1 (1962), pp. 194—199.

"Dukhovnaya tsenzura v Rossii v XIX—nachale XX v.," chap. 16 of *Tserkov v istorii Rossii (IX v.—1917 g.)*, resp. ed. N. A. SMIRNOV, Moscow: Nauka, 1967, pp. 298—313.

LEBEDEV, V. K., "Borba dukhovnoy pechati protiv izdaniya proizvedeny L. N. Tolstogo dlya naroda," *Uchenyye zapiski Leningradskogo gosudarstvennogo pedagogicheskogo instituta imeni A. I. Gertsena*, Vol. 414 (1971), pp. 273—287.

CHUDNOVTSEV, M. I., *Tserkov i teatr. Konets XIX—nachala XX v.*, Moscow: Nauka, 1970.

CENSORSHIP OF PUBLIC LIBRARIES IN RUSSIA
AND THE SOVIET UNION

SLEVTSCVA, M., "Tsenzura posle tsenzury," pp. 217—223 of *V zashchitu slova. Sbornik,* St. Petersburg: Klobukov, 1905.

VALDENBERG, D. V., *Spravochnaya kniga o pechati vsey Rossii,* St. Petersburg: T-vo Khudozhestvennoy Pechati, 1911, p. 603.

Apropos of Krupskaya's purging of libraries in the early 1920's (section [c] of footnote 4 in the introduction to the present volume), see ABRAMOVICH, RAPHAEL, *The Soviet Revolution, 1917—1939,* London: Allen and Unwin, 1962, pp. 306—309; MAXIMOFF, G. P., *The Guillotine at Work. Twenty Years of Terror in Russia (Data and Documents),* Chicago: The Chicago Section of the Alexander Berkman Fund, 1940, pp. 221—223; and McNEAL, ROBERT H., *Bride of the Revolution. Krupskaya and Lenin,* London: Victor Gollancz Ltd., 1973, pp. 200—202.

FUTRELL, MICHAEL, "Banned Books in the Lenin Library," *Library Review* (Autumn, 1959), pp. 184—186.

HORECKY, PAUL L., *Libraries and Bibliographic Centers in the Soviet Union,* Indiana: Indiana University Publications, 1959, pp. 155—161.

POSTAL CENSORSHIP IN RUSSIA AND THE SOVIET UNION

GOGOL, N. V., *Revizor,* Act 1, scene 2 and Act 5, scene 8.

ROZENBERG, V. and YAKUSHIN, V., *Russkaya pechat i tsenzura v proshlom i nastoyashchem,* Moscow: Sabashnikovy, 1905, pp. 183—187.

"Iz vospominany M. Ye. Bakaya. O chernykh kabinetakh v Rossii," *Byloye,* No. 7 (1908), pp. 119—133.

KANTOR, R., "K istorii 'chernykh kabinetov,'" *Katorga i ssylka,* No. 37 (1927), pp. 90—99.

KOROLENKO, V. G., "O chernykh kabinetakh i perlyustratsiyakh," *Russkiya Vedomosti,* No. 174 (1913).

For other works on this period see footnote 3 of the introduction to the present volume. Mail sent to Soviet national servicemen is thought to be censored: see *Sever,* No. 10 (1971), p. 79. On current postal regulations see "Tamozhenny kontrol za mezhdunarodnymi pochtovymi otpravleniyami," from section 2 of the *Tamozhenny kodeks Soyuza SSR, Vedomosti Verkhovnogo Soveta SSR,* No. 20 (1964), p. 377, and "Ob utverzhdenii Ustava svyazi Soyuza SSR," *Sotsialisticheskaya zakonnost,* No. 10 (1971), pp. 81—83. See also footnote 233 of the text in the present volume.

EDITORIAL CENSORSHIP AND REWRITING IN THE SOVIET UNION

MILCHIN, A. (ed.), *Redaktor i kniga,* No. 3, Moscow: Iskusstvo, 1962.

KUZMINA, E. and MILCHIN, A. (eds.), *Redaktor i kniga,* No. 4, Moscow: Iskusstvo, 1963.

REILLY, ALAYNE, *America in Contemporary Soviet Literature,* New York-London: New York University Press—University of London Press Ltd., 1971. (On KATAYEV see especially pp. 133 and 168; on V. NEKRASOV see pp. 86—107.)

NEKRASOV, VIKTOR, "O vulkanakh, otshelnikakh i prochem," *Grani,* No. 74 (1970), pp. 25—86.

TWAROG, LEON, "A Novel in Flux: V. Kostylev's *Ivan Groznyj,*" *The American Slavic and East European Review,* Vol. 14, No. 3 (1955), pp. 359—370.

See also footnotes 5, 6, and 8 of the introduction to the present volume and footnotes 6, 22, 24, 26, 29, 50, 68, 103, and 153 to the text.

THEATRE AND FILM CENSORSHIP IN RUSSIA
AND THE SOVIET UNION
(GLAVREPERTKOM)

DRIZEN, BARON N. V., *Dramaticheskaya tsenzura dvukh epokh 1825—1881* [Petrograd]: Prometey, 1917.

PETROVSKAYA, I. F., *Istochnikovedeniye istorii russkogo dorevolyutsionnogo dramaticheskogo teatra*, Leningrad: Iskusstvo, 1971, pp. 28—32 and 52—56.

REVYAKIN, A. I., "A. N. Ostrovsky i tsenzura," *Stranitsy istorii russkoy literatury*, resp. ed. D. F. MARKOV, Moscow: Nauka, 1971, pp. 348—356.

CHUDNOVTSEV, M. I., *Tserkov i teatr. Konets XIX—nachalo XX v.*, Moscow: Nauka, 1970.

KUSHAKOVA, O. A., "Doneseniya tsenzorov o zapreshchenii postanovki pyes v gody stolypinskoy reaktsii," *Sovetskiye arkhivy*, No. 3, 1972, pp. 98—101.

BALUKHATY, S. D., "Dramaturgiya M. Gorkogo i tsarskaya tsenzura," pp. 195—256 of *Teatralnoye naslediye*, No. 1, resp. ed. K. N. DERZHAVIN, [Leningrad]: Gosudarstvenny akademichesky teatr dramy, 1934.

GRIDNEVA, O. V. and NAZAROV, B. A., "K voprosu ob otstavanii dramaturgii i teatra," *Voprosy filosofii*, No. 5 (1956), pp. 85—94 (and also No. 6 [1956], pp. 7—9).

See also footnotes 139 and 209 to the text of the present volume.

On prerevolutionary cinema censorship see VALDENBERG, D. V., *Spravochnaya kniga o pechati vsey Rossii*, St. Petersburg: T-vo Khudozhestvennoy Pechati, 1911, pp. 21 and 603—604.

LENIN, V. I., "Direktivy po kinodelu," *Polnoye sobraniye sochineny* (5th ed.), Vol. 44, Moscow: Izdatelstvo politicheskoy literatury, 1964, pp. 360—361 and 579.

"Zapreshchennyye kinofilmy," *Khronika tekushchikh sobyty*, No. 19 (pp. 15—16 of *Posev*, ninth special issue, 1971). This contains a list of recently banned films.

See also E. RADZINSKY's play *Snimayetsya kino*, *Teatr*, No. 1 (1966), pp. 157—192, and footnotes 171 and 172 of the text of the present volume.

On GLAVREPERTKOM see: *Teatralnaya entsiklopediya*, Vol.1 (1961), column 1184, and Vol.2 (1963), columns 237—238. MIKHAIL BULGAKOV frequently alludes to the work of GLAVREPERTKOM (e. g., in *Bagrovy ostrov* and *Teatralny roman*), and so does ILYA EHRENBURG (in *Burnaya zhizn Lazika Roytshvantsa*). See also Mayakovsky's *Banya*, Act 3. For an example of GLAVREPERTKOM's disregard for expert opinion in the 1920's see: ASKOLDOV, A., "Vosem snov," *Teatr*, No. 8 (1957), pp. 62—63.

See also footnote 163 to the text of the present volume.

CENSORS IN RUSSIA AND THE SOVIET UNION
(GLAVLIT)

For numbers and names of prerevolutionary censors see: FEOKTISTOV, YE. M., *Za kulisami politiki i literatury 1848—1896*, Leningrad: Priboy, 1929; RIGBERG, BENJAMIN, "The Efficacy of Tsarist Censorship Operations, 1894—1917," *Jahrbücher für Geschichte Osteuropas*, Vol. 14 (1966), pp. 339—341; MAYSKY, S., "Cherny kabinet," *Byloye*, No. 7 (1918), p. 188; and VALDENBERG, D. V., *Spravochnaya kniga o pechati vsey Rossii*, St. Petersburg: T-vo Khudozhestvennoy Pechati, 1911, pp. 225—258. See also footnote 3 of the introduction to the present volume and the following sections of the present bibliography: "Censorship in Russia, 1917—1922," "Censorship in the Soviet Union, 1922—1931," "Censorship in the Soviet Union, 1931—1964," and "Censorship in the Soviet Union, 1964—1972."

On the first head of GLAVLIT (1922—1931), P. I. LEBEDEV-POLYANSKY, see the various editions of the *Bolshaya sovetskaya entsiklopediya* and *Malaya sovetskaya entsiklopediya*. See also: *Literaturnaya entsiklopediya* (under "Polyansky," Vol. 9 [1935], columns 124—128); the Granat *Entsiklopedichesky slovar* (7th ed.), supplement to Vol. 41, Part 1, columns 285—289; *Literaturnoye nasledstvo*, Vol. 55 (1948), pp. 575—584 and 611—626; and *Literaturnaya gazeta*, No. 4 (1972), p. 7. For some idea of his views and interests, see his contributions to: *Proletarskaya Kultura*, Nos. 1—17/19 (1918-1920); *Krasny arkhiv*, No. 3 (10) (1925), pp. 286—299 and *Novy mir*, Nos. 5 and 7 (1928), pp. 224—233 and 195—204.

The head of GLAVLIT from 1931—1935 was B. M. VOLIN (FRADKIN), on whom see: *Bolshaya sovetskaya entsiklopediya*, Vol. 12 (1928), column 727; *Literaturnaya entsiklopediya*, Vol. 2 (1929), columns 280-281; *Malaya sovetskaya entsiklopediya* (2nd ed.), Vol. 2 (1934), column 632.

VOLIN was succeeded as the head of GLAVLIT in 1935 by S. B. INGULOV, on whom see: *Malaya sovetskaya entsiklopediya* (2nd ed.), Vol. 4 (1936), column 694, and *Bolshaya sovetskaya entsiklopediya*, Vol. 28 (1937), column 64. *Vsya Moskva. Adresno-spravochnaya kniga. 1936 god*, Moscow: Moskovsky rabochy, 1936, p. 43, gives INGULOV's chief assistants as M. L. REMEZ (secretariat and operations squad); A. P. TANYAYEV (deputy head); A. S. SAMOKHVALOV (inspection section); P. A. KAZANSKY (section for political and economic literature); N. L. SPASSKY (section for belles-lettres); I. N. CHESNOKOV (section for agricultural literature); and D. YA. BORSHCHEVSKY (section for foreign literature).

For the names of other leading censors up to this date see such handbooks as *Vsya Moskva* (for 1923, column 55 of Section 1; for 1927, pp. 93 and 119; for 1929, pp. 101 and 127; for 1931, pp. 58 and 68); *Ves Petrograd* (for 1923, p. 231 and insert); *Ves Leningrad* (for 1924, pp. 55 and 283); *Vsya Sibir* (for 1924, pp. 170, 209, 270 and 343); and *Vsya Srednyaya Aziya* (for 1926, p. 400).

The head of GLAVLIT for the last sixteen years has been P. K. ROMANOV, on whom see: *Prominent Personalities in the USSR*, Metuchen, N. J.: The Scarecrow Press, 1968, p. 523. For part of an order signed by ROMANOV on May 24, 1971, calling for the removal from sale and from libraries of books by R. L. BAUMVOL, I. B. KERLER, and Z. I. TELESIN (all of whom had legally emigrated to Israel), see: *Nasha strana* (Tel-Aviv), August 19, 1971.

On GLAVLIT see the references in footnote 5 of the introduction to the present volume and footnotes 4, 5, 21, 89, 90, 91, 97, 99, and 100 to the text. See also *Malaya sovetskaya entsiklopediya*, Vol. 2 (1929), columns 513—514, and successive issues of *Moskva. Kratkaya adresno-spravochnaya kniga*. The 1965 issue of the last-mentioned work gives the address of *Mosoblgorlit* as 25/1, Oruzheyny pereulok (p. 56), and the address of the USSR State Committee for the Press (including GLAVLIT of the USSR) as No. 7, Kitaysky proyezd. This building seems to be mainly occupied by the *Ministerstvo stroitelstva elektrostantsiiSSSR*, replaced in 1962 by the *Ministerstvo energetiki i elektrifikatsii SSSR*. (See, for example, the 1962 edition of *Moskva. Kratkaya adresno-spravochnaya kniga*, p. 23.)

On the GLAVLIT permission letters printed in most Soviet books and journals see: GOROKHOFF, B. I., *Publishing in the USSR*, Indiana: Indiana University Press, 1959, Supplement 46, "Censorship Symbols," p. 257. The letters and numbers run from A-00000 (e.g., ANNA AKHMATOVA, *Stikhotvoreniya*, Moscow: Goslitizdat, 1958) upwards, and are occasionally changed (e.g., in N. K. GEY, *Iskusstvo slova*, Moscow: Nauka, 1967, from T-03922 to A-02510) and sometimes omitted (e.g., in books by BREZHNEV, the *Zhurnal Moskovskoy Patriarkhii*, and books mainly intended for foreign consumption, such as FRANZ KAFKA, *Roman. Novelly. Pritchi*, Moscow: Progress, 1965). Sometimes years elapse after a work is set up in type (*sdano v nabor*), which does not require permission from GLAVLIT before a GLAVLIT plenipotentiary signs the stamp allowing it to be printed (*podpisano v pechat*, sometimes *podpisano k pechati*). For instance, APOLLON GRIGORYEV's *Stikhotvoreniya i poemy*, Moscow-Leningrad:

Sovetsky pisatel, 1966, was *sdano v nabor* on February 2, 1963, but not *podpisano v pechat* until January 6, 1966. Not infrequently the *podpisano v pechat* date is for some reason earlier than the *sdano v nabor* date (e.g., *L. N. Tolstoy v portretakh, illyustratsiyakh, dokumentakh*, eds. A. I. POPOVKIN and N. P. LOSHCHININ, Moscow: Uchpedgiz, 1961), and occasionally both dates are omitted altogether (e.g., *Literaturnaya Armeniya*, No. 4—5 [1969]). The *sdano v nabor* entry is often left out, and GLAVLIT's final permission to distribute the work (*razreshayetsya v svet*) is always omitted.

See also the end of footnote 5 of the introduction to the present volume and p. 58 of the text.

Index of Personal Names

(Excluding references to participants in the symposium and references in the footnotes)

Soviet Newspapers and Periodicals Mentioned in the Text